International Research on Poverty Reduction

Series Editors

Xiaolin Wang, Beijing, China

Qianqian Liu, Beijing, China

This book series covers poverty reduction practices and experience, knowledge mobilization, poverty reduction strategy analysis, and comparative research of different poverty reduction models. By analyzing China's poverty reduction approaches and experiences, and comparing them with those of other countries, this book series provides policy makers, researchers and practitioners in poverty reduction with theoretical and technical support, as well asproviding a new channel for sharing experiences as well as facilitating collaboration and communication in poverty reduction development fields between China and the rest of the world. Poverty remains a crucial development issue for the world, and China has become an important player in the global endeavor in poverty reduction and development. China has made a substantial contribution to the achievement of the Millennium Development Goals (MDGs) by reducing half of its poverty population.

Fang Cai
Editor

Income Inequality and Poverty Governance in China

Springer

Editor
Fang Cai
Chinese Academy of Social Sciences
Beijing, China

ISSN 2195-9781 ISSN 2195-979X (electronic)
International Research on Poverty Reduction
ISBN 978-981-95-5062-3 ISBN 978-981-95-5063-0 (eBook)
https://doi.org/10.1007/978-981-95-5063-0

Jointly published with Social Sciences Academic Press

The print edition is not for sale in China Mainland. Customers from China Mainland please order the print book from: Social Sciences Academic Press.International Research on Poverty Reduction

Translated title

Translation from the Chinese language edition: “中国收入差距与贫困治理” by Fang Cai, © Social Sciences Academic Press 2022. Published by Social Sciences Academic Press. All Rights Reserved.

This Springer imprint is published by the registered company Springer Nature Singapore Pte Ltd.
The registered company address is: 152 Beach Road, #21-01/04 Gateway East, Singapore 189721, Singapore

Contents

Contents

Chapter 1
Economics of the Poor: Ideas, Practices and Contribution of China's Poverty Alleviation

Fang Cai

Abstract China's economic reform has broken down institutional barriers that had prevented the movement and allocation of production factors, facilitated an exodus of laborers from low-productivity employment sectors and the movement of labor between rural and urban areas, across regions, and among industries, improved allocative efficiency, thereby not only creating the necessary conditions for rapid economic growth, but also increasing the income of rural households by enhancing their participation in nonfarm sectors, and achieving development and shared prosperity. In parallel with this, the Chinese government launched a dedicated rural poverty alleviation and development strategy. As the stage of development and the nature of poverty change over time, the strategy has also evolved, reflecting shifting priorities. The strategy effectively addressed the diminishing marginal utility of poverty alleviation efforts, and achieved widely recognized success in poverty reduction. By reviewing the process of China's reform and development over the past 40 years from the perspective of poverty reduction, this paper first reveals the sources of China's economic growth and illustrates that sharing is inherent to development. It then reviews the implementation of the national strategy of rural poverty alleviation to show how it reflects the people-centered development approach. It summarizes the good practices and experience of China's poverty alleviation campaign and what other countries can learn from these. In conclusion, it points out new challenges faced by China's poverty alleviation after the country eliminates poverty as defined by the current standard by 2020, and puts forward corresponding policy recommendations.

Keywords Sharing · Poverty reduction · Chinese program · Significance to the world

F. Cai (✉)
Chinese Academy of Social Sciences, Beijing, China
e-mail: lvqs@ssap.cn

F. Cai (ed.), *Income Inequality and Poverty Governance in China*, International Research on Poverty Reduction, https://doi.org/10.1007/978-981-95-5063-0_1

1.1 Introduction

During his visit to Japan in 1978, Deng Xiaoping took the famous Shinkansen high-speed train. Later, when reporters asked him how he felt about this experience, his response was succinct and sincere: "It's fast, really fast!"[1] During the next 40 years, China's reform and opening-up policy, enacted by Deng himself, created a miracle in the world history of economic development, poverty alleviation, building national strength, and improving living standards. When commenting on this miracle, any observer would, as if they were admiring China's high-speed railway today, find Deng's simple words apt,

China's achievements in economic development have drawn praise from researchers and casual observers alike. However, while few dispute how fast China's economy has grown, there is no consensus on what made this possible, how this has been achieved, and what it will bring. Biases and misconceptions are not difficult to find.

For example, because many economists failed to accurately grasp the nature of China's economic reform, and even underrated the importance of some basic conditions for economic growth, they misjudged the sustainability of China's growth. Experts also disagree on whether China's economic development is fully inclusive and universally beneficial. Some scholars deny that it is, given the changes in income inequality and other indicators. These two misconceptions have led some researchers to arrive at dubious conclusions about the demand-side factors of China's economic growth, denying the importance of domestic demand, especially consumer demand, and even drawing questionable implications or policy suggestions. Thus, even those observers who sincerely admire China for its achievements in poverty reduction are unable to see China's poverty reduction and economic development as an integral and coherent whole.

John Maynard Keynes has a famous quote: "Practical men, who believe themselves to be quite exempt from any intellectual influence, are usually the slaves of some defunct economist." Indeed, two late economists, widely cited by contemporary scholars, have produced highly influential theories about China's economic development experience, which, unfortunately, have largely been proved invalid by China's reform and opening-up process and achievements during the past 40 years, as they, regardless of the origin, tend to misinterpret the facts when applied to explain the modern Chinese experience. Nevertheless, these theories do have their academic value, as they are capable of inspiring more in-depth discussions, sometimes in unexpected ways.

Let's talk about Friedrich Hayek's influence first. It is said that one of this Austrian economist's contributions lies in broadening the space of our ways of thinking. On the basis of the traditional dichotomy that divides all social phenomena into those that are independent of human intervention and those that result from

[1] See Vogel, E.F. (2013). *Deng Xiaoping and the Transformation of China*. trans. Feng, K. Beijing: SDX Joint Publishing Company, 303.

human activities, he added a third category, namely, unintended consequences of human activities (Hayek, 1967). Either by citing Hayek directly, or because they have been influenced by his ideas, economists such as Huang Yasheng, Steven N. S. Cheung, Ronald Coase, and Wang Ning, who speak glowingly of China's reform and its achievements, all see China's experience as an excellent example of the third category.[2] That is to say, whether it was because they are outsiders, or because they are blinded by prejudices, these economists failed to grasp the fundamental intent behind China's reform.

At the very moment Xiaoping Deng was marvelling at how "really fast" the Shinkansen high-speed train was, he already drew an important conclusion, that poverty is not socialism. Obviously, the original intent behind and the abiding driving force of China's reform has been to eradicate poverty and to continue to improve the Chinese people's living standards. Later in his famous Southern Tour Speeches, Deng Xiaoping proposed three criteria as forming the overarching principle of China's reform: "promotes the growth of the productive forces in a socialist society, increases the overall strength of the socialist state and raises living standards" (later known as "the three favorables"). China has adhered to these criteria throughout the reform process. Since the 18th CPC National Congress, socialism with Chinese characteristics has entered a new era and people-centered development has become a cornerstone of the economic ideas of Xi Jinping Thought of Socialism with Chinese Characteristics for a New Era. The people are the main players in reform and development, the people are to share the benefits of development, and the people are the ultimate beneficiary of development. Evidently, there is nothing unintentional about the reform process in the past 40 years, nor the miracles it created in economic growth and poverty reduction.

Many economists have noticed that indicators for income inequality, such as the Gini coefficient, have, tended to increase for China. They have therefore concluded that in China the benefits of development have not been widely shared. Not only is this conclusion incoherent theoretically, it is also statistically erroneous and misleading. Moreover, without a proper understanding of how China's development benefits the whole population, a coherent explanation of China's poverty reduction achievements would simply be impossible. More importantly, the facts and their underlying logic in poverty reduction are the most powerful evidence that China's reform practices are clearly goal-oriented and intentional. This paper will clarify and illustrate this point in detail.

Now, let's discuss Hollis Chenery's influence. As the former chief economist at the World Bank, Chenery believes that certain development conditions, even in the absence of other conditions, can by themselves promote economic development in the short turn (Chenery & Strout, 1966). This theory has led some scholars to delineate all the basic condition of China's economic development and assign a tried to

[2] For example, see Huang, Y. (2008). *Capitalism with Chinese Characteristics: Entrepreneurship and the State*. Cambridge, New York: Cambridge University Press; Cheung, S. (2009). *The Economic System of China*. Beijing: China CITIC Press; Coase, R. & Wang, N. (2012). *How China Became Capitalist*. Palgrave Macmillan.

argue that each one contributes differently to economic growth, and therefore, reforms aimed at creating different development conditions would create different kinds of outcomes of significance.[3] Based on this belief, some researchers went so far as to claim that during China's reform in the early 1980s, rural reform centered on the household contract responsibility system was the only policy of great importance, and not other reform measures mattered.[4] Although they observed correctly that reforms solve certain problems by providing incentives that stimulate economic growth, their failure to appreciate the underlying logic of the reforms and the relationships between them meant they were unable to understand the prerequisites of economic growth during the reform. They rushed to the conclusion that the growth brought about by the reform is a one-time return to the production possibility frontier, and that such economic growth would not be sustainable in the long term.[5]

In fact, those who apply, inappropriately, neoclassical growth theory to explain the development of China's dual economy due to their failure to see that China's reform and opening up temporally coincided with a special window of opportunity offered by demographic factors, will not only underestimate the potential and sustainability of China's economic growth from the supply side, but also overlook the important role of consumer demand, or are otherwise unable to provide a consistent explanation for the relevant demand side factors.

Scholars and observers at home and abroad generally agree that the Chinese economy has achieved high-speed growth since the launch of the reform and opening-up. They also acknowledge that reform measures aimed at improving incentive mechanisms play a critical role in such growth. The international community has also recognized the significance of China's poverty reduction achievements during the same period. Yet, because reforms in other areas have so far received relatively little research attention, especially measures intended to improve resource reallocation, scholars have been unable to establish logically coherent connections between reform and shared development, or explain why China's poverty reduction efforts have been so successful. This is also why publications on economic transformation, economic growth, or poverty reduction and development do not seem to speak to one another.

Whether it is because they are unaware of it, or have forgotten it, these scholars have also failed to heed the advise of another late economist, Karl Marx, who once said: "But what distinguishes the worst architect from the best of bees is this, that

---

[3] For example, see Brandt, L. & Rawski, T.G. (2008). "China's Great Economic Transformation". In Brandt, L. & Rawski, T.G. (eds). *China's Great Economic Transformation*. Cambridge, New York: Cambridge University Press, 9.

[4] For example, Huang, Y. (2008). *Capitalism with Chinese Characteristics: Entrepreneurship and the State*. Cambridge, New York: Cambridge University Press.

[5] Krugman and Young are advocates of this theory. See Young, A. (2003). "Gold into the Base Metals: Productivity Growth in the People's Republic of China during the Reform Period". *Journal of Political Economy*, 111(6), 1220–1261; Krugman, P. (2013). "Hitting China's Wall". *New York Times*, July 18.

the architect raises his structure in imagination before he erects it in reality."[6] Each and every step in the reform process, as well as each and every achievement made in shared development, constitutes the best evidence for this insight and fully reflect the "three favorables" and the people-centered development approach.

This paper will explain how the reform translated both the historical legacy of insufficient employment and the demographic transition into sources for economic growth, illustrate how reform helped China maintain high-speed growth for 40 years, while bringing benefits to all and achieving huge successes in poverty reduction. This paper begins by revealing that China's economic development, characterized by labor reallocation, promoted employment and increased workers' income, and that this fact by itself ensures shared development. This is followed by an examination of how, guided by the people-centered development philosophy, the Chinese government has sought to improve people's living standards through reform, and continued to adapt the targeted poverty alleviation strategy to the changing needs of the country at different development stages, and successfully overcome diminishing marginal utility of poverty alleviation. In conclusion, this paper attempts to tease out the implications of China's poverty reduction ideas and practices for the world, offer future outlook for poverty reduction efforts, and put forward policy recommendations.

1.2 Widely Sharing the Benefits of High-Speed Growth

Over the nearly four decades from 1978 to 2016, China's gross national income (GNI) grew by an average of 9.6% a year, labor productivity increased by 17 fold, and consumption among urban and rural residents by 16 fold. Such incredible achievements did not come into being *ex nihilo*; instead, they not only are in line with the general pattern of economic development, but also distinctly reflect the uniqueness of the Chinese experience. Although neither theoretically nor empirically can we claim that economic growth inevitably leads to poverty reduction, we have to admit that making the pie bigger necessarily makes it easier to share it. For example, the international comparisons below show clearly that, while China's high-speed economic growth came together with significant poverty reduction; upper-middle-income countries (excluding China) achieved only limited results in poverty reduction as they saw moderate economic growth (Fig. 1.1).

For 30 (1980–2010) of the 40 years of China's reform and development, China went through an unique process of demographic transition, whereby the working age population of those aged 15–59 maintained high growth rate (1.68% on average

[6] Marx, K. (1975). *The Capital, Volume 1*. Beijing: People's Publishing House, 202. Of course, not all economists have ignored this assertion. In fact, Wu Jinglian quoted this same sentence in his introduction to a book, explaining the internal logic of the reform and opening up of China. See Fan, G., Yi, G., Wu, X., Xu, S. & Cai, F. (eds.) (2018). *20 Years for 50 People*. Beijing: CITIC Publishing House.

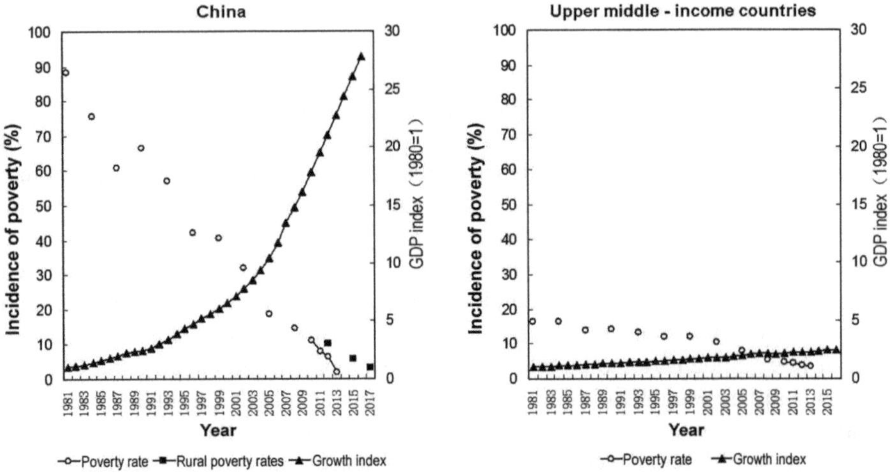

Fig. 1.1 International comparison of the relationship between economic growth and poverty reduction. Source: World Bank database, https://datacatalog.worldbank.org/dataset/poverty-and-equity-database; National Bureau of Statistics. *China Statistical Yearbook*, China Statistics Press; Keqiang Li. *Report on the Work of the Government 2018*

per annum); while the dependent population outside of this age range largely remained the same, dropping slightly at an average rate of 0.01% per annum. This unique phenomenon is in sharp contrast to the situations in both developed countries and other developing countries, since the former showed an average annual working-age population growth rate of 0.44% and an annual dependent population growth rate of 0.47%, while the latter had an average annual working-age population growth rate of 2.44% and an average rate of 1.43% for dependent population. This demographic features means that China was in a window of opportunity in demographic terms, which was beneficial to economic growth since there were more people generating economic output than consuming them.

In the early days of the reform, and even long after that, apparently no one realized the existence of this potential demographic dividend. On the contrary, scholars and policy makers had long considered the large population and surplus labor as a historical baggage, and a huge challenge. In hindsight, although such a view has historical limitations, the relevant policy measures and corresponding reform initiatives did hit the targets and bring positive results. Here, I do not intend to judge the merits and demerits of the strict family planning policy or its actual effects. After all, the family planning policy, at least to a certain extent, accelerated the demographic transition from a period of rapid growth resulted from a high birth rate plus a low death rate to a period of slow growth resulted from a low birth rate plus a low death rate. By facilitating this transition, it released the demographic dividend relatively early. The family planning policy is not the focus here. Instead, the focuses is on reform that promoted economic growth and expanded employment by facilitating labor transition.

During the early days of reform, poverty was widespread in rural areas, and the implementation of the household contract responsibility system led to a surplus in rural labor. Therefore, the primary effect of the reform carried out in rural areas then was facilitating the release of production factors in labor-centered rural production from industries in which they were low in productivity and return and redirecting them to those that were higher in both. In some sense this has always been the fundamental objective of China's reform, until this day.

First of all, the most thorough major rural reform was the abolition of the people's commune system that had been in place for more than 20 years. Along with the swift adoption of the household contract responsibility system across the nation, in the revised *Constitution of the People's Republic of China* promulgated at the end of 1982 the village committee was officially identified as an organization of villager self-rule; in 1983, the CPC Central Committee and the State Council issued *Circular on Separating Government Administration from Commune Management and Establishing Township Governments*, requiring separation of government administration from commune management and the establishment of township governments. Accordingly, administrative villages replaced production brigades, and of villager groups were set up on the basis of production teams. The villager self-rule system, together with the basic rural administration system with the household contract responsibility system at its core, provided fundamental guarantee that under collective land ownership, individual farmers have the right to allocate production factors as they fit, so as many as possible can benefit from rural reform, and over the long term.

Secondly, policies that placed restrictions on the allocation of labor were gradually eased, and obstacles to labor mobility across different production activities, the three industrial sectors, and between rural and urban areas were removed. Instead of engaging exclusively in farming, farmers were now also taking up forestry, animal husbandry and food processing and fishery. Many also found jobs in village enterprises, before moving on to nonfarm employment in small, medium-sized and even large cities. In the process of implementing the household contract responsibility system, the word "may" in documents issued by the CPC Central Committee played a key role (e.g., farm output quotas may be fixed for each household). In the same vein, institutional barriers to labor mobility were eliminated through a series of other policies where the word "allowed" also appeared frequently. For example, starting from 1983, farmers were allowed to engage in long-haule transportation and sales of agricultural products, thus breaking the geographic restrictions on employment for the first time in history. Starting from 1988, farmers were "allowed" to seek employment in nearby towns and cities if they could provide their own food. The barriers to migration for employment were torn down. By the early 1990s, all rationed coupons such as food coupons had been abolished, and with this, rural labor were *de facto* allowed to reside and work in cities of all levels and sizes.

Thirdly, as reform of the household registration, or *hukou*, system and of related institutions progressed, the scope of labor mobility and transfer expanded. This reform was carried out mainly in two areas: First, the government undertook reforms of state-owned enterprises and the urban and rural employment system, boosting the development of the labor market. Second, the social security system that treated people with rural and urban household registration status differently began to phase out that distinction. The employment reform in the late 1990s was aimed at breaking the "iron rice bowl" (a secure permanent job) in state-owned enterprises. While it did cause large-scale unemployment and lay-offs, as well as serious urban poverty, as the country made adjustment, it was able to China achieved the transition in its labor distribution that corresponded to the shift from a planned economy to a market economy. At the same time, the urban social security system was also established. All these reform initiatives produced a chain effect: On one hand, rural migrant workers could seek employment opportunities through fair competition, and on the other hand, social security gradually expanded to rural areas, greatly boosting development with coordinated planning.

In hindsight, a clear logic can be found in all the above mentioned reform initiatives: a large labor force moved out of low-productivity employment in rural areas and some urban enterprises, migrated between rural and urban areas, across regions, and among industries and enterprises, completing the process of labor reallocation to high-productivity fields. Through the accumulation of factors and the reallocation of resources, demographic dividends were transformed into high-speed economic growth. A research shows that, during 1978–2015, out of the labor productivity growth of 16.7 times (measured by GDP per worker), 44% came from these types of labor reallocation (Cai, 2017).

When we review the reform process and its effect on promoting economic growth, we see clearly how reform progressively eliminated the systematic obstacles that deter the migration of production factors, how the reform turned rural surplus labor into abundant workers in enterprises in urban areas, converting one of the legacies of the planned economy into a positive growth factor, how more generally, the reform transformed the favorable demographic conditions in a transition period into demographic dividends, and then cashed them into high-speed economic growth. The whole process of such economic growth was accompanied by a rising nonfarm participation rate, and by the expansion of employment. Through this kind of redistribution effect and economies of scale, workers and their families harvested higher income amid economic growth, and their living standards improved.

Needless to say, the Chinese society indeed experienced periods when the income gap widened. At the same time, we have to point out that the relevant statistics have overestimated components related to statistical factors. Besides, this paper concentrates on the holistic shared development of the economic growth in the reform and opening-up process, so we need to analyze stage problems separately from the trend problems. Only by doing so, can we avoid underrating our achievements, or ignoring the problems and challenges. Expenditure methods show labor remuneration percentage in GDP decreases, and based on this, some researches draw the conclusion that income distribution worsens. This indicator does show downward trend since 2003, and reached its lowest point in 2011 (45.8%). However, after that, it has been increasing every year, and returned to 51.1% in 2015. Other scholars claim that the decline of this indicator is at least partially due to the fact that the agricultural percentage decreases and since the labor remuneration occupies a larger percentage in agriculture, decline of such indicator doesn't necessarily mean the worsening of income distribution (Bai & Qian, 2009). Their observation reminds us that we should consider agricultural percentage decline as a regular change factor, and with this additional consideration, we can rethink and study the shared nature in the reform and development process.[7]

With economic development, agricultural output value and employment percentage will decline irreversibly. This is a widely accepted rule and even an inexorable law. While the share of agriculture in the economy is declining, both the past experience of developed countries and the current reality of developing countries show the following characteristic: Agricultural employment declines later than the share of agricultural output (Barrett et al., 2010). In China, due to the existence of institutional factors such as the household registration system, this phenomenon is even more prominent. Even so, the percentage of agricultural labor eventually reduced significantly. According to data from the National Bureau of Statistics, the percentage of agricultural labor declined from 70.5% in 1978 to 27.7% in 2016. According to my research findings, the actual share is probably 10 percentage points lower than the official figure.[8] Obviously, this is the result of the mass migration of rural labor to urban nonfarm industries.

Achieving such large-scale labor transition in relatively short time facilitates the formation of a typical Lewis dual economic development process. Migrant workers get jobs that pay more than farming, thus reducing rural poverty generally and narrowing the urban-rural income gap. On one hand, even if the salary rate remains the same, the increasing scale of labor migration alone would increase significantly farmer household income. On the other hand, poor farmers are able to significantly increase their household net income per capita by taking advantage of labor migration opportunities. One research shows that migrant villagers can increase their household net income per capita by 8.5% to 13.1% (Du et al., 2005). Now we are going to summarize several important facts about reducing poverty through labor migration.

First of all, before 2013, household surveys inside the official statistical system were conducted independently and separately at rural and urban areas. Due to this practice, those rural families that relocate to cities and those rural household members who seek work elsewhere are often excluded from urban research samples since they are outside the sampling range; at the same time, most of them are also outside the coverage of rural research samples since they live elsewhere most of the time and are not considered rural residents any more. Some researchers use data from certain regional research, and estimate more accurately the income of these migrant workers who are ignored or omitted by both the rural and urban household surveys. Their researches indicate that, problems in the sampling and definition in

---

[7] For example, in terms of the main needs of economic growth, because the proportion of agricultural output value, the proportion of agricultural labor force and the rural population have all dropped significantly, the decline in the contribution of rural residents' consumption is reasonable.

[8] See Cai, F. (2016). *China's Economic Growth Prospects: From Demographic Dividend to Reform Dividend.* Cheltenham, UK: Edward Elgar.

the household survey conducted by official statistical systems lead to overestimation of the disposable income for urban residents by 13.6%, while those same problems cause underestimation of the net income for rural residents by 13.3%. Therefore, the urban-rural income gap is overrated by an average of 31.2% (Gao et al., 2011).

We all know that income gap is caused by various factors; accordingly, indicators of income inequality can be statistically broken down. When attempting to do the breakdown, some studies discovered that the contribution of the urban-rural difference to the overall income gap was 40–60%, measured by the Theil index.[9] Therefore, if we can use statistical tools to correct the overestimation of urban-rural income gap, the overall income inequality ratio (showing on Gini coefficient) should decrease accordingly.

Secondly, some studies estimate extremely high values for income inequality indicator, causing public interests on the issue.[10] These studies may have their own special value, but they utilize methods that focus on unearthing statistical outliers, thus their conclusions are much less reliable. Generally speaking, income distribution follows normal distribution, and statistical surveys usually have difficulties to gather accurate information when they try to collect data from the two end sampling areas, with one being the richest population, and the other, the poorest. This difficult statistical problem is shared by national statistical systems all over the world. Obviously, we cannot compare China's data obtained from this special calculation method with official statistics from other countries; we cannot make general inferences from such data either (Cai et al., 2009).

Moreover, although salaries of rural migrant workers did not increase significantly within a certain period, since labor participation rate of nonfarm industry grows and rural labor is more fully employed, the amount and the percentage of wage inside farmers' total income grows consequentially. For example, during 1997–2004, the salary of migrant workers virtually did not increase, but because migrant labor increased from less than 40 million to over 100 million, the sum of migrant workers' wage achieved an average annual growth rate of 14.9%. Even being underestimated, wage related income as a percentage of farmer's net income increased significantly from 24.6 to 34.0%.

[9] For example, see Kanbur, R. and Zhang, X. (2004). "Fifty Years of Regional Inequality in China: A Journey through Central Planning, Reform, and Openness". *United Nations University WIDER Discussion Paper*, No. 2004/50, 87–106; Wan Guanghua (2007). "Understanding Regional Poverty and Inequality Trends in China: Methodological Issues and Empirical Findings". *Review of Income and Wealth*, Series 53, No. 1, March, 25–34.

[10] For example, Xiaolu Wang focuses on discovering the huge hidden income of those high-income people who are not included in statistics; however, Li Gan estimates the Gini coefficient as high as 0.61. See Wang, X. (2013). "Grey Income and National Income Distribution: Report of 2013". *Comparative Studies*, Issue 5; Gan, L. et al. (2012). *Chinese Household Finance Survey Report 2012*. Chengdu: Southwestern University of Finance and Economics Press.

Thirdly, after China's economy experienced the Lewis Turning Point in 2004,[11] some characteristics of the dual economy have been gradually disappearing; because labor deficit becomes a constant, workers gain more negotiation power in the job market, and both wages of ordinary worker and income of low-income household rise in an accelerated pace. For example, during 2003–2016, migrant worker's actual salary increased at a rate of 10.1%. Wage increase for ordinary workers is the characteristic of Lewis Turning Point, pushing the income gap to reach its peak value. If such trend continues, it may become the Kuznets Turning Point of income distribution. The income gap between urban and rural residents calculated at constant prices (the ratio of urban residents' income to rural residents' income) decreased from the peak of 2.67 in 2009 to 2.35 in 2017, a 12.3% reduction over the years; the Gini coefficient of national income reduced from the highest point of 0.491 in 2008 to 0.467 in 2016, a total reduction of 4.9%.

Finally, at the same time when Lewis Turning Point arrived, central and local governments remarkably strengthened the implementation of re-distribution policies. By advancing the fullness and equalization of the supply of the basic public services, shared benefit of economic development was further deepened. There has been significant increase in social security coverage for urban workers and residents. Since 2004 when the government expanded the social security focus to rural areas, urban social security policy has been gradually benefiting more and more migrant rural workers and their accompanying family members, as well as unemployed population. The construction of labor market system and social security system speed up, and economic and social development become more coordinated, highlighting the broad inclusiveness of Chinese experience.

1.3 Poverty Reduction Practices and Effect in the Reform

Reform promotes rural economic development and rapid growth of the overall national economy, driving the employment expansion and better labor compensation, and such economic development undoubtedly constitutes a critical measure in solving the poverty problem. Nevertheless, although economic development is a necessary condition for better income distribution, it is not a sufficient condition. Economists have observed the following phenomenon worldwide, that is, while economic development indeed leads to poverty reduction, it won't necessarily lead to the "trickle-down effect". Therefore, implementing a specific poverty relief strategy is indispensable in order to achieve shared development and poverty reduction goal. China's poverty reduction achievements link closely to the implementation of specific poverty relief strategies and their effects. During the 40 years of reform period, the journey of poverty reduction in China's rural areas can be divided into

[11] For the definition of the Lewis Turning Point and discussion on its arrival time, see Cai, F. (2015). *Demystifying China's Economy Development*. Beijing, Berlin, Heidelberg: China Social Sciences Press and Springer-Verlag.

three phases, including the unannounced actual phase and the clearly announced phase of strategy implementation.

The first stage of poverty reduction runs from early 1980s to mid-1980s. During this period, there were no clearly announced poverty reduction strategies available. The overall reform of the rural economic system became the main engine that advanced the rapid development of both the rural and national economies. The overall income growth of rural residents constituted the main factor for poverty reduction. Reform of the basic operation system in rural areas largely mobilized farmers' production enthusiasm. Along with the increased price of agricultural products, the accelerated adjustment of agricultural structure, and the industrialization of rural areas, the reform comprehensively enhanced the vitality of the rural economy, and provided more opportunities for the rural labor force with higher capabilities to expand their employment horizon, to overcome poverty and to achieve prosperity.

During the 1978–1985 period, national agricultural added value increased by 55.4%, agricultural labor productivity was up by 40.3%, and the comprehensive purchase price index of agricultural product rose by 66.8%. Over the same period, accompanied by the rapid increase in production of various agricultural products, farmers' net income per capita increased by 2.6 times. Their calorie intake per capita increased from 2300 kcal per person per day in 1978 to 2454 kcal in 1985. At the same time, after the poverty standards doubled, rural population living below the absolute poverty line decreased from 250 million to 125 million, and their percentage was down to 14.8%. On average, the poor rural population decreased by 17.86 million every year.

The period between mid-1980s to the end of twentieth century can be considered as the second implementation phase of poverty reduction, and was also the first time that a poverty relief strategy was announced officially. The government set up special poverty relief agencies, arranged special funds from multiple channels, established related preferential policies, made radical reform on the traditional relief-based methods, and established the new poverty relief policy focusing on development. Through a whole series of policies and measures, planned, organized and large-scale poverty relief efforts aimed at development and progress were carried out. The poverty relief work done at this stage is considered official efforts to alleviate poverty by targeting specific rural populations, and it has two special experiences that deserve mentioning.

First, after the general idea of regional and development-oriented poverty relief policy is determined, in order to centralize the use of poverty relief funds and assist the poor population efficiently, the Central Government selects several priority poor counties requiring key support through development of uniform standards. According to these standards, if the average annual net income of a farmer in a county is less than RMB 1150 in 1985, it qualifies as a priority county. Government established 592 national priority poor counties that needed key support in 1986. They accounted for almost 1/5 of the county-level administrative units across the nation. Later, this standard has been adjusted in a timely manner as economy develops and especially as economic conditions in poor regions improve.

Second, in 1993 the Government developed and implemented the "National 'Eight Seven' Poverty Relief Plan", which strives to concentrate all resources to ensure adequate food and clothing for the then 80 million rural poor population during the last 7 years of the twentieth century. This plan works in a unique way as it attempts to achieve the biggest poverty relief effects in a relatively short time by taking advantage of the rather powerful mobilization and high consensus that Chinese society enjoys. During the 3 years between 1997 and 1999, 8 million poor people saw their food and clothing problem resolved every year, thus achieving the fastest pace of poverty reduction since 1990s, and driving the relief effort in the second stage to their climax.

The implementation outcomes indicate that during those 7 years, rural poor population decreased by 50 million, and rural poverty rate reduced from 8.7 to 3.4%. From 1986 to 2000, the net income per capita of farmers in the poverty relief priority counties increased from RMB 206 to RMB 1338, and national poor population decreased from 131 million to 32.09 million. Various social undertakings in poverty-stricken areas improved and progressed. For example, thanks to the efforts made during this time, infrastructure access indicators in poor area such as those of transportation, communications, electricity, and school are close to those in non-poor areas.

The "National 'Eight Seven' Poverty Relief Plan" drew to its end and it mostly achieved expected goals. The official poverty relief strategy entered into its third stage in 2001. The relief efforts made by government during the previous stage significantly changed the overall distribution of rural poverty, and the regional disparities became more obvious. In the economically developed eastern regions, the incidence of poverty decreased remarkably; while poverty was concentrated in some central and western regions with harsh natural conditions. Based on such distribution, the Central Government identified 592 key counties for poverty relief and development in central and western regions. In 2002, those counties counted for 62.1% of the national absolute poor population and 52.8% of national low-income population.

Since 2000, the incidence of poverty in rural areas mostly remains the same, and during the 10 years after 2000, poor population was reduced by 5.21 million. Considering the fact that government invests ever more funds each year in poverty relief, this means that regional development plan has ceased to produce obvious poverty relief effects as it did before. Marginal poverty, the long-term poverty caused by natural conditions such as geography and climate, and by family background and personal abilities, becomes the main characteristic of rural poverty.

This new situation requires big adjustments in poverty management, since regional development, or promotion of local industries in poor areas can hardly benefit this marginalized poor population. Even inside the same poor county, the spatial separation between the poor and the non-poor becomes more and more obvious. Whether regional economic growth can actually benefit poor population, or whether the use of poverty relief funds targets the real poor, increasingly becomes a question that requires to be answered seriously. Therefore, in order to bring poverty relief resource to the real poor, we must enhance the focus of poverty relief policy and measures, as well as improve the efficiency of poverty relief funds.

In 2001, the CPC Central Committee and State Council developed and announced *Outline of Rural Poverty Relief and Development in China (2001–2010)*. One notable feature of this Outline is relief efforts in the village level, and its corresponding implementation method is called "poverty relief strategy across the whole village". Since 2001, a new policy that treated county as its basic unit and poor villages as its base has been implemented. According to various indicators of economic and social conditions, influenced by production, living situation and geographical environment, priority poor villages besides poor counties were identified. A total of 148,000 priority poor villages across the country were identified. In this way, our policy not only targets the poor regions, but also screens more thoroughly the poor population, thus improving the efficiency of precision poverty alleviation.

During this period, the whole village poverty relief policy obtained evident effects. In the process of implementing the Outline, the income growth rate of farmers who resided in those priority villages was significantly higher than the average growth rate of priority poor counties, and it was also higher than the national average rate. Among all priority villages, the income growth rate of farmers whose villages implemented the whole village poverty relief policy was higher than the rate of those not implementing the same policy by 8 to 9%. During the same period, great progress was recorded in various undertakings in poor regions. The same remarkable improvements in production related infrastructure and living service facilities were registered in priority poor villages, and the related indicators improved significantly above the average level of priority poor counties.

By the end of 2010, the national poor population further decreased and China became the first country to achieve one of the United Nations Millennium Development Goals to halve the poor population. China immediately started to implement *Outline of Rural Poverty Relief and Development in China (2001–2010)*. Government identified concentrated areas with extreme poverty as priority areas of poverty relief, providing poverty relief efforts in those areas with stronger policy guarantees and financial support. Meanwhile, government raised China's poverty relief standards above the international common ones, thus indicating government put more responsibility on itself by bringing more low income rural population into poverty relief scope, and offering more support to poor regions and the poor population.

Since the 18th CPC National Congress, treating poverty alleviation effort as fighting a new tough battle, China has increased its effort to implement poverty alleviation projects, carrying out precise poverty relief, precise poverty alleviation, support for poor households by category, and have harvested new achievements in the field. Even under the higher poverty standards, rural poor population decreased from 122 million in 2011 to 43.35 million in 2016, reduced by an average of 15.81 million per year. This result breaks the diminishing marginal poverty relief effect "Law" in this field. The 13th Five-Year Plan that started in 2016 set up an even more ambitious poverty alleviation goal, which is, under the current poverty standard adjusted by factors such as prices, by 2020 China will eliminate poverty for all rural poor population whose annual income per capita is less than RMB 4000; it will help all poor counties get out of poverty, and it will eradicate regional poverty. In fact, in 2016 alone, 28 poor counties were able to exit the poverty list through legal procedures, achieving the breakthrough of zero poor county exits, and marked a good start to ultimately meet its goal of zero rural poverty by 2020.

1.4 Contributions to the World

Since the reform and opening-up, China not only achieves the world's fastest economic growth and maximally improves people's living standards, but also achieves the world's largest poverty relief and reduction. In 1978, calculated by the government's poverty standards at that time, which was RMB 100 per person per year, rural poor population who lacked food and clothing was 250 million, which counted for 30.7% of the total rural population. In 1984, poverty standards rise to RMB 200 per person per year, while the poor population reduced to 128 million, and incidence of poverty was down to 15.1%. Since then, the government has started to implement the official poverty relief and development strategy. While the poverty standard keeps rising, the poor population keeps falling. Calculated by the 2010's poverty relief standards of RMB 1274, the rural poor population reduced from 94.22 million in 2000 to 26.88 million in 2010, and the corresponding incidence of poverty decreased from 10.2 to 2.8% (Fig. 1.2).

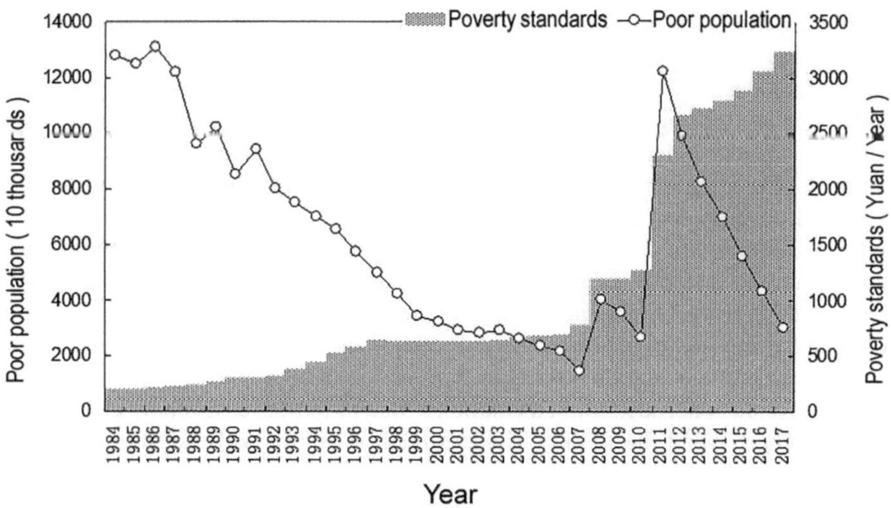

Fig. 1.2 Change of poverty standards and poor population. Source: National Bureau of Statistics, *China Statistical Yearbook*, China Statistics Press; Keqiang Li, *Report on the Work of the Government 2018*

In 2011, the Central Government substantially raised the national poverty standard to RMB 2300, calculated by the constant prices of 2010, a 92% increase from 2009. This new standard increased the number and the coverage of the national poor population from 26.88 million in 2010 to 128 million. According to the international comparable PPP (purchasing power parity), this new standard is equivalent to average of USD 1.8 per person per day, which exceeds the international poverty standard of USD 1.25 per day, set by the World Bank in 2008. Under the new standard, the rural poor population continues decreasing substantially (as shown in Fig. 1.2). During the National People's Congress, Premier Li Keqiang in his *Government Work Report* points out that, in the 5 years from 2012 to 2017, a total of more than 68 million rural poor population exited poverty, and the poverty rate in accordance with this new standard reduced from 10.2 to 3.1%.

China achieves its Millennium Development Goals ahead of time, this, together with the incredible success in its poverty relief and development efforts, receive unanimous praise and admire globally. The general consensus is that China's poverty relief achievements deeply impact the whole world, for they not only contribute quantitatively to the international poverty reduction, but also provide a referential model for other developing countries and the rest of the world. During 1981 to 2013, the world's poor population, calculated by the World Bank's standard of less than GKD 1.9 (constant price of 2011), decreased form 1.893 billion to 0.766 billion, while over the same period, China's poor population reduced from 878 million to 25.17 million, meaning that China contributes 75.7% of the world's poverty relief. In this way, China makes enormous contributions to the cause of international poverty relief and development as well as to the cause of human civilization and progress.

Proven knowledge and ideas are special kinds of public goods. Therefore, upgrading China's successful practices and Chinese story into China's wisdom, and introducing Chinese solution to other developing countries as one possible development route available to choose from, undoubtedly becomes the main way for China to make even greater contributions to humanity. Obviously, the least questionable Chinese wisdom reflects in China's successful poverty reduction practice. The criteria of "Three Favorables" proposed by Deng Xiaoping, as well as the people-centered development ideas upheld by Xi Jinping, fundamentally guarantee that reform, opening-up, development and sharing become one integrated entity, connected among one another by internal logics and essential causalities. Inside this overall relationship, implementation of poverty relief strategy constitutes a key component in order to achieve shared development and to improve people's livelihood. Such implementation is the conscious action of the Chinese people, instead of an unconscious one; such implementation is due to initiatives taken by government and society, beyond the market trickle effects. Now we will use the example of breaking the law of diminishing marginal effect of poverty relief to explain the reason why people-centered development ideas deserve to be the core of Chinese wisdom and Chinese solution.

In the practice of poverty relief in countries around the world, both researchers and practitioners observe a diminishing marginal effect, some even call it "law", which is, as poverty relief efforts move forward, the poor population decreases until the last remaining, smaller chuck of poor population faces notable difficulties to exit out of poverty because geographically, they generally live in areas with poor ecological, production and living conditions, and demographically many of them suffer from disabilities, other illnesses, aging and low level of education, making them lack of labor capability. Therefore, the last mile in the poverty alleviation journey becomes the most difficult to complete; therefore, most developing countries, even many developed countries are stuck trying to conquer this stubborn fort.

The practices during the reform and opening-up period also similar patterns: the diminishing marginal effect keeps appearing while China's rural poor population is in the process of continuous reduction. As shown by Fig. 1.2, while poverty relief standards keep rising, and at each stage so far, the relief efforts have been strengthening, yet the last remaining rural poor population, although much smaller, has never exited poverty completely. Take the increase of the special poverty relief fund from the state revenue and their effects in recent years as an example, for every RMB 100 million from the special fund, the poverty reduction number decreased from 878 thousand in 2011 to 317 thousand in 2014, and decreased even more in 2017 to 68 thousand (Zhu & He, 2018).

Investment activities in material production field usually will stop and move to other areas once they encounter the diminishing marginal effect. Nevertheless, unlike other investment activities, poverty relief is an investment in people, and it should not follow the law of material investment. The most notable Chinese characteristic in this field is manifested by this distinction. Between 2010 and 2017, poverty relief fund provided by state revenue continued to grow steadily at an annual average of 21.3%. Only under the fundamental guidance of people-centered development epistemology, can China make such unremitting efforts to alleviate poverty and such solemn promise to eradicate poverty. Following the same logic, poverty reduction constitutes the return from poverty relief effort, an investment in people, and the "law" of diminishing marginal effect does not apply in China. As the 2020 target of building a moderately prosperous society in all respects approaches and "no one left behind" task becomes more difficult and realistic, the CPC Central Committee makes the solemn promise of zero rural poverty under the current standard, and establishes the corresponding strategic and tactical deployments.

Under the guidance of people-centered development principle and inside the shared development process of reform and opening-up, China implements special rural poverty relief strategy. We summarize China's poverty relief and reduction achievements and experiences with the following aspects.

First, implement all-round and whole society poverty relief by taking full advantage of the national system and maximizing social mobilization. As early as mid-1980s, a standing institution that leads the poverty relief effort was established at the central government level, making poverty relief not only an established strategy but also a continuous practice. In the forms of the "National 'Eight Seven' Poverty Relief Plan" and 10-year Outline of Rural Poverty Relief and Development, every phase has its own special key tasks and goals. Special funds for poverty relief are integrated into the central and provincial government budgets, with ever rising scales. Moreover, social security system such as urban and rural minimum living security system and social assistance is established; meanwhile charity is growing and its corresponding poverty relief mechanism is improving. All these works together with poverty reduction strategies and complement those strategies. Since the reform, especially since the 18th CPC National Congress, China mobilizes the strength of the whole Party, the whole country and the whole society, adhering to the targeted poverty relief and targeted poverty alleviation, and becomes a social intervention experiment that attracts worldwide attention.

Second, as the stage of economic development changes, poverty relief focus is constantly adjusted, and the policy and measures concentrate more on the poor population. As the poor population distribution changes from widely distributed across the country to increasingly concentrated in vulnerable areas and among disadvantaged families, the corresponding poverty relief strategy transforms accordingly, from the initial regional poverty relief and development, to the present stage where every poor family is registered and has their own file, and support measures directly target specific individuals. According to the different situations of marginalized poor population, government utilizes multiple initiatives and measures, such as assisting poor population with production and employment, helping migrants with moving and resettlement, providing official minimum guarantee policy for low income insurance recipients, and offering medical assistance. Besides, since 2000, certain coordinated regional development strategies, such as the Western Development Strategy, are implemented, eliminating the obstacles against poverty alleviation through more macro-level regional development, human resources, infrastructure, mechanisms and institutional efforts.

Finally, a constantly improving working mechanism is formed by absorbing all the experiences and lessons learned from previous stages into the next stage of poverty relief strategy. Looking at the overall and final goals, the Chinese Government's poverty relief efforts suffer many hardships but harvest outstanding results. It is a journey of exploration with successful experiences and lessons to learn. These experiences and lessons are fully reflected before they are absorbed into the new round of strategic ideas. In this way, an effective working mechanism is gradually formed. Since the 18th CPC National Congress, China establishes a working mechanism led by the Central Government, organized by provincial governments, and implemented by city and county level administrative units. The responsibility mechanism where Party and Government leaders take final and overall responsibility is strengthened. The working mechanism adheres to the overall pattern of poverty relief, focuses on combining poverty relief with ambition inspiration and with intellectual training, deepens the poverty relief cooperation between the eastern and western regions, and concentrates on overcoming poverty alleviation in severely poor areas.

1.5 Conclusions and Outlook

Under the background of reform and opening-up, through shared economic development and implementation of special poverty relief strategies, China has achieved the largest poverty reduction in human history in the past 40 years, making tremendous contributions in reducing the world's poor population. In his keynote speech delivered at the World Economic Forum's Annual Meeting in 2017, President Xi Jinping quoted from Dunant, founder of the International Red Cross: "Our real enemy is not the neighboring country; it is hunger, poverty, ignorance, superstition and prejudice." Even in today's world, this sentence still resonates well and hits the target.

According to World Bank, in 2013, 766 million people worldwide still earn less than USD 1.9 per day (purchasing power parity 2011), and 36.4% of them live in those low-income countries that account for only 8.4% of the world. Therefore, in the *2030 Agenda for Sustainable Development* published in 2015, "end poverty in all its forms worldwide" is still ranked first among the 17 sustainable development goals. As a result, China's practice in poverty relief and poverty alleviation undoubtedly becomes a successful exploration into the law of development in human society, and the Chinese story, Chinese wisdom, and Chinese solution formulated from such practice should become a common spiritual asset for China and numerous other developing countries.

Practice has no end and exploration never stops. We firmly believe that, as long as we stick to the right guiding ideology and follow the established working methods, we are bound to steadily alleviate the last remaining rural poor population out of poverty and "leave no one behind", one of the goals in building a moderately prosperous society before 2020. Nevertheless, there's no end to safeguarding and to improving people's livelihood, only a continuous set of new starting points. The same happens for poverty relief and alleviation. We should work on the following issues in order to explore and to plan ahead for the upgraded post-2020 version of poverty relief and alleviation strategies.

First of all, we must maintain policy stability and sustainability in order to consolidate the poverty alleviation achievements. The work we do during the last phase of achieving total poverty alleviation in rural areas undoubtedly will be the hardest and we must give all we have. After we achieve the zero poverty goal, we must keep on working arduously in order to consolidate our success, and to prevent substantial return to poverty. Reaching poverty alleviation target is one thing, while obtaining the solid poverty alleviation capacity is another. For those farmers with income level close to the poverty line, a high probability of returning to poverty is expected. For example, in 2016, the disposable income per capita for those famers in the lowest 20% group is RMB 3006, only slightly above the poverty line in that year.[12] Both the long-term factors, such as the slower growth of migrant workers due to changes in

[12] See Li, P., Wei, H., Wu, G. (eds) (2017). *China's Poverty Relief Report 2017*. Beijing: Social Science Academic Press, 59–60.

demographics of rural population, and the periodic factors, such as price fluctuations of agricultural products, may lead the farmers in this group back to poverty. Therefore, the key policy must control the dynamic balance between poverty alleviation and return to poverty, keeping the poverty alleviation rate higher than the return rate.

Second, we should pay close attention to and proactively tackle new causes of poverty. With the deepening of aging population degree, the number of elders and people with disabilities continue to expand, leading to increased disabled population, who become the new source for poor population. Aging population by itself and problems of disability derived from aging lead to loss or weakening of labor capacity. Since the young labor force migrate from countryside to cities, the aging problem in rural areas becomes more severe than in urban areas, posing serious challenges to consolidate the achievements of poverty alleviation. We need to consider these new challenges in our strategies to address population aging; at the same time, our previous experience and working mechanism in poverty relief have to evolve with new times and new problems.

Third, we should cope with risk shock poverty. Generally speaking, periodic shocks such as financial crises are inevitable, and the resulting poverty will occur repeatedly; therefore, we cannot afford to slack even one bit in our anti-poverty war. Farmers are particularly vulnerable facing various risks, and those low-income farmers with income levels close to poverty line are even more vulnerable and sensitive to external impacts. For example, besides those periodic macro-economic phenomena, poor farmers are also particularly vulnerable to natural risks from agriculture, risks related to agricultural products, labor migration environment and changes in relationship between labor supply and demand.

Finally, we should explore long-term sustainable poverty reduction strategies. It may not exist for ever, but we have to admit that poverty will persist for a long time. There are endless arguments in the theoretical community around the absolute or relative nature of poverty. One theory divides poverty into the absolute type and the relative type. For post-2020 China, relative poverty will be a long-standing problem, and its coping mechanism differs from that for absolute poverty; therefore, we need to transform our institutions and methods through innovation. Another theory advocates different absolute poverty standards based on development stage or income level. For example, since October 2017, using different purchasing power parity income standards based on constant prices in 2011, the World Bank has set up absolute poverty lines for low-income countries, lower-middle-income countries, upper-middle-income countries and high-income countries, as USD 1.9, 3.2, 5.5 and 21.7 per day respectively (Ferreira & Sanchez, 2017).

We need to point out that, the reason we set up separate poverty standards for middle-income and high-income countries is not because of the higher poverty alleviation standards, but because of the fact that higher the development stage is, higher cost there is to achieve the same poverty alleviation effects. According to the World Bank, China's GNI per capita in 2016 was current USD 8260, making China one of the upper-middle-income countries. If we use the poverty standard of USD 5.5 PPP, we would face a more difficult task in poverty reduction even after we meet the goal of zero poverty in rural area by China's current standards (between USD 1.9 and 3.2). If by 2020, China's GNI per capita exceeds the number that divides middle-income and high-income countries (for example USD 12,055),[13] we would face even tougher challenges.

References

Bai, C., & Qian, Z. (2009). Who's squeezing residents' income? Analysis on China's National Income Distribution Pattern. *Social Sciences in China (Zhongguo Shehui Kexue), 5*, 99–115.

Barrett, C. B., Carter, M. R., & Timmer, C. P. (2010). A century-long perspective on agricultural development. *Am. J. Agric. Econ., 92*(2), 447–468.

Cai, F. (2017). Analysis of the effects of China's economic reform: A perspective of labor reallocation. *Economic Research Journal (Jingji Yanjiu), 52*(7), 4–17.

Cai, F., Du, Y., Gao, W., & Wang, M. (2009). *Labor economics: Theory and China's reality*. Beijing Normal University Press, 220

Chenery, H. B., & Strout, A. M. (1966). Foreign assistance and economic development. *The American Economic Review, LVI*(4), 679–733.

Du, Y., Park, A., & Wang, S. (2005). Migration and rural poverty in China. *Journal of Comparative Economics, 33*(4), 688–709.

Ferreira, F. & Sanchez, C. (2017, October 13). A richer Array of international poverty lines. *Let's talk development*, Accessed Aug 29, 2018, from http://blogs.worldbank.org/developmenttalk

Gao, W., Zhao, W., Cheng, J. (2011). Impact of rural labor mobility on statistics of income gap between urban and rural residents. In Cai, F. Report No.12 on China's population and labor issues—challenges during the 12th Five-Year period: Population, employment and income distribution., Social Sciences Academic Press, 228–242

Hayek, F. (1967). *Studies in Philosophy, Politics and Economics*. Routledge and Kegan Paul.

Zhu, L., & He, W. (2018). Rural poverty alleviation in the process of industrialization and urbanization. *Studies in Labor Economics, 4*, 4–32.

Fang Cai, research fellow at Chinese Academy of Social Sciences.

[13] Regarding the classification standards, see World Bank Data Team. New country classifications by income level: 2018–2019, July 1, 2018, http://blogs.worldbank.org/opendata/new-country-classifications-income-level-2018-2019

Chapter 2
Hierarchy of Cities and the Income Gap among Urban Residents

Chuliang Luo and Jinjun Xue

Abstract Based on data from Urban Household Survey (2009), this paper analyzes the regional income gap among urban residents from the perspective of hierarchy of cities. The main findings include: large income gap exists among residents in cities of different hierarchical levels, and the hierarchical gap among cities amounts to about 11% of the overall gap, larger than the hierarchical gap among the three major economic regions (eastern, central and western); regression analysis shows that hierarchy of cities plays an important and significant role in income determination, even when other variables that affect income are controlled. The impact of hierarchy of cities on income gap is different on the different quantiles on income distribution. Generally speaking, the importance of hierarchy of cities increases as the quantile of income distribution get higher, yet at the highest quantile, its importance decreases. Furthermore, this paper decomposes the income gap among cities of different hierarchical levels in terms of mean value and relevant quantiles. Generally speaking, the income gap among cities of different hierarchical levels is caused by the disparity of income determination mechanism (coefficient), especially by the constant term; on the contrary. The impact of the variables representing characteristics of different populations is relatively low, and this fact is reflected when the income determination mechanism shows fragmentation among cities of different hierarchical levels.

Keywords Income gap · Hierarchy of cities · Regional gap

C. Luo
Capital University of Economics and Business, Beijing, China

J. Xue (✉)
Nagoya University of Japan, Nagoya, Japan
e-mail: lvqs@ssap.cn

F. Cai (ed.), *Income Inequality and Poverty Governance in China*, International Research on Poverty Reduction, https://doi.org/10.1007/978-981-95-5063-0_2

2.1 Introduction

The rapid rise in income gap among Chinese residents has become an indisputable fact, and researchers are eager to interpret it from various perspectives. The detailed analysis of groups of people with different incomes draws the following general conclusions: the income gap among urban residents rises faster than that among rural residents, and the regional income gap plays a very important role in explaining the internal income gap among urban and rural residents. Publications on regional gap usually emphasize income gap among different provinces, or among the eastern, central and western economic regions. These gaps are attributed to the horizontal gap among regions. It is called horizontal gap because such theories believe that different regions have the same economic status in economic resource allocation decisions. Yet this view fails to capture the unique phenomenon inside China's economic structure, that is, differences exist among different types of regions in resource control and in resource allocation competence, and governments at different levels in the hierarchy have unequal status in economic decision-making, as the economic behaviors of lower-level governments need to obey policy of higher authorities. In the pyramid structure of government agencies, those on upper levels usually have greater capabilities to mobilize resources; therefore, as micro-economic entities, they enjoy more opportunities to collect benefits. In terms of the flow of production factors, both labor and investment have a clear tendency to cluster towards higher administrative levels. The direct cause for such clustering tendency is monetary, since higher administrative regions make it easier to make money, providing higher salary income and more employment opportunities. This may signify that among regions of different administrative levels inside the hierarchy, there is income gap that leads to labor mobility. This kind of income gap based on different administrative levels can be called the vertical gap among regions; compared to research on horizontal gap, study on vertical inequality is relatively rare.

There has been a considerable body of work on the trends in China's regional gap and its possible causes. During the reform and opening-up period, China's regional gap experienced a process of gradual reduction to continuous expansion, that is, in the early days of reform, regional gap gradually diminished; yet since 1990s, they continue to widen (Li & Xu, 2006; Fan & Zhu, 2002). Researchers tend to focus on the regional gap characteristics in the second stage, the continuous expansion stage. Government issued a series of economic policies and initiatives in order to reverse this trend. For example, the Western Development Strategy and the Revitalization of the Old Industrial Base in Northeast China were initiated in the late 1990s. Although such political interventions provide preferential policies to improve economic development in under developed regions, and have boosted the economic development in some less developed regions. But generally speaking, the development disparities among regions still persist and the overall pattern of underdeveloped areas lagging relatively behind has not been radically changed.

Facing this trend of regional gap, many researchers attempted to reveal its cause from different angles. Liu et al. (1994) and Hu et al. (1995) attribute the causes of widening regional gap to a low starting point for economic development, market failure, policy failure, decline of central financial resources, widening gap between workers and farmers and between urban and rural areas, different developmental models and so on (Dong, 2004). Among the discussions of some more specific determining factors, Cai and Du (2000) emphasize the impacts of human resources; while Wang and Fan (2004) believe that differences in productivity and the resulting capital flows are the main factors; in those discussions on the efficiency of resource allocation, Gong and Xie (2004) discover that while the regional disparities in capital marginal productivity remain basically stable, the differences in marginal productivity of labor force are gradually increasing. In those detailed discussions of institutional factors, the regional tilt of central government's investments (Yang, 1994; Wei, 1992), the regional disparities in the development of township enterprises (Zhang, 1999; Wan, 1998; Rozelle, 1994), enhanced local power (Raiser, 1998), regional differences in the degree of openness (Wei & Wu, 2001; Jian et al., 1996), and the regional disparities in infrastructures such as transportation (Demurger, 2001) are also among the factors stressed by researchers. As we already mentioned before, all the above literature are focused on the horizontal gap among different regions, and on the developmental disparities or income gaps among regions of different hierarchical levels. Huang and Wu (2008) and Ning (2014) realize the impacts of the hierarchy or size of cities on wage determination, but they draw two totally opposite conclusions. Huang and Wu (2008) find that workers with similar characteristics in provincial capitals earn 14% more than those in non-provincial capital cities; while Ning (2014) finds that big cities hold no income advantage in determining the income of migrant workers.

This paper attempts to analyze the income gap among regions at different levels in the administrative hierarchy by using the data from China's urban household survey. Our discussion is based on the administrative levels of the cities where participated households reside. Most analyses about regional gap within cities utilize provinces in the eastern, central or western region or county territories as their research objects; while we divide households into different groups according to different administrative levels. Based on China's administrative organization, we divide the all regions into five types: municipality directly under the Central Government (hereinafter referred as "municipality"), provincial capital or city specifically designated in the state plan, prefecture-level city (municipal district), county-level city and county.[1] We discuss the impact of city hierarchy on the income gap among urban residents. We hope this paper will help answer the following questions: How big a role does the administrative hierarchy play in the income gap of urban residents? What are the distribution characteristics of the income gap among regions of different administrative hierarchical levels? What are the manifestations

[1] The most ideal approach is to describe in detail the economic decision-making power for these five regional types in order to provide the corresponding institutional frameworks, but from publicly available information, we find it difficult to determine clear boundaries for the respective powers. Prefecture-level cities include those cities with municipal districts and Dong Guan of Guangdong province.

of such gap among populations with different characteristics? The rest of this paper is constructed as follows: the second part offers a descriptive analysis on income gap of urban residents in cities of different administrative hierarchical levels by using the data from household survey; third part provides a quantitative analysis on income gaps of urban residents caused by hierarchy of cities; it then decomposes the income gaps among cities of different hierarchical levels by the Oaxaca-Blinder method and by Unconditional Quantile Regression analysis, both based on the Income Function, in order to discuss the impacts of various factors on income gap at different quantiles; the final part draws the conclusions.

2.2 Data Illustration and Description of Income Gap among Cities of Different Hierarchical Levels

This paper uses data from urban household survey of 2009 in China, which collected data from 40,570 households and 117,620 individual samples in sixteen cities.[2] To serve this paper's purpose, we divide the samples into five classes based on their residence at the time of survey: municipality directly under the central government (including Beijing, Shanghai and Chongqing), provincial capital or city specifically designated in the state plan,[3] prefecture-level city, county-level city and county. The basic income indicator used is the disposable income of urban residents, including wage, business income, property income and transfer income. We make weighted adjustments for all these income indicators in their calculation processes in the form of family income per capita. It is necessary to point out that data in this paper is not adjusted for purchasing power parity (PPP) among regions.[4] We know intuitively that there are serious disparities among regions in their monetary PPP. Unfortunately, research on inter-regional monetary PPP is relatively rare, and they all concentrate on the province level; therefore, they have limited use for this paper. Further and more in-depth evaluations and adjustments on monetary PPP indexes in different cities within the same province would be more significant for this paper, yet current research cannot provide useful references on such adjustments.

[2]The sixteen provinces and cities include: Beijing, Shanxi, Liaoning, Heilongjiang, Shanghai, Jiangsu, Anhui, Jiangxi, Shandong, Henan, Hubei, Guangdong, Chongqing, Sichuan, Yunnan, and Gansu.

[3]Cities specifically designated in the state plan referred in this paper include Dalian, Qingdao, and Shenzhen.

[4]An important reason for making currency purchasing power parity adjustments is to obtain an income measure that is closer to people's true welfare. However, non-monetary income are among the factors that constitute this true welfare, and they are very important for urban residents of different regions, yet currently it is almost impossible to accurately measure the true welfare disparities caused by the supply of public goods and public services. Therefore, this paper continues to use the currency income as the main analysis object.

Table 2.1 shows the individual sampling characters, income per capita levels and income structures for cities of different hierarchical levels. In terms of sampling compositions, prefecture-level cities account for the largest proportion with 48.93%, representing almost half of the samples; while both county-level cities and counties account for less than 10%. We cannot find relevant statistics for the overall population distribution among cities of different hierarchical levels so we cannot determine the differences between our samples and the population. In terms of income levels, municipalities have the highest income per capita, while counties have the lowest; in terms of the mean income value, the former is twice as much as the latter. Generally speaking, residents in high-level cities usually have higher income per capita levels. This holds true for the most itemized incomes; for wage income and pension income, this trend is extremely strong. Wage income per capita of municipalities is more than RMB 10,000 higher than that of county-level cities or that of counties, more than double of the latter, while the former's pension per capita is also more than double that of the latter. We need to point out that the wage and pension per capita are calculated based on the average value of all household members, not limited to working members or retirees. Research on residents' income distribution usually assumes that income from all sources is equally shared among all household members.

Table 2.2 lists details of wage and pension per capita when we limit samples to working age population and to population over 60 years old respectively. The distributions for these two incomes among cities of different hierarchical levels are similar to those shown in Table 2.1, while Table 2.2 seems to have narrowed income gaps between different hierarchical levels. For example, among the population over 60, most individuals in municipalities can claim pensions, while at county level this percentage is only 71%, 25 percentage points lower than the former. This shows that cities in higher hierarchical level have better social security systems. This characteristic is also illustrated by the last column of Table 1, which lists the social security expenses. As a component of disposable income, social security expenditure is usually deducted automatically, so its nature and function are more similar to the forced savings for the future. Table 1 shows that social security expenses of residents in municipalities are 3.7 times to those of residents in counties. In terms of relative levels, the former accounts for 10.85% of the disposable income, while the latter accounts for merely 5.84%.

In order to compare the income levels of residents who occupy the same positions in the income distribution of different city types, Fig. 2.1 shows the relative income levels at different quantiles in various hierarchical regions. In Fig. 2.1, the income levels of county residents are standardized to 1. We observe a very interesting trend: the relative incomes of "provincial capitals or cities specifically designated in the state plan", of "prefecture-level cities", and of "county-level cities" that relative to counties' show clear increasing tendencies as the quantiles rise. Among the high-end people in the income distributions of various regions, the relative income advantage of cities at higher hierarchical level is more obvious. Yet this trend is absent in municipalities, where changes in relative income show no obvious trend, instead they seem rather stable. This means among residents in municipalities, those in low-end income groups have bigger relative

Table 2.1 Income levels and compositions of cities of different hierarchical levels

	Proportion of population	Income per capita (RMB)	Wage income (RMB)	Business income (RMB)	Property income (RMB)	Pension (RMB)	Other transfer income (RMB)	Personal income tax (RMB)	Spending on social security (RMB)
Municipality	16.27	25,290.39	19,983.48	1119.95	490.82	5962.19	1004.40	−526.23	−2744.23
Provincial capital or city specifically designated in the state plan	19.32	19,772.97	14,108.99	1679.27	603.59	4653.75	748.03	−184.31	−1836.36
Prefecture-level city	48.93	15,827.41	11,371.42	1318. 83	366.22	3435.32	802.47	−62.34	−1404. 52
County-level city	6.80	14,191.46	9826.85	1648.86	226.24	2960.98	595.83	−40.25	−1027.04
County	8.67	12,609.82	8832.08	1471.13	228.30	2257.06	573.55	−15.84	−736.47
Ratio of municipalities to Counties	–	2.01	2.26	0.76	2.15	2.64	1.75	33.22	3.73
Total	100	17,739.39	12,976.53	1391.79	410.88	3947.51	790.90	−155.86	−1622.36

Source: Calculated based on data from 2009 household survey in urban China

Table 2.2 Wage and pension details of specific population

	Wage per capita (16–60 working age population)		Pension per capita (population above 60)		Proportion of population above 60 who collect social security (percent)
	Number of samples (person)	average value (RMB)	Number of samples (person)	Average value (RMB)	
Municipality	10,657	35,000.72	2409	22,617.16	96.47
Provincial capital or city specifically designated in the state plan	11,144	28,094.23	3386	20,148.39	90.67
Prefecture-level city	27,924	22,766.83	7863	15,836.87	83.47
County-level city	3718	20,385.05	1148	13,777.78	75.52
County	4637	18,818.92	1263	11,552.79	71.26
Ratio of municipalities to counties	–	1.8599	–	1.9577	–
Total	58,080	25,566.13	16,069	17,278.02	85.41

Source: Calculated based on data from 2009 household survey in urban China

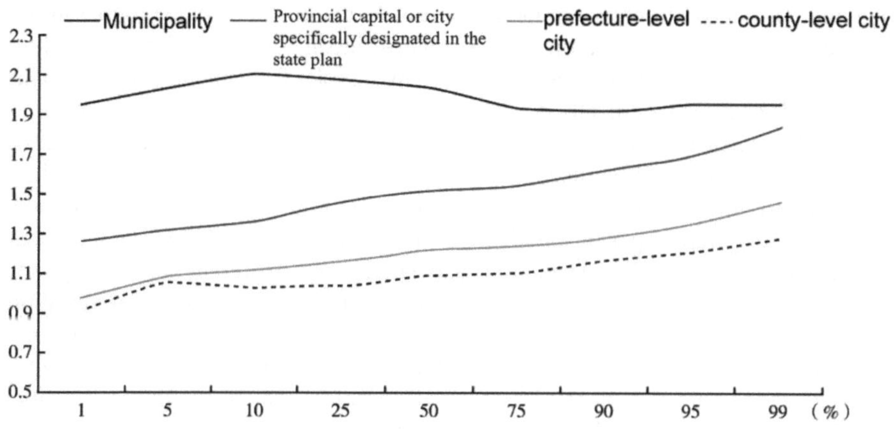

Fig. 2.1 Relative income levels at different quantiles (county = 1). Source: Calculated based on data from 2009 household survey in urban China

advantages. We need to remind readers that such a trend of relative incomes in municipalities may be caused by sampling deviation in the household survey. High-income households may be more resistant to the survey, and such resistance may have led to insufficient sampling of high-income households. Sampling deviation caused by this type of resistance may be more prominent in the samples of, municipalities discussed in this paper, because usually high-income populations tend to reside in such regions. At the same time, these regions attract the majority of migrant workers from countryside. Current urban household surveys lack effective coverage for migrant workers and this in turn leads to overestimation of income levels for local low-income populations.

Table 2.3 equally sorts all samples into 10 groups according to the personal income from low to high, and lists the distribution characteristics of individual samples at each city level in each income group, as well as the relative levels of income per capita by city level within each income group. In terms of income group structure, municipality residents are mostly concentrated in high-income groups, as 19% and 22% of them are inside group 9 and the highest group respectively. These figures are much higher than those in other urban areas of the hierarchy: for example, provincial capitals or cities specifically designated in the state plan only have 12% and 13% of their residents inside the top two income groups, 7 and 9 percentage points lower than the former respectively. Only 2% of municipality residents are inside the lowest two income groups, and the number for provincial capitals or cities specifically designated in the state plan for the two lowest groups is 7%. Residents of the counties or county-level cities have the opposite distributions: 16% of their individual samples are inside the lowest group that is 10% of all income samples, while only 2.37% of county samples and 4.94% of county-level cities' samples are among the highest income groups. The distributions of residents of different hierarchical levels inside income groups are consistent with the distributions of the income per capita level of the residents at cities of different hierarchical levels. In terms of the relative income of different samples within each income group, the income levels of different samples in the middle-income groups are relatively close, while in the low-end and high-end groups of the income distribution, there is a large difference in income levels. In the lowest income group, samples from county-level cities have the highest relative income, slightly higher than those from counties; while in the highest income group, samples from municipalities, provincial capitals or cities specifically designated in the state plan have higher incomes.

The degree of inequality of income distribution inside each hierarchical level also shows obvious differences (see Table 2.4). In terms of Gini coefficient, Municipality and county have relatively small internal gaps, while other regions have relatively high disparities, with Gini coefficient at around 0.33. The latter also have high MLD (Mean Log Deviation) and Theil index. Different income gap indicators offer slightly different relative rankings. In terms of coefficient of variation, cities of higher hierarchical level seem to have greater internal income gap. Nevertheless, county-level cities usually show relatively low internal income gap in terms of various measurements. Based on all samples from 16 provinces and cities in this paper, the urban Gini coefficient is 0.3448, which is slightly higher than 0.335, the Gini coefficient of cities and towns nationwide (Zhang & Wu, 2004).

Table 2.5 shows the relative importance of inter-group inequality among cities of different hierarchical levels. We use MLD and Theil index to decompose the overall inequality into inter-group inequality and intra-group inequality.[5] Based on

[5] Theil index and mean log deviation are two special cases of the generalized entropy (GE) index. The GE index is decomposable among groups. We can decompose the overall gap into inter-group gap and intra-group gap $GE(\alpha) = GE_b(\alpha) + GE_w(\alpha)\alpha$: $GE(a) = GE_b(a) + GE_w(a)$, where a α is sensitivity coefficient, usually taken as 1 or 0, representing Theil index or Mean logarithmic deviation $GE_w(\alpha) = \underset{i}{?} p_i GE_i(\alpha) GE_b(\alpha) = \underset{i}{?} p_i \log(p_i / p_i)$., $GE_b(a) = \sum_i \pi_i \log(\pi_i / p_i)$, where π_i $p_i p_i$ is population share, $GE_i(\alpha)$ $GE_i(a)$ $GE_i(\alpha)$ is GE index, and p_i p_i p_i is income share for its group respectively.

Table 2.3 City hierarchy composition in each income group and relative income of each income group

	Share (percent)					Relative income (county = 1)				
All samples income groups	Municipality	Provincial capital or city specifically designated in the state plan	Prefecture-level city	County-level city	County	Municipality	Provincial capital or city specifically designated in the state plan	Prefecture-level city	County-level city	County
Lowest group	2.19	7.05	11.71	16.01	16.87	0.9807	0.9577	0.9680	1.0085	1
Group 1	2.49	7.58	11.76	13.85	16.53	1.0051	0.9970	0.9968	0.9944	1
Group 2	3.18	7.78	11.88	12.67	15.01	1.0038	1.0027	0.9999	1.0007	1
Group 4	5.48	9.31	11.12	11.72	12.31	1.0069	1.0028	0.9995	1.0006	1
Group 5	7.20	10.15	10.77	10.36	10.32	1.0059	1.0015	1.0008	1.0004	1
Group 6	9.45	10.78	10.13	9.85	8.70	1.0052	1.0006	1.0020	1.0002	1
Group 7	12.68	11.03	9.56	8.12	6.62	1.0033	1.0000	0.9988	0.9974	1
Group 8	15.77	11.58	8.44	6.36	7.27	1.0100	1.0054	1.0060	1.0106	1
Group 9	19.09	11.86	7.85	6.12	4.00	1.0101	1.0133	1.0034	1.0026	1
Highest group	22.47	12.88	6.77	4.94	2.37	1.1345	1.1504	1.1177	1.1009	1
Total	100	100	100	100	100	2.0056	1.5681	1.2552	1.1254	1

Source: Calculated based on data from 2009 Household survey in urban China

Table 2.4 Income gap within different hierarchical regions

	Gini coefficient	Coefficient of variation	Mean log deviation (MLD)	Theil index
Municipality	0.2938	0.8807	0.1505	0.1657
Provincial capital or city specifically designated in the state plan	0.3375	0.7295	0.1962	0.1986
Prefecture-level city	0.3346	0.7155	0.1920	0.1948
County-level city	0.3332	0.7040	0.1876	0.1915
County	0.3012	0.5951	0.1526	0.1510
All samples	0.3448	0.8176	0.2042	0.2087

Source: Calculated based on data from 2009 household survey in urban China

hierarchy of cities, inter-group inequality usually is about 11%, that is, income gap among cities of different hierarchical levels accounts for about 11% of the overall urban income gap. To facilitate comparison, Table 2.5 also lists the inter-group Theil indexes based on the traditional eastern-central-western economic regions and on provinces, as well as their contribution shares to the overall income gap. Hierarchical gap among cities has higher relative contribution share than the regional inequality based on eastern-central-western regional division, and slightly lower share than the provincial gap based on provinces. Therefore, the hierarchical gap among cities plays a very important role in the overall income gap among urban residents.

2.3 Regression Analysis of Income Inequality among Cities of Different Hierarchical Levels

2.3.1 Basic Ideas and Description of Variables

We can use the following equation to perform regression analysis of the impact of city hierarchy on residents' income:

$$\ln Y = a + \gamma citylevel + \beta X$$

Here, $\ln Y$ is the income logarithm, *citylevel* is a group of virtual variables representing the hierarchical level of cities, and X is other control variable. As shown in Fig. 2.1 and Table 2.3, the impact of city hierarchy on income may change with the different quantiles of income distribution. Therefore, we adopt the re-centered

Table 2.5 Relative importance of inter-group inequality of hierarchy of cities

	Hierarchy of Cities	Eastern-central-western region	Province
Theil index of inter-group	0.0226	0.0163	0.0290
Share of Total Theil index (percent)	10.86	7.81	13.90
MLD index of inter-group	0.0219	0.0166	0.0279
Share of Total MLD index (percent)	10.71	8.15	13.64

Source: Calculated based on data from 2009 household survey in urban China

influence function (RIF) proposed by Firpo et al. (2007, 2009) to perform unconditional regression analysis, in order to discuss the impacts of the relevant variables on different quantiles of income distribution.

Refocusing influence function at quantile τ r τ is defined as

$$\mathrm{RIF}(\mathrm{Y};\mathrm{q_t}) = \mathrm{q_t} + \frac{\mathrm{t} - \mathrm{I}(\mathrm{Y} = \mathrm{q_t})}{\mathrm{f_Y}(\mathrm{q_t})} \; RIF(Y;q_\tau) = q_\tau + \frac{\tau - I(Y \le q_\tau)}{f_Y(q_\tau)} \; \mathrm{RIF}(\mathrm{Y};\mathrm{q_t}) = \mathrm{q_t} + \frac{\mathrm{t} - \mathrm{I}(\mathrm{Y} = \mathrm{q_t})}{\mathrm{f_Y}(\mathrm{q_t})},$$

where q_τ must satisfy the condition $P(Y \le q_\tau) = \tau$ $(0 < \tau < 1)$, $P(.)$ is the probability distribution, $I(.)$ is indicator function, and f_Y is marginal density function of Y. From τ and the definition of indicator function $I(.)$, we know that $\mathrm{E(RIF(Y;q_t))} = \mathrm{q_t}$ $E(RIF(Y;q_r)) = q_r$. If $E(RIF(Y;q_\tau)|X) = X\beta$ then $q_\tau(Y) = E(X)\beta_\tau$, β_τ is the marginal effect of explanatory variables on the income level at the quantile τ.

Oaxaca-Blinder method is usually used to decompose and analyze the income determinations of different groups, as it can decompose the differences in average income levels of different populations or different points of time into various specific factors. In order to decompose the income disparities among cities of different hierarchical levels into various factors, this paper estimates the corresponding income function at each city level, and performs the decomposition using the Oaxaca-Blinder method. Selecting different reference groups in the equation will lead to differences in decomposition results, and this paper chooses the following decomposition method:

$$\ln Y^s - \ln Y^g = \left(\mathrm{X^s} - \mathrm{X^g}\right)\frac{\left(\beta^s + \beta^g\right)}{2} + \frac{\left(X^s + X^g\right)}{2}\left(\beta^s - \beta^g\right) \tag{2.1}$$

Here the superscripts are used to mark different groups of people; the first item on the right side of the Eq. (2.1) demonstrates the differences in variables between two groups and their impacts on income disparities; the second item demonstrates the differences of the income function coefficients between two groups and their impacts on income gaps, showing that even though individuals in different groups may share the same characteristics, but the mere fact that they belong to different groups causes disparity among their incomes. Yet the above equation can only be used to decompose mean values, so in order to decompose the all characteristics of income distribution, this paper performs decomposition analysis on income disparities of various income distribution quantiles based on the quantile regression method.

Based on the result of quantile regression, the difference on quantile τ of $q_t(ln\mathrm{Y})$ between s and g group can be decomposed as:

$$q_r\left(\ln Y^s\right)-q_r\left(\ln Y^g\right)=\left(X^s-X^g\right)\frac{\left(\beta_r^s+\beta_r^g\right)}{2}+\frac{\left(X^s+X^g\right)}{2}\left(\beta_r^s-\beta_r^g\right) \quad (2.2)$$

The first item on the right hand side of Eq. (2.2) represents the variable (endowment) feature variation effect, the second item depicts how the changes of coefficient returns impact the income of given groups.

To estimate the income function, beside the variable representing city hierarchy, we include several other explaining variables and their mean values in cities of different hierarchical levels. Table 6 shows these variables such as age of head household, their education level, and employment status of household members. In terms of age of head of household, the mean age of all samples is 48.76, and there is no significant difference among cities in different hierarchical levels. Those who reside in provincial capitals or cities specifically designated in the state plan are oldest with mean age of 49.55, while those in counties are youngest with a mean age of 47.80. Roughly speaking, household heads in samples from municipalities, provincial capitals, or cities specifically designated in the state plan are relatively older, while those from other regions are younger.

The education levels of household heads show rather significant differences among cities of various hierarchical levels. Overall, in all city types, junior high school and high school graduates have the highest share of all samples, accounting for about 60%. County-level cities have the highest percentage of junior high school or high school graduates at their household heads, at 65%; while provincial capitals or cities specifically designated in the state plan have the lowest percentage of 57%. The difference between the two types is eight percentage points. The higher the city level, the higher the average level of education of the household heads is. This characteristic is more prominent among people with higher education or with primary school or lower level education. As shown in Table 2.6, the proportion of heads of household with primary school education and below gradually increases from municipalities to counties. They account for 3.61% in municipalities, and 9.74% in county samples, a six percentage point difference between the two types of cities. Heads of household with bachelor degree or above account for about 10% of samples in county-level cities and counties, while 17.49% of samples in municipalities have the same education levels. The rest are provincial capitals (16.73%) and prefecture-level cities (12.42%). This difference in the distribution of education levels

Table 2.6 Mean values of other explaining variables of income function

	Municipality	Provincial capital or city specifically designated in the state plan	Prefecture-level city	County-level city	County	All Samples
Age of household heads	49.09	49.55	48.50	48.79	47.80	48.76
Household heads with primary school education or lower	0.0361	0.0644	0.0811	0.0924	0.0974	0.0727
Household heads with junior high school education	0.2672	0.2519	0.2872	0.2979	0.2870	0.2778
Household heads with high school education	0.3228	0.3201	0.3274	0.3507	0.3204	0.3262
Household heads with college degree	0.1990	0.1964	0.1802	0.1638	0.1949	0.1865
Household heads with bachelor degree or above	0.1749	0.1673	0.1242	0.0952	0.1003	0.1367
Family size (person)	3.0352	3.0908	3.1100	3.1848	3.2687	3.1130
Proportion of male members in a household	0.4934	0.4966	0.4953	0.4986	0.5000	0.4959
Proportion of employment in competitive sectors	0.1089	0.1245	0.1182	0.1045	0.1055	0.1159
Proportion of employment in monopoly sectors	0.2298	0.1761	0.1766	0.1887	0.2366	0.1913
Proportion of the person-in-charge	0.0217	0.0228	0.0196	0.0194	0.0245	0.0210
Proportion of the professionals and technical personnel	0.1464	0.1186	0.1091	0.1112	0.1094	0.1172
Proportion of clerks	0.1563	0.1435	0.1383	0.1337	0.1608	0.1439
Proportion of state-owned sectors	0.2836	0.2267	0.2370	0.2199	0.2461	0.2422

(continued)

Table 2.6 (continued)

	Municipality	Provincial capital or city specifically designated in the state plan	Prefecture-level city	County-level city	County	All Samples
Proportion of private sectors	0.0919	0.1238	0.1336	0.1550	0.1599	0.1287
Coverage rate of pension	0.7094	0.7257	0.6371	0.5456	0.3975	0.6390
Eastern region	0.8518	0.4885	0.4913	0.5437	0.3486	0.5406
Central region	0.0000	0.3040	0.3844	0.2842	0.3314	0.2949
Western region	0.1482	0.2075	0.1243	0.1721	0.3200	0.1645

Source: Calculated based on data from 2009 household survey in urban China

is similar to the relative status of income distribution among cities of different hierarchical levels.[6]

Although family size has similar mean values for cities of different hierarchical levels, it also shows certain patterns. Municipalities have the smallest family size, while county samples have the biggest. The difference between the two is only 0.13 person. Generally speaking, family size is increasing from municipalities to counties. In terms of mean values among cities of different levels, male members usually account for about 50% of the household in all levels of cities.

Employment status of household members plays an important role in determining the family income per capita. This paper describes the employment structure of household members from the following three aspects: the competitiveness of the industry, career types, and ownership of the industry. Industry competitiveness is determined by its type.[7] Provincial capitals and specific plan cities have the highest percentage of household members who work in competitive sectors with 12.45%, while counties have the lowest percentage in competitive sectors; counties and municipalities have the top two percentages of household members who work in monopoly sectors, while other types of cities have lower percentages. In terms of career types, the percentage of household members who are persons-in-charge is similar across different levels of cities, representing around 2%; municipalities have 3 percentage points more of household members who are professionals and

[6]Differences in education levels among samples from cities of different hierarchical levels are more pronounced in the working-age population (between 16 and 60 years).

[7]Competitive industries include agriculture, forestry, animal husbandry, fishery, mining, construction, accommodation and catering, leasing and business services, resident services and other service Monopoly industries include the following sectors: production and supply of electricity, gas and water, financial industry, scientific research, technical service and geological exploration, water conservancy, environmental and public facilities management, education, health, social security and social welfare, culture, sports, entertainment, public management and social organization, among others. Other industries are between these two types and are used as the reference. This classification is borrowed from ideas of Bian and Zhang (2002).

technical personnel than all the other city types; municipalities and counties have relatively more family members who are clerks.[8] In terms of ownership, municipalities have the highest percentage of members who work at state-owned sectors, followed by county samples, with county-level cities as the lowest. The difference between the highest and lowest regions is about 6 percentage points. As for private sectors, counties have the highest percentage, and municipalities have the lowest. Generally speaking, the lower the city hierarchical level, the higher the percentage of residents employed in private sectors.

The last group contains control variables describing regional characteristics that are divided into two types: one uses the commonly division of eastern-central-western region; the other uses the pension insurance coverage rate, measured by the proportion of people who have pension insurance among all employees, and reflects the social security situation from the standard degree of the employment market. We see from Table 6 that, municipalities, provincial capitals, or cities specifically designated in the state plan have the highest pension insurance coverage rates with 70% or above, while counties have the lowest with less than 40%. In terms of the three regional divisions, county samples are more evenly distributed in all three regions, with each around one third; while other city types seem to tilt toward the eastern region, and their presence in the western region is significantly lower.

2.3.2 Overall Impact of City Hierarchy on Income Distribution

Table 2.7 lists the regression results of income gap of urban residents at different city levels. In Table 2.7, two types of classification are used to represent city hierarchy: the first puts municipalities, provincial capitals or cities specifically designated in the state plan into one type called metropolis; the second continues the same five hierarchical levels as before and uses municipalities as the reference group. The estimated results consider the different scenarios of controlling separately other income determining variables listed at Table 2.6. The explained variable is the family income per capita. We assume that family income is evenly distributed among all family members and weighted adjustment by family size.

Results from the first two columns of Table 2.7 show that "metropolis" has significant impact on its residents' income. If we do not control other variables depicting individual characteristics, the relative advantage of income per capita of residents in metropolis is 47%[9]; if we control those variables, the relative advantage caused by metropolis reduces to 28%. The last two columns of Table 2.7 divide cities into five hierarchical types and use municipalities as reference group. The estimated coefficients for regional variables of all other hierarchical types are

[8] According to the household survey, clerks include administrative staff, political security staff, postal and telecommunication staff, other clerks and related personnel.

[9] Because the estimation uses a logarithmic model, we calculate by using the equation of exp. (b)-1, where b is the estimated coefficient.

Table 2.7 Impact of city hierarchy on income

	All Samples	All Samples	All Samples	All Samples
Metropolis	0.3881 (103.55) ***	0.2467 (73.13) ***		
Provincial capital or city specifically designated in the state plan			−0.2912 (48.92) ***	−0.1989 (37.98) ***
Prefecture-level city			−0.5097 (100.67) ***	−0.3449 (75.92) ***
County-level city			−0.6145 (76.07) ***	−0.4122 (58.47) ***
County			−0.6981 (93.85) ***	−0.4214 (60.93) ***
Other control variables	No	Yes	No	Yes
Sample size	117,579	117,579	117,579	117,579
F statistics	10,723.02	3361.63	3592.41	3024.08
Adjusted R^2	0.0836	0.3519	0.1089	0.3613

Note: ***, **and * show significance at 1%, 5% and 10% respectively; numbers inside parenthesis are t statistics; reference group is municipalities; estimated results from constants are omitted
Source: Calculated based on data from 2009 household survey in urban China

significantly negative, meaning that the relative income levels of urban residents in those regions are significantly lower than the reference group. The estimated coefficients are also related to whether we control other individual characteristic variables that determine income. When we add those controlled variables, the estimated coefficients of hierarchy variable declined. Compared with the reference group, the provincial capitals or cities specifically designated in the state plan have the smallest gaps in income per capita. When other variables are not controlled, the latter is 25% lower than the former. When other variables are controlled, the difference still amounts to 18%. Counties have the biggest gap in income per capita. Their value is 50% lower than the reference group with uncontrolled variables. But this difference drops to 34% when other variables are controlled. When we compare the estimated results from the last column of Table 7, we can see that whether to control other individual characteristic variables that affect income or not has great difference in the impact on the change of estimation coefficient of each city hierarchy. Roughly speaking, whether to control other income affecting variables or not has the least effect on the change of the estimated coefficient of "provincial capital or city specifically designated in the state plan", and has the greatest impact on "county". This situation shows the relevance between income inequality among city hierarchy and other control variables that affect income. The results from the last column of Table 7 show that after other income affecting variables are controlled, there is no significant difference between "county-level city" and "county".

Figure 2.2 shows the influence coefficients on different quantiles of income distribution based on quantile regression of city-level variables. In most cases, the absolute values of the estimated coefficients for all hierarchy variables show an

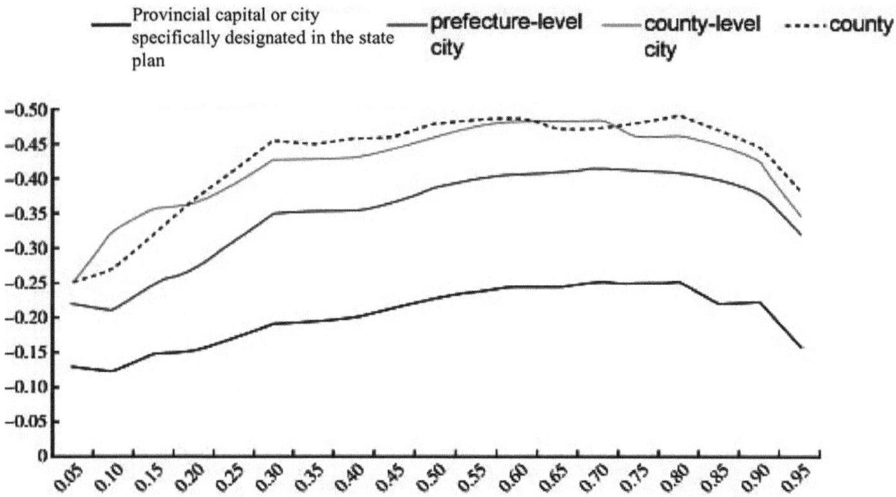

Fig. 2.2 Estimated coefficients of city hierarchy at different quantiles of income distribution (other variables controlled). Source: Calculated based on data from 2009 household survey in urban China

increasing trend with the rise of the quantiles, and such trend only changes at the 85% quantile. This phenomenon means that, generally speaking, hierarchy variables have greater impacts on high-income residents. Since the Y-axis is ordered on the absolute value of the regression coefficient, we can see that provincial capitals or cities specifically designated in the state plan have the smallest gap from the reference group (municipalities), while the regression coefficient curves of all other hierarchy variables are located above the provincial capitals' curve. Even if we control other variables that impact urban residents' income, results from Fig. 2 still show that residents in lower-level cities have lower income. When we control other variables in the income function, county-level cities and counties show certain differences of relative income advantages at different quantiles, but overall, the two curves are quite close.

2.3.3 *Disparities in the Mean Income of Cities of Different Hierarchical Levels and Their Decomposition*

In order to perform the decomposition analysis on income gaps among cities of different hierarchical levels, we decompose various factors that cause such gaps based on the income functions of samples from different city levels. Table 2.8 lists the estimated results of income functions from different city levels. The last two columns combine the first five city levels into two types: "metropolis" includes

Table 2.8 Income functions of cities of different hierarchical levels

	Municipality	Provincial capital or city specifically designated in the state plan	Prefecture-level city	County-level city	County	Metropolis	County and city area
Age of household head	0.0017 (0.84)	−0.0142 (7.12)***	−0.0033 (2.46)***	0.0046 (1.38)	0.0143 (5.03)***	−0.0035 (2.43)***	−0.0001 (0.09)
Square of the age of household head /100	0.0097 (4.77)***	0.0215 (11.44) ***	0.0142 (10.91) ***	0.0055 (1.74)*	−0.0029 (1.07)	0.0132 (9.45) ***	0.011 (9.90)***
Head of household with junior high school education	0.2624 (13.64) ***	0.0652 (3.95) ***	0.1501 (16.51)***	0.2241 (10.38)***	0.1482 (8.54) ***	0.1531 (12.16) ***	0.1579 (20.61) ***
Head of household with high school education	0.3307 (17.05) ***	0.183 (11.08) ***	0.2774 (30.25) ***	0.303 (13.86) ***	0.2354 (13.29) ***	0.2449 (19.39) ***	0.2727 (35.24) ***
Head of household with college degree	0.4405 (21.95) ***	0.3436 (19.34) ***	0.4306 (41.89) ***	0.4249 (16.63) ***	0.3699 (18.03) ***	0.3734 (27.93) ***	0.4235 (48.41) ***
Head of household bachelor degree or above	0.6081 (29.42)***	0.4947 (26.65) ***	0.54 (47.87) ***	0.5038 (17.14)***	0.408 (16.89)***	0.5294 (38.15) ***	0.5274 (54.26)***
Family size	−0.0914 (22.90)***	−0.0999 (25.55)***	−0.1145 (49.73)***	−0.1452 (27.07)***	−0.1173 (25.84)***	−0.1004 (35.34)***	−0.1187 (61.22)***
Proportion of male members	0.0923 (4.67) ***	0.0866 (4.02) ***	0.1208 (8.76) ***	0.0895 (2.49)**	0.0799 (2.70) ***	0.0835 (5.57) ***	0.1121 (9.39) ***
Proportion of employment in competitive sectors	0.0666 (3.73) ***	−0.0225 (1.22)	−0.0297 (2.57)**	−0.0337 (1.08)	−0.021 (0.81)	0.0236 (1.80)*	−0.0184 (1.83)*
Proportion of employment in monopoly sectors	0.2361 (14.13) ***	0.2107 (10.55) ***	0.2417 (19.03) ***	0.1656 (4.63) ***	0.1774 (5.62) ***	0.2455 (18.52) ***	0.2217 (19.79) ***

Proportion of person-in-charge	0.6412 (17.24)***	0.4312 (10.65) ***	0.595 (22.37) ***	0.6623 (9.42)***	0.5202 (9.47)***	0.5108 (18.15)***	0.5893 (25.76)***
Proportion of the professionals and technical personnel	0.4425 (24.63) ***	0.3085 (14.54) ***	0.439 (32.05) ***	0.5287 (14.82) ***	0.4635 (13.87) ***	0.3739 (26.34) ***	0.4496 (37.48) ***
Proportion of clerks	0.3763 (21.77) ***	0.2765 (14.50) ***	0.3628 (29.31) ***	0.3208 (9.36) ***	0.42 (14.25) ***	0.3103 (23.60) ***	0.3648 (33.59) ***
Proportion of state-owned sectors	0.0112 (0.75)	0.175 (9.91) ***	0.1239 (10.77) ***	0.2233 (6.84) ***	0.2 (6.59) ***	0.1205 (10.28) ***	0.1309 (12.81) ***
Proportion of private sectors	0.1443 (7.46) ***	0.2985 (15.99) ***	0.1399 (12.25) ***	0.2874 (10.40) ***	0.2666 (11.45) ***	0.2202 (16.18) ***	0.1723 (17.71) ***
Coverage rate of pension	0.6183 (13.30) ***	0.2504 (7.15) ***	0.4401 (36.71) ***	0.5449 (18.62) ***	−0.0099 (0.45)	0.1083 (4.68) ***	0.4298 (46.22) ***
Central region		−0.2596 (29.02) ***	−0.1337 (26.92) ***	−0.1721 (12.30) ***	−0.1456 (11.52) ***	−0.3765 (53.99) ***	−0.1282 (29.31) ***
Western region	−0.3888 (39.74) ***	−0.241 (17.92) ***	−0.1652 (22.75) ***	−0.1635 (10.33) ***	0.045 (3.69) ***	−0.3509 (47.84) ***	−0.114 (19.66) ***
Constant	8.9241 (143.42)***	9.6302 (154.45)***	8.9039 (238.70)***	8.6914 (93.67)***	8.5736 (110.51)***	9.4861 (221.14)***	8.825 (276.90)***
Sample size	19,139	22,719	57,523	7999	10,199	41,858	75,721
F statistics	518.33	457.70	1326.39	237.16	276.52	1017.95	1797.49
Adjusted R^2	0.3149	0.2657	0.2932	0.3470	0.3272	0.3043	0.2993

Note: ***, **and * show significance at 1%, 5% anc 10% respectively; numbers inside parenthesis are t statistics
Source: Calculated based on data from 2009 household survey in urban China

municipalities, provincial capitals or cities specifically designated in the state plan, and the other three levels left are merged into "county and city area".

There are obvious differences in the relationship between the age of head of household and the family income per capita among different types of cities. For those samples from municipalities, county-level cities and counties, there is a positive relationship between the two; while for prefecture-level cities, provincial capitals or cities specifically designated in the state plan, although the estimation coefficients of both the age of household head and its square are significant, in terms of the value of the estimated parameters, there is no non-linear relationship between the age of household head and the family income per capita. The family income per capita increases with the increase of the age of head of household. When all samples are divided into "metropolis" and "county and city area", there is still an incremental relationship between the "age" and the "income".

In the estimated results from coefficients of the educational level of heads of household, we use the junior high school and lower educational level as reference group. The estimated coefficients of the educational level variable of heads of households of all city levels are all significant, and they increase with the increase of the educational levels. Yet the estimated coefficients of the educational variable level of head of household vary significantly among cities of different hierarchical levels. Municipalities have the highest estimated coefficient with the variable of junior high school educational level. Except for county-level cities, municipalities' coefficient is much higher than all other city levels, especially higher than provincial capitals or cities specifically designated in the state plan. Municipalities also have the highest estimated coefficient with the variable of high school educational level. By comparing the disparities between coefficients of junior high school and high school level, we can measure the additional benefits of the latter over the former. From such a comparison, we found that municipalities receive the least from this additional benefit. When we performed similar comparisons, we found that in prefecture level cities, provincial capitals or cities specifically designated in the state plan, junior college yields the highest benefits; while college and above educational level give municipalities, provincial capitals or cities specifically designated in the state plan the most benefits. On the contrary, heads of household with college and above degree at counties and county-level cities do not have obvious income advantages. From the comparison between "metropolis" and "county and city area", we discover that latter enjoys higher educational returns than the former. The estimated results from educational variables in municipalities show that lower-end and higher-end educational levels have higher returns, while middle levels have relatively low returns; samples from counties or county-level cities show that gains from mid-level education seem to be higher instead.

Family size has significant negative impact on family income per capita, and the absolute value of the estimated coefficient in "county and city area" samples is higher than that in "metropolis". The proportion of male members in a household always has a significant positive effect on family income per capita, and samples in prefecture-level cities have the biggest estimated coefficient.

In terms of the competitiveness and monopoly nature of employment units of household members, the impact of the percentage of employment in competitive sectors on income varies widely among cities of different hierarchical levels. In most cases, it is not significant. Although it is significant in municipalities and prefecture level cities, the signs of the estimated coefficients are opposite, one positive, the other negative. The impact of the employment percentage in monopoly sectors on income is significantly positive for all region types, although there are some disparities among estimated coefficients of different city levels; and for all city levels, their estimated coefficients are higher than those of competitive sectors. Municipalities, provincial capitals or cities specifically designated in the state plan, and prefecture-level cities have higher estimated coefficients for monopoly sectors than county-level cities or counties. All three variables that measure the employment structures of household members have significant estimated results under all circumstances, and their corresponding estimated coefficients in "county and city area" are higher than in "metropolis". The proportion of employment in state-owned institutions has the highest coefficient on county-level samples, while its impact on municipality samples is negligible. The proportion of employment in private sectors has significantly positive impact on family income per capita among all city levels, while their coefficients are slightly lower in municipalities and prefecture-level cities.

In terms of estimated results of regional variables, in areas with higher pension coverage among employed residents, the income per capita of local families will be higher. On one hand, the high pension coverage variable may mean more regulated local labor market that facilitates higher income from employment; on the other hand, the high pension coverage variable may signify better social security and social protection. The corresponding estimated coefficient in municipalities and county-level cities is relatively higher than in other region types; while it is not significant in county samples. Table 2.6 also shows that counties have the lowest pension coverage rate.

In terms of the commonly used eastern-central-western division, under normal circumstances income level in eastern region is significantly higher than those in central or western region. Therefore, Table 2.8 shows that the estimated coefficients of variables for central and western regions are mostly very negative. We need to point out that there are disparities of the income comparison between western and central regions among different city levels. For provincial capitals or cities specifically designated in the state plan, and county-level cities, estimated coefficients show lower incomes in the central region than in the eastern region, but the difference between the western region and the central region is not obvious; after we control other variables, western region is slightly higher than the central region. Nevertheless, county samples show very different regional characteristics: income in the central region is significantly lower than in the eastern region, yet income per capita in the western region is significantly higher than the eastern region by about 4.5%.

Based on the regression results of income functions for various city levels on Tables 2.8, and 2.9 lists the decomposition results by Oaxaca-Blinder method as

Table 2.9 Decomposition result of difference in income mean value (%)

	Municipality & provincial capital[a]		Provincial capital & prefecture-level city		Prefecture-level city & county-level city		County-level city & county		Metropolis & county and city area	
	Coefficient	Variable	Coefficient	Variable	Coefficient	Variable	Coefficient	Variable	Coefficient	Variable
Age of household head	165.29	−3.26	−156.01	5.67	−154.46	−2.82	−305.85	12.87	−29.07	2.45
Education level of household head	47.59	2.92	−34.69	10.66	−23.94	13.15	76.02	−5.26	−5.04	7.11
Family structure	9.97	1.89	13.38	1.59	107.04	8.45	−101.17	14.62	11.24	2.58
Industry	5.33	3.95	−1.81	0.00	12.68	−2.35	−4.09	−9.94	2.45	0.90
Occupation	13.06	4.81	−13.61	2.95	−4.69	0.47	−5.26	−14.04	−4.91	3.36
Ownership	−19.93	−0.52	14.74	−1.59	−41.78	−1.41	9.94	−7.60	0.90	−1.03
Regional characteristic	82.65	37.80	−83.90	13.38	−46.01	35.68	236.26	65.50	−81.91	20.16
Constant	−251.55	0.00	329.25	0.00	200.00	0.00	138.01	0.00	170.80	0.00
Total	52.41	47.59	67.35	32.65	48.83	51.17	43.86	56.14	64.47	35.53

Note: The "provincial capital" in this table include city specifically designated in the state plan

Source: Calculated based on data from 2009 household survey in urban China

[a]Since there are no municipalities in the central region, in the decomposition between municipalities and provincial capitals, the income function of both uses the eastern region as the reference group, and the regional variables adopted are called "central-western region"

well as the relative contribution shares of various variables. Overall, income disparities among cities of different hierarchical levels due to differences in variables are relatively small in most cases, and they are largely caused by differences in regional variables. As shown in Table 2.9, except for the regional characteristic variables, the highest explaining share among all other variables that explain of the income gap among cities of different hierarchical levels is less than 20%. In fact, those descriptive results from Table 2.6 also demonstrate that the difference in the mean value of income function control variable among cities of different hierarchical levels is not obvious. This also means the main factor that causes the income gap among cities of different hierarchical levels is not the difference in demographic distributions, but the difference in the corresponding income determining mechanism. In spite of this observation, we cannot conclude that such difference in income determining mechanism is directly linked to the disparities in economic decision-making power among cities of different hierarchical levels. In terms of the coefficient difference, we found that except for the first column showing the decomposition results between municipalities and provincial capitals, constants have very high explanatory shares in all other cases, reflecting the importance that pure location factors have on explaining income gaps among cities of different hierarchical levels.

The decomposition results between municipalities and provincial capitals show that the contribution of the constant is negative. We see from the regression results in Table 2.8 that the constant term regression coefficient of the latter is greater than the former. The coefficient return difference between the two city types is mainly due to differences in characteristics of household heads (including age and education level) and regional characteristics. The decomposition results between provincial capitals and prefecture-level cities show that the explaining share of variable differences is only 32.65%, and is mainly caused by regional characteristics and education level of household heads; on the contrary, the explaining share of coefficient differences is up to 67.35%, the highest among all decomposition results. The decomposition results between "metropolis" and "county and city area" show the similar trend: the overall contribution of variable differences to the income gap reaches to 35.53%, of which regional characteristics contributes to 20 percentage points. Other than that, head of household's education level has relatively high contribution share and its coefficient is up to 64.47%; the most important contribution factor comes from the constant term. The decomposition results of income gap between prefecture-level cities and county-level cities show that head of household's education level has a contribution share of 13.15%, higher than all other variables. Besides the constant, the coefficient difference of family structure plays an important role in explaining the income gap between the two city levels. The decomposition results between county-level cities and counties show that, the regional differences, family structure and the age of household head are the first three contribution variable factors, while the constant, regional characteristics and the education level of household head are the three biggest contribution coefficients. We need to point out that the contribution of regional factors to the decomposition results of the income gap between county-level cities and counties is higher than all other results, both in terms of variable difference and coefficient difference. In fact, county-level cities are mostly distributed in the developed eastern region, while counties are concentrated in the relatively less-developed central or western regions. The regional disparities caused by this distribution play an important role in income gap between the two city types. Besides, the difference in household head's educational returns contributes more in explaining the income gap between the two city types than in other decompositions. When we compare the estimated results of income functions between county-level cities and counties listed in Table 2.8, we see that the estimated coefficients of all education variables in county-level cities are obviously higher than those in counties, in other words, educational returns and yield rates in county-level cities are higher and better. Nevertheless, the descriptive results from Table 2.6 show no obvious difference in the distribution of education level between the two city types, especially in terms of the percentage of higher education levels for head of household. Therefore, the disparities of educational returns between the two are probably caused by the economic structure and the degrees of economic development.

2.3.4 *Decomposition of Income Gap by Quantile*

Figure 2.1 shows large difference in income gaps among cities of different hierarchical levels at various income distribution quantiles. Therefore, we will decompose income gaps of different groups at various quantiles based on the quantile regression results from the recentralized influence function.[10] Table 2.10 lists the decomposition results, and for each case, decomposition results for the 10%, 25%, 50%, 75% and 90% quantiles are reported.

The most significant feature in the decomposition results between municipalities and provincial capitals is that the explanatory share of variables to the income gap at a particular distribution quantile rises as the quantile number rises, while the explanatory share of coefficients declines as the quantile rises. This phenomenon may be related to the fact that low-income residents in municipalities receive better social security and social protection. Similar to the decomposition results of the mean value, among all variables, regional characteristic variable is the main factor of influence, and the contribution shares of the regional variable increase as the quantile rises. The other important factor whose contribution share rises as quantile rises is the industry variable. These two trends mean that, among high-income residents in municipalities and provincial capitals, Eastern region advantage and

[10]The decomposition of the income gap at various quantiles in the income distribution of different groups needs to be based on the quantile regression of the income function. The report of related regression results has been omitted here. This paper did not make weighted adjustments to the income distribution of different groups to obtain the counterfactual distribution before the decomposition of the quantile regression. Readers can refer to the comparison instructions by Fortin et al. (2011) to understand the difference between quantile regression decomposition based on counterfactual distribution by weighted adjustments and unweighted decomposition.

Table 2.10 Decomposition results of income gaps at various quantiles (%)

	Municipality & provincial capital		Provincial capital & prefecture-level city		Prefecture-level city & county-level city		County-level city & county	
	coefficient	variable	coefficient	variable	coefficient	variable	coefficient	variable
10 percent quantile								
Age of head of household	88.82	−1.90	−2.68	8.16	−537.23	−5.67	109.13	62.09
Education level of head of household	33.18	1.64	−125.45	9.42	−257.42	16.60	123.53	−6.80
Family structure	28.69	0.68	3.89	1.48	99.86	10.49	66.28	52.39
Industry	−0.54	0.81	10.22	−0.14	70.06	−4.21	−228.32	−3.11
Occupation	−3.77	2.25	−30.15	3.53	−92.46	1.90	−24.46	−76.93
Ownership	−12.56	1.17	−3.70	−2.80	−129.36	−2.73	−183.88	−58.77
Regional characteristic	24.83	13.85	−37.78	16.15	−85.17	61.28	1378.84	221.70
Constant	−77.12	0.00	249.86	0.00	954.05	0.00	−1331.70	0.00
Total	81.51	18.49	64.21	35.79	22.34	77.66	−90.58	190.58
25 percent quantile								
Age of head of household	169.40	−2.66	−89.18	6.30	99.45	−3.32	−1664.67	39.14
Education level of head of household	40.01	2.49	−70.51	9.89	−119.94	14.09	−85.76	−16.10
Family structure	4.95	1.47	14.76	1.70	262.42	10.00	−303.93	52.06
Industry	3.81	2.38	−4.29	−0.09	39.97	−1.91	−104.13	−14.01
Occupation	7.63	3.84	−18.23	3.04	−33.24	1.05	−211.58	−61.45
Ownership	−16.26	0.83	10.08	−1.88	−74.40	1.32	120.44	−29.42
Regional characteristic	77.72	34.53	−62.17	15.45	−41.51	42.78	675.55	186.27

(continued)

Table 2.10 (continued)

	Municipality & provincial capital		Provincial capital & prefecture-level city		Prefecture-level city & county-level city		County-level city & county	
	coefficient	variable	coefficient	variable	coefficient	variable	coefficient	variable
Constant	−230.14	0.00	285.14	0.00	−96.76	0.00	1517.57	0.00
Total	57.13	42.87	65.59	34.41	35.99	64.01	−56.50	156.50
50 percent quantile								
Age of head of household	270.54	−3.61	−215.66	5.68	−319.19	−3.23	−228.86	15.17
Education level of head of household	35.41	3.26	−16.90	11.76	−65.64	14.37	61.17	−6.32
Family structure	−76.88	2.87	13.04	1.91	292.53	10.18	−215.49	19.79
Industry	9.93	5.09	−3.15	−0.08	23.40	−3.72	−61.41	−16.10
Occupation	35.02	6.51	−13.26	3.15	−8.40	0.76	−32.25	−15.07
Ownership	−23.70	−0.82	19.59	−1.29	−61.50	0.37	7.29	−9.07
Regional characteristic	110.30	55.78	−95.98	14.71	−61.66	35.59	217.40	67.49
Constant	−329.69	0.00	376.47	0.00	246.17	0.00	296.26	0.00
Total	30.92	69.08	64.16	35.84	45.70	54.30	44.12	55.88
75 percent quantile								
Age of head of household	272.91	−4.69	−218.11	4.70	77.96	−2.51	−378.33	10.65
Education level of head of household	66.54	4.13	17.16	12.15	−8.30	9.89	53.34	−4.95
Family structure	−102.78	4.00	2.31	1.82	55.88	6.96	−0.23	12.12
Industry	40.59	9.86	−6.85	−0.21	−17.05	−2.87	21.60	−14.99
Occupation	68.57	10.29	−1.69	3.27	10.19	0.48	0.31	−8.59

Ownership	−41.61	−5.31	14.01	−1.41	−8.59	−1.10	−30.79	−5.26
Regional characteristic	64.12	74.10	−116.24	13.43	−11.35	25.72	143.80	49.26
Constant	−360.72	0.00	375.66	0.00	−35.33	0.00	252.06	0.00
Total	7.62	92.38	66.26	33.74	63.42	36.58	61.76	38.24
90 percent quantile								
Age of head of household	700.81	−5.43	−218.77	3.61	−18.83	−2.57	−113.78	5.31
Education level of head of household	162.05	5.86	17.75	10.63	1.20	10.63	50.63	−2.99
Family structure	−76.08	5.48	−67.11	1.44	−14.32	6.21	37.11	5.33
Industry	73.73	21.46	−4.30	−0.26	−14.00	−2.55	36.81	−6.70
Occupation	104.03	13.63	−0.28	3.01	7.89	0.62	25.89	−4.67
Ownership	−55.86	−13.38	11.54	−0.93	−8.24	−4.88	−33.71	−2.07
Regional characteristic	32.21	97.54	−92.54	12.28	7.51	22.88	54.02	30.20
Constant	−966.05	0.00	423.93	0.00	108.45	0.00	18.61	0.00
Total	−25.15	125.15	70.23	29.77	69.66	30.34	75.57	24.43

Note: Provincial capitals in this table include cities specifically designated in the state plan
Source: Calculated based on data from 2009 household survey in urban China

monopoly industries play an important role in explaining the income gap. Other variables, such as education level of head of household, employment ownership of household members, occupation of household members, do not show such significant trend. In terms of coefficients, contributions of the constant are always negative, and its absolute values increase as quantile rises. Age and education level of head of household, industry where household members are employed, occupation of household members all have contribution shares that rise with quantiles; while contribution shares for family structure and industry ownership decrease as quantile rises. The regional disparities have higher explanatory effects on the income gap at the middle end of the income distribution.

In the decomposition results between provincial capitals and prefecture-level cities, contribution shares of variable difference and coefficient difference are relatively stable, as neither shows obvious tendency to change with the quantile change. In terms of specific explaining factors, the contribution of variable difference at various quantiles shows no obvious regularity either. The explanatory shares of regional variable only slightly decline as quantile rises. At the lowest quantile of 10%, its contribution share is 16.15%; while at the highest income distribution quantile of 90%, contribution share of the regional variable also reaches to 12.28%. In terms of contribution share of coefficients, two changes are worth noting: first, at low quantiles of income distribution, coefficient contribution of head of household education is negative, while it changes to positive at high quantiles. This shows that disparities in education return play an important role in explaining the income gaps among high-income residents in these two regions; second, contribution of the constant increases progressively as quantile rises, and its contribution at any quantile is significantly important.

The decompositions of the last two regional types (one is between prefecture-level cities and county-level cities, and the other between county-level cities and counties) share the following common character: contributions of all variables in the income gap decrease progressively as the quantile rises, and the main source for variable contributions comes from the regional variable. The explanation shares of the regional variable also decrease as quantile rises. We need to point out that the contribution of educational variables plays almost the opposite role in these two types of decompositions. In the decomposition between prefecture-level cities and county-level cities, educational variables have higher explanation shares at lower quantiles, and their values at any quantile are all positive; while in the decomposition between county-level cities and counties, explanation shares of educational variables at any quantile are all negative.. In terms of the explanation shares of coefficients for the income gap between county-level cities and counties, regional variables' shares show a clear downward trend as quantile rises. Although in the same decomposition, the explanation shares of coefficients show upward trend as quantile rises, those shares in the low-end of income distribution are negative, that is, coefficient returns are more beneficial for low-income groups. This differs from the decomposition result between prefecture-level cities and county-level cities.

2.4 Conclusions

Using the household survey of 2009 in urban China, this paper discusses the income gap among urban residents in terms of hierarchy of cities. The main findings include: there is a relatively high-income gap among urban residents among cities of different hierarchical levels, and the hierarchical gap among cities amounts to 11% of the total gap, larger than the gap among the commonly used three major economic regions of the east, central and west; regression analysis shows that hierarchy of cities plays an important and significant role in income determination, even when other income affecting variables are controlled. The importance of hierarchy of cities varies at different quantiles of income distribution. Generally speaking, the hierarchical importance increases as quantile increases, but its importance decreases at the top of income distribution.

We decompose the income gap among cities of different hierarchical levels at the mean value and at various quantiles. We found out that the income gap among cities of different hierarchical levels is mainly caused by disparities in income determination mechanism (coefficient), especially by the constant, while variables depicting residents' characteristics have relatively low explanatory impacts. This finding reflects to a certain extent that the income determination mechanism among cities of different hierarchical levels is fragmented. This finding is also consistent with the trend that production factors concentrate at and flow to cities and regions of higher hierarchical level. Although this paper does not further extrapolate inequalities in income determination mechanism to other bigger factors such as regional disparities in economic decision-making power or regional gaps in the degree of economic development, the income gap among cities of different hierarchical levels analyzed in this paper is consistent with the vertical allocation features of China's current economic decision-making power.

Needless to say, the results of this paper need to be further improved and refined. Firstly, this paper did not take into account the disparities in cost of living index or in purchasing power of currencies among regions, which made currency income likely overvalued in high-income regions and undervalued in low-income ones; we certainly did not consider the regional inequalities in social security benefits and other non-monetary benefits. Secondly, as shown in Fig. 2.1, there may be some degree of deviation in the income distribution of municipalities, which may lack effective coverage of low-income and high-income people in this type of region. This in turn, may underestimate the internal income gap within municipalities. This is only an intuitive assumption. It is not easy to determine how much impact this potential distribution deviation has on the overall income distribution characteristics. This paper treats municipality samples separately, reducing to a certain extent the impact of such potential deviation on our analysis.

References

Bian, Y., & Zhang, Z. (2002). Marketization and income distribution: Analysis of urban household income surveys in 1988 and 1995. *Social Sciences in China, 5*, 97–111.
Cai, F., & Du, Y. (2000). Convergence and difference of economic growth in China: Enlightenment to the strategy of Western development. *Economic Research Journal, 10*, 30–37.
Dong, X. (2004). On the regional income gap in China: 1952-2002. *Economic Research Journal, 9*, 48–59.
Fan, J., & Zhu, G. (2002). Evolution of regional differences in China and its structural decomposition. *Management World, 7*, 37–44.
Gong, L., & Xie, D. (2004). Analysis of differences in factor flows and marginal productivity among China's provinces. *Economic Research Journal, 1*, 45–53.
Hu, A., Wang, S., & Kang, X. (1995). *China's regional difference report*. Liaoning People's Publishing House.
Huang, F., & Wu, C. (2008). A study on wage premium of China's provincial capitals. *Journal of Finance and Economics, 9*, 71–80.
Li, S., & Xu, Z. (2006). The changing trend of China's regional differences in recent years. *China Development Review, 1*, 106–116.
Liu, S., Li, Q., & Xue, T. (1994). *Research on Regional Economic Development in China*. China Statistics Press.
Ning, G. (2014). Are wages high in China's Metropolis? *China Economic Quarterly, 3*, 1021–1046.
Wan, G. (1998). An empirical study on the changing disparities of residents' income in rural China. *Economic Research Journal, 5*, 36–41.
Wang, X., & Fan, G. (2004). Trends and determining factors of regional differences in China. *Economic Research Journal, 1*, 33–44.
Wei, H. (1992). On the change pattern of China's regional income disparities. *Economic Research Journal, 4*, 61–65.
Yang, K. (1994). Research on the changes of regional economic disparities in China. *Economic Research Journal, 12*, 28–33.
Zhang, J., & Wu, G. (2004). Regional disparities in China: Metrics and causes. *World Economic Papers, 4*, 60–81.
Zhang, P. (1999). Regional income inequality and non-agricultural employment of China's rural residents. In R. Zhao, S. Li, & C. Riskin (Eds.), *Further study on income distribution of Chinese residents: Income distribution during economic reform and development* (pp. 290–312). China Finance and Economic Press.
Demurger, S. (2001). Infrastructure development & economic growth: An explanation for regional disparities in Chinas? *Journal of Comparative Economics, 29*(1), 95–117.
Firpo, S., Fortin, N., & Lemieux, T. (2007). *Decomposing wage distribution using recentered influence function regression*. University of British Columbia.
Firpo, S., Fortin, N. & Lemieux, T. (2009). "Unconditional quantile regression". Econometrics, 77(3), 953–973
Fortin, N., Lemieux, T., & Firpo, S. (2011). Decomposition methods in economics. In O. Ashenfelter & D. Card (Eds.), *Handbook of labor economics* (Vol. 4, pp. 1–102). Elsevier.
Jian, T., Sachs, J., & Warner, A. (1996). Trends in regional inequality in China. *NBER Working Paper, 5412*.
Raiser, M. (1998). Subsidizing inequality: Economic reforms, fiscal transfers and convergence across Chinese provinces. *Journal of Development Studies, 34*(3), 1–26.
Rozelle, S. (1994). Rural industrialization and increasing inequality: Emerging patterns in China's reforming economy. *Journal of Comparative Economics, 19*, 362–391.
Wei, S., & Wu, Y. (2001). Globalization and inequality: Evidence from within China. *NBER Working Paper, 8611*.

Chuliang Luo, professor at Capital University of Economics and Business.

Jinjun Xue, professor at Nagoya University of Japan.

Chapter 3
Informal Employment in Urban Labor Market and its Effects on Poverty Reduction

Yang Du and Guanghua Wan

Abstract By using data from China Urban Labor Survey (CULS), this paper thoroughly evaluates poverty among urban residents and migrant workers. Our results show that based on family income per capita, the total poverty incidence rate for urban residents is 4.15%, while for migrant workers, this number reaches 5.65%, 1.8 percentage points higher than local urban residents. Although the proportion of rural migrant workers in in standard employment is declining, they still form the buck of the in standard employment in the urban labor market. For those families at the bottom of income distribution, income from the labor market, especially from in standard employment plays an essential role in poverty reduction. For policymakers, this implies that in standard employment should be fully utilized rather than simply formalized in the urban anti-poverty process.

Keywords In standard employment · Poverty reduction · Migration

3.1 Introduction

Although the welfare meaning of in standard employment varies at different stages of economic development, this type of employment exists widely from the underdeveloped countries to the developed OECD countries (OECD, 2009). In the case of a dual economy with unlimited labor supply, although in standard employment is often associated with low level of social protection and working conditions, due to

Y. Du
Institute of Population and Labor Economy, Chinese Academy of Social Sciences, Beijing, China

G. Wan (✉)
Yunnan University of Finance and Economics, Kunming, China
e-mail: lvqs@ssap.cn

F. Cai (ed.), *Income Inequality and Poverty Governance in China*, International Research on Poverty Reduction, https://doi.org/10.1007/978-981-95-5063-0_3

shortage of standard employment opportunities, in standard employment becomes an important tool of poverty elimination. When the wage level in the market increases gradually, and workers receive certain level of social security, some of them will choose in standard employment voluntarily.

As a developing country, in standard employment accounts for a large proportion of total urban employment in China. Although data on the total size of in standard employment is not available in the formal statistical system, we can use the measurement method proposed by Cai and Wang (2004) and estimate that approximately the informal sector accounted for about 40% of total urban employment in 2012.

The changing trend of in standard employment in urban China is not only related to the transformation of the labor market system, but also depends on the scale of rural migrant workers who migrate from rural to urban areas. Before the reform and opening-up period, China's labor market was completely divided between urban and rural areas. By limiting the flow of rural labor to cities, urban workers could not only obtain stable jobs, but also receive comprehensive social welfare. Therefore, in standard employment was negligible in the urban labor market. And similarly, poverty was mainly concentrated in rural areas.

Since the mid-1990s, the reform of the state-owned economy has caused the reorganization of the urban economy and led to large-scale layoffs and unemployment. The loss of formal jobs is especially severe in the state-owned economic sector (Cai et al., 2005). Since the same time period, the Chinese government has been working hard to build a safety net in the labor market to protect the laid-off and unemployed workers. Meanwhile, in standard employment, as an important supplement to the government's proactive employment policy, starts to play a positive role in alleviating urban poverty. We have observed that this is exactly an important reason why the proportion of in standard employment has increased since the beginning of this century.

The labor force that migrates from rural to urban areas also forms an important part of urban in standard employment. With the gradual relaxation of restrictions on labor mobility, the rural labor force guided by the labor market signal has become the main supplement to the new employment in China's urban labor market. In 2013, the sum of rural migrant workers reached 166 million, and most of them were employed in an informal way.

We should point out that the flow of rural labor not only changes the composition of in standard employment in the urban labor market, but also makes the poverty alleviation efforts more complicated. If in standard employment fails to enable migrant workers to eradicate poverty effectively, the flow of labor force may also bring poverty from rural to urban areas. Since China's anti-poverty system has always focused on rural poverty, regional poverty relief often ignores poverty accompanied by labor migration. More importantly, the current social assistance system is associated with the household registration system. Once rural migrant workers fall into poverty in the city, it will be hard for them to obtain support from the urban social assistance system. Due to limited data, this new poor group is seriously neglected.

The impact of in standard employment on poverty alleviation keeps changing with the changes in the labor market. In recent years, the institutional changes in the labor market and the changes in the relationship between supply and demand have dramatically reversed the situation of in standard employment. *The Labor Contract Law* implemented in 2008 has significantly improved the level of employment protection and effectively solidified the regulations of labor market. *The Labor Dispute Mediation and Arbitration Law* implemented in the same year provides a system guarantee for workers to safeguard their employment rights and interests. All these institutional changes help to regularize the labor market.

In addition, demographic changes promote the transformation of labor market (Cai, 2010), as well as objectively promotes the process of labor market regularization. Due to the increasing scarcity of labor, labor shortage occurs frequently, and the wages of ordinary workers rise rapidly. This has undoubtedly improved their bargaining position in the labor market, and market forces have spontaneously reduced the proportion of in standard employment. For example, in 2013, the average monthly wage of migrant workers reached RMB 2609, which is not only far higher than the poverty line (in rural areas), but also much higher than the minimum life insurance standard of urban cities. As workers have more job options, they naturally favor the more formal jobs.

Under this background, this paper hopes to use extensive micro data to measure the incidence of urban poverty in China and its composition among different groups, as well as to observe the impact of labor market behavior, especially the in standard employment, on poverty alleviation.

3.2 Data

This paper uses data from China Urban Labor Survey (CULS) conducted by the Institute of Population and Labor Economics, Chinese Academy of Social Sciences in 2001, 2005 and 2010. Each round of survey includes five cities, Shanghai, Wuhan, Shenyang, Fuzhou and Xi'an, and Guangzhou was added in 2010. The main analysis of this paper utilizes the third round of survey data, but when making cross period comparison, we have to use those five cities in all three rounds of surveys to ensure comparability.

For all three rounds of survey, we use a similar sampling method, namely the probability proportion sampling. 70 communities were selected in each city, and 15 households were randomly selected in each community, among which 10 households were investigated, and the other 5 were used as backup samples in case of refusals. The valid samples in 2010 include 3637 migrant families and 4273 local families. In each round of survey, we also conducted research the community situation. According to the information on community size, urban population, and composition of migrant population and local population, we calculated the sampling weight of community level, and adjusted the representativeness of samples accordingly.

CULS questionnaire contains rich personal and family information, including demographic characteristics, employment characteristics, social protection, income and expenses, among others. What's special about this data is that we can collect very specific job information, which enables us to identify the informality of employment at the individual level. Moreover, CULS collected information about income and consumption, enabling us to precisely measure the poverty status of different groups.

What's more, CULS may be the only sample survey database that collected the information of migrant population and local population under a unified sampling framework. Since rural migrant workers are the most important component of urban poverty and of in standard employment in urban labor market, understanding their behavior and situation should be the focus of this paper.

3.3 Trend of Urban Informal Employment

In standard employment is a typical feature of labor market in developing countries. Since the market-oriented reform began in China, the informal trend of the labor market has been in constant change. As mentioned earlier, both rural to urban labor mobility and state-owned economic reform have impacted the trend of in standard employment. However, due to insufficient data, it has been difficult to clearly measure the size of in standard employment in urban China. Cai and Wang (2004) proposed a simple approximate measurement method to observe changes of the in standard employment scale in urban labor market. The total urban employment published by the National Bureau of Statistics is based on the survey of urban households, including various forms of employment. While the number of employments divided by ownership system is based on the reporting system, covering only standard employment. The difference between the two can be approximately regarded as the scale of in standard employment in urban China. If we go a step further and include the self-employed in the second statistical model into the in standard employment, based on the data published by the National Bureau of Statistics, we can get the changes of the proportion of in standard employment to total employment, as shown in Fig. 3.1.

The two definitions basically show similar trend of in standard employment. For most of the 1990s, the total size of in standard employment in the urban labor market was relatively small. Since then, due to the restructuring of the state-owned economy and the continuous expansion of rural labor mobility, the scale of in standard employment is also increasing. By 2002, the proportion of in standard employment in the broad sense accounted for 48% of the total urban employment. In recent years, due to the improvement of labor market conditions, the informal trend has gradually weakened, and by 2012, it has dropped to 39.6%.

In terms of the composition of in standard employment, rural migrant workers occupy the main part. Although it is difficult for us to directly measure how many rural migrant workers are employed in the informal sector, if we define the rural migrant workers without labor contracts and those self-employed rural migrant workers as informal employees, the number of them in 2009 accounted for about

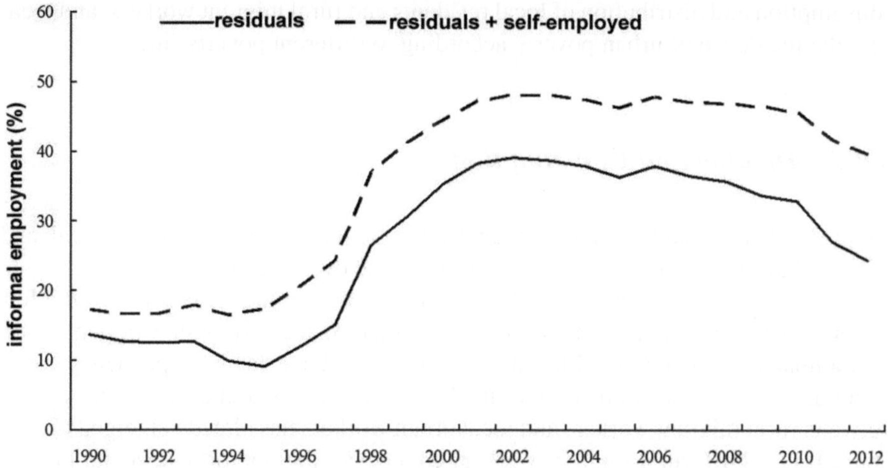

Fig. 3.1 Trend of in standard employment in China's urban labor market. Source: National Bureau of Statistics, *China Statistical Yearbook 2013*, China Statistics Press, 2013

60% of the total rural migrant workers. However, since most household surveys do not involve more specific information on measuring in standard employment, it is hard for us to obtain nationally representative micro data to infer the overall size of in standard employment, and it is even more difficult to distinguish its distribution between rural migrant workers and local urban workers. As an alternative, we use three rounds of CULS data to examine changes in the size and composition of in standard employment. As shown in Table 3.1, the total size of in standard employment in the sample cities increased from 2001 to 2005 and decreased significantly in 2010. This is consistent with the trend shown in Fig. 3.1.

3.4 Measuring Urban Poverty

China has been carrying out large-scale poverty relief and development projects for more than 20 years, but these projects are mainly aimed at rural areas afflicted by poverty. With the deepening of reform on urban economic system, especially the large-scale flow of labor from rural to urban areas, urban poverty has become increasingly prominent. Next, we will use micro data to observe the income,

Table 3.1 Proportion of informal employment calculated by CULS (%)

	Local workers	Rural migrant workers	Overall
2001	13.4	87.3	30.2
2005	30.6	86.5	37.5
2010	29.0	53.5	30.1

Source: Calculated according to CULS data. Samples were weighted by sampling ratio consumption and distribution of local residents and rural migrant workers, and measure the incidence of urban poverty according to different poverty lines.

3.4.1 *Income and Consumption*

Table 3.2 lists separately the consumption and income per capita of local and migrant families in sampling cities. In term of the overall sample, the consumption per capita and income per capita of migrant families are higher because of the following reasons. First, migrant families are smaller. As the current flow of population is dominated by labor mobility, migrant families have lower dependency ratio. Second, as China's economy crosses the Lewis turning point, the wage convergence between rural migrant workers and local urban workers has already emerged (Cai & Du, 2011). Third, rural migrant workers cannot get the appropriate social protection. In order to obtain a living standard comparable to that of local urban workers, they must have more cash for consumption.

In terms of cities, in Shanghai, Shenyang and Fuzhou, migrant families have higher income per capita, while local families in other cities have higher income level. Consumption per capita of local families in Wuhan and Fuzhou is higher.

3.4.2 *Poverty Line*

In the study of urban poverty, what kind of poverty line we should use as the standard to measure poverty has long been controversial. The Chinese government has set a unified poverty line for rural poverty, but has yet to promulgate one for urban poverty. In practice, people use different standards to measure urban poverty.

Table 3.2 Family income and consumption Per Capita (RMB)

	All samples		Local families		Migrant families	
	Consumption	Income	Consumption	Income	Consumption	Income
Total	1453 (1809)	2194 (3063)	1376 (1927)	2139 (2110)	1543 (1654)	2261 (3899)
Shanghai	1437 (1243)	2259 (1958)	1221 (917)	2109 (1504)	1697 (1507)	2438 (2381)
Wuhan	1008 (1128)	1397 (1892)	1082 (1403)	1514 (2445)	921 (685)	1258 (896)
Shenyang	968 (799)	1421 (1420)	867 (701)	1374 (1620)	1092 (897)	1479 (1142)
Fuzhou	1525 (1574)	1693 (1495)	1558 (1845)	1701 (1480)	1486 (1179)	1683 (1522)
Xi'an	1049 (1154)	1485 (1711)	1084 (1299)	1516 (1896)	1007 (971)	1449 (1489)
Guangzhou	1623 (2322)	2586 (4127)	1626 (2744)	2491 (2395)	1620 (1704)	2698 (5504)

Note: Weighted by sampling weight. Data in brackets show standard deviation

Many studies regard the urban minimum living security line as the urban poverty line. With the gradual improvement of the urban social assistance system, the minimum living allowance system has become the most important system of urban assistance. The minimum living allowance system project started in 1999. In 2003, the Ministry of Civil Affairs claimed that the project had covered all the urban population (household registration). However, because the minimum living allowance system project was designed based on household registration system, this means that although rural migrant workers have been counted as urban permanent residents, they are still excluded by the urban social assistance system.

In order to implement the minimum living allowance system, local governments define their own minimum living standards. However, as a tool to measure poverty, the basic living allowance line is often challenged, because it is mostly determined on the local financial resources, rather than the actual poverty status. There are many studies that determine the urban poverty line based on the minimum consumption level or on the cost-of-basic-needs (CBN) method (Ravallion, 1994; Meng et al., 2005). However, as a major policy tool, it is still of great policy value when we discuss the scale of poverty and its distribution among the migrant population and the local population based on the minimum living standard. Therefore, this paper continues to use the minimum living standard to measure and analyze poverty. Column 1 in Table 3.3 lists the minimum living standards of each city in the sample.

In addition, the poverty line proposed by the World Bank has also been widely used. That is to say, according to 1993 Purchasing Power Parity (PPP), USD 1.08 per person per day was defined as poverty line. Converted into RMB in 2003 would be RMB 888 per person per year in rural areas and RMB 1124 per person per year in urban areas in 2003. In practice, the poverty lines proposed by the World Bank, such as USD 1, USD 2 and USD 3 per day, have often been used to measure poverty. Although the poverty standards proposed by the World Bank are not specific to each country and lack clear theoretical basis, they are still a useful gauge when we need to compare poverty internationally. According to this standard, the inter-regional price level is adjusted according to the regional price deflator proposed by Brandt and Holz (2004). The corresponding results are shown in the last two columns of Table 3.3.

3.4.3 Poverty Incidence Rate

Table 3.4 reported the poverty incidence of income and consumption weighted by sampling ratio of each city. We measure poverty on the basis of family income per capita as well as family consumption per capita. Our sample includes both urban local and migrant families. In terms of overall samples, the incidence of poverty measured by the minimum living standard was 4.15%, while at USD 2 and USD 3 per day, this number was 2.94% and 4.47% respectively. Interestingly, even though minimum living allowance system plays a pillar role in urban social assistance (Du

Table 3.3 Poverty line of sample cities

	The minimum living standard	USD 2 per day	USD 3 per day
Shanghai	450	282	422
Wuhan	360	227	341
Shenyang	340	219	329
Fuzhou	290	235	352
Xi'an	240	224	337
Guangzhou	398.75	282	423

Note: All poverty lines are adjusted according to the regional price index of Brandt and Holz (2004)

Table 3.4 Incidence of income and consumption poverty (%)

	All samples	Shanghai	Wuhan	Shenyang	Fuzhou	Xi'an	Guangzhou
Income poverty							
The minimum living standard							
Local	3.84	2.89	4.36	6.02	4.90	2.72	4.26
Migrant	5.65	6.03	4.07	11.56	8.24	9.00	3.80
All samples	4.15	3.31	2.04	6.47	5.64	3.09	4.07
USD 2 per day							
Local	2.65	1.91	1.84	3.62	4.64	2.57	3.47
Migrant	4.41	4.40	2.47	9.39	7.68	8.56	2.75
All samples	2.94	2.24	13.67	4.08	5.31	2.92	3.18
USD 3 per day							
Local	4.19	2.89	3.83	5.34	6.11	5.59	4.44
Migrant	5.86	5.69	3.47	11.26	8.94	11.99	4.17
All samples	4.47	3.26	19.13	5.82	6.74	5.97	4.33
Consumption poverty							
The minimum living standard							
Local	3.27	2.11	6.99	6.38	0.73	2.49	1.67
Migrant	2.66	2.49	8.10	3.19	0.96	2.94	2.25
All samples	3.16	2.16	7.09	6.13	0.78	2.52	1.91
USD 2 per day							
Local	0.94	0.44	1.48	0.96	0.36	2.49	0.49
Migrant	0.85	0.49	3.48	0.75	0.66	2.16	0.61
All samples	0.92	0.44	1.67	0.94	0.42	2.47	0.54
USD 3 per day							
Local	3.53	1.37	5.91	5.04	1.47	7.91	2.28
Migrant	2.78	1.27	7.55	3.19	2.03	8.30	2.62
All samples	3.41	1.36	6.06	4.89	1.59	7.93	2.42

Note: The incidence of poverty is weighted by sampling ratio

& Park, 2007), more than 4% of the families in our sample still live below the minimum living standard. In addition, although migrant families have higher average income and consumption level, for those at the low-end of income and consumption distribution, the probability of living under the minimum insurance level is higher.

No matter what poverty standard is used, migrant families show higher probability of falling into poverty. Since China is still in the process of urbanization, the continuous flow of rural population to cities will continue to challenge the existing social assistance system. The incidence of poverty measured by income varies among different cities, and migrant samples show higher variation.

The incidence of consumption poverty in all samples was 3.16%, about one percentage point lower than that of income poverty. Interestingly, if we measure poverty by consumption, the probability of migrant population falling into poverty decreases. One possible explanation is that migrants do not have access to urban social protection or public services, so if they want to have a standard of living comparable to that of urban residents, they must spend more. We also see that poverty measured by consumption is more sensitive to the poverty line. For example, based on the USD 2 per day line, the incidence of poverty in the whole sample is less than 1%; while measured by USD 3 per day line, this number rises to 3.4%.

3.4.4 Poverty Characteristics

It is of direct policy value to understand the characteristics of poor families. First of all, if urban poor families share similar characteristics, then we can target the corresponding poor families according to these characteristics when implementing poverty alleviation policies. Secondly, we also need to know whether there are different characteristics between urban local families and migrant families.

Our sample shows that the phenomenon of "working poverty" of migrant families is more significant. Among poor migrant families, the proportion of family members who work is still very high, even higher than that of non-poor families. Moreover, poor families have larger workloads. Since those migrant population who hardly have access to employment in urban labor market are more likely to return to the countryside, without the counter-flow of labor force, the phenomenon of working poverty may be even more serious. In addition, simply pursuing standard employment alone cannot eliminate urban poverty, especially for the migrant population. The comparison of poor and non-poor families shows that in standard employment is not necessarily associated with poverty. For poor and non-poor families, the proportion of family members with formal jobs is roughly the same. Non-poor families even have more family members working in the informal sector. The positive role that human resources play in poverty reduction is in line with our expectations. For the local urban families, the education years of the head of household of poor families are 2.94 years less than those of non-poor families; while for migrant families, this gap is 2.3 years.

3.5 Informal Employment and Poverty Reduction

3.5.1 Composition of in Standard Employment

According to the definition of International Labour Organization, in standard employment includes the following forms of employment: (1) domestic workers, (2) the self-employed, (3) employers and employees in the informal sector. The data used in this paper contains detailed information in order to measure in standard employment, so that we can meticulously measure the composition of in standard employment in urban China, as shown in Table 3.5.

For local workers, the main component of in standard employment is informal employees. For example, workers without contracts account for 47% of in standard employment. For rural migrant workers, although the proportion of employees in informal sectors is similar to that of local workers, the proportion of the self-employed in in standard employment is larger, reaching 43%. The difference of in standard employment among cities is very large, and the proportion of in standard employment in economically developed cities such as Shanghai and Guangzhou is significantly lower. In addition, the proportion of in standard employment of rural migrant workers in different cities is higher than that of local workers.

3.5.2 Role of in Standard Employment in Income Determination

We use the following model to examine the impact of in standard employment on income, as shown in Eq. (3.1). In this model, y_i represents family income per capita, and the determinants of family income per capita include the proportion of family members in standard employment and the proportion of family members in in standard employment, represented by N_i and F_i respectively; as well as a series of control variables representing family characteristics, such as family size S_i, years of education received by the head of household E_i, the proportion of children in the family K_i, the proportion of family members over 64 years old O_i, age of the head of household A_i, whether is migrant family or not M_i and so on. c_j is a set of urban virtual variables to control the impact of labor market location on income, and ε_i is a random disturbance term.

$$\ln y_i = \alpha_1 N_i + \alpha_2 F_i + \beta_1 S_i + \beta_2 E_i + \beta_3 K_i + \beta_4 O_i + \beta_5 A_i + M_i + \mathbf{c}_\mathbf{j} + \varepsilon_i \quad (3.1)$$

Because the effect of in standard employment on income determination may vary at different income levels, we use quantile regression to observe the regression coefficient α_1 of in standard employment N_i and its changes relative to α_2. Table 3.6 shows the regression results. For the sake of brevity, we only report the regression results of the two most important variables N_i and F_i. The three columns in Table 3.6 are migrant population sample, urban resident sample and all samples.

Table 3.5 Informal employment and its composition

	Local	Migrant	All samples
Informal employment and its composition			
Proportion of in standard employment (percent)	29.0	53.5	30.1
Domestic workers	1.21	3.13	1.20
The self-employed	7.63	22.90	7.95
The informal sector	5.73	11.61	5.76
Without work contracts	13.76	13.77	13.48
Employers in the informal sector	0.67	2.14	0.67
Proportion of in standard employment in different cities (percent)			
Shanghai	4.64	43.57	11.95
Wuhan	16.66	87.38	34.67
Shenyang	22.45	75.13	53.23
Fuzhou	15.73	63.59	33.57
Xi'an	15.59	69.38	34.95
Guangzhou	14.03	48.21	31.21

Note: The proportion of in standard employment is weighted by sampling ratio

The regression results show that both formal and in standard employment play a positive role in income determination. Compared with local urban residents, the coefficient of in standard employment of migrant workers is significantly larger in most income quantiles. In terms of the poor families, the regression coefficient of in standard employment is as high as 0.76 at low quantile. It's not hard to understand that migrants depend more on employment income because they cannot get urban social protection and their non-labor income is lower.

In addition, compared to migrant workers, the effects of in standard employment on local workers' income vary less between different income levels. As shown in Fig. 3.2, for the migrant population, as income level rises, income elasticity gradually decreases *vis-à-vis* informal and standard employment. However, local residents do not exhibit the same characteristics. The income elasticity of employment for them shows a lower degree of variability than that for the migrant worker sample. This implies that urban, local residents may rely on non-labor income for their livelihoods. Another characteristic observed in the local-resident sample is that the elasticity of in standard employment takes on a U-shaped distribution as income level changes, implying those in the higher income brackets may opt for in standard employment.

3.5.3 In Standard Employment and Poverty Reduction

How would in standard employment affect poverty reduction? In Table 3.7 we use Probit regression to examine the determinants of urban poverty. We have primarily focused on the marginal effect of informal and standard employment on poverty determination. From the results, we see that when the other household variables, the

Table 3.6 Quantile regression of income determination

	(1)	(2)	(3)
Explained variable: logarithm of family income per capita	Migrant	Local	All samples
Q10			
Proportion of family members in standard employment	0.922***	0.495***	0.529***
	(0.113)	(0.079)	(0.061)
Proportion of family members in in standard employment	0.762***	0.245***	0.397***
	(0.097)	(0.077)	(0.057)
Q30			
Proportion of family members in standard employment	0.759***	0.459***	0.468***
	(0.070)	(0.039)	(0.040)
Proportion of family members in in standard employment	0.606***	0.124***	0.274***
	(0.069)	(0.040)	(0.039)
Q50			
Proportion of family members in standard employment	0.665***	0.414***	0.438***
	(0.078)	(0.059)	(0.039)
Proportion of family members in in standard employment	0.454***	0.056	0.192***
	(0.070)	(0.076)	(0.036)
Q70			
Proportion of family members in standard employment	0.558***	0.455***	0.467***
	(0.065)	(0.060)	(0.043)
Proportion of family members in in standard employment	0.317***	0.140***	0.169***
	(0.055)	(0.049)	(0.035)
Q90			
Proportion of family members in standard employment	0.400***	0.533***	0.525***
	(0.099)	(0.062)	(0.043)
Proportion of family members in in standard employment	0.156*	0.197***	0.209***
	(0.086)	(0.061)	(0.041)
Observed value	3519	4211	7730

Note: The observed values are weighted by the sampling ratio. Standard deviations are listed in brackets. *, **, and *** represent that result is significant at 10%, 5% and 1% respectively

dummy variable of the city surveyed and the status of household registration (*hukou*) are controlled, the two main variables that we are concerned with would have significant effects on poverty. Similar to the regression results for income determination, the employment variable has a stronger marginal effect on poverty reduction for the migrant population. *Ceteris paribus*, for every one percentage-point increase in standard employment, the poverty incidence rate decreases by 0.14 percentage point in migrant households and only by 0.05 percentage point in local households. For every one percentage-point increase in in standard employment the poverty incidence rate decreases by 0.1 percentage point in migrant households and only around 0.048 percentage point in local households. Clearly, where social protections are lacking, in standard employment is an indispensable means for migrant workers seeking to lift themselves out of poverty.

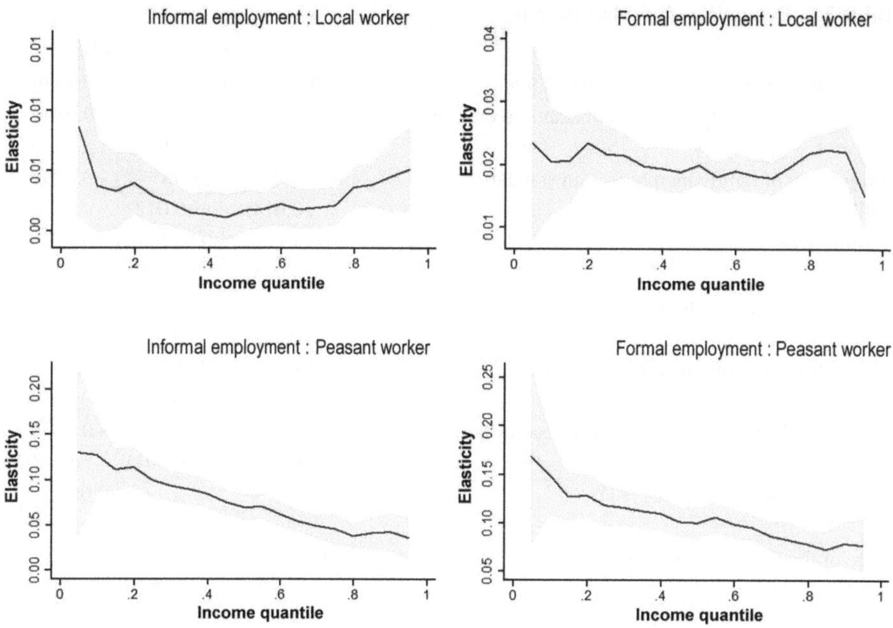

Fig. 3.2 The income elasticity of employment. Source: Numbers calculated based on CULS data

To confirm that the effect of our observations is robust, we redefined poverty using the World Bank's "USD 2 per day" and "USD 3 per day" poverty lines, and used the same model to observe the determinants of poverty. For brevity, we omit other control variables and only report the regression results of the two employment variables that we are most concerned about, as shown in Table 3.8. The regression results obtained by using different poverty standards show that both formal and in standard employment have stable effects on poverty reduction. But when the lower poverty line is used, the marginal effect is smaller.

3.6 Conclusions

In standard employment accounts for a large proportion in China's urban labor market. In the past 20 some years, due to the institutional transformation of the labor market and the labor flow from rural to urban areas, the overall trend of in standard employment has shown an inverse U-shaped change. Along this course, the first turning point comes mainly from large-scale layoffs and unemployment caused by urban economic restructuring, while the second transition is led by the recent strengthening of labor market regulation and driven by the Lewis turning point. Both the analysis of aggregate data and our micro survey data show the same trend.

Table 3.7 Determinants of urban poverty

Explained variable: family poverty or not	(1) Migrant	(2) Local	(3) All samples
Proportion of family members in standard employment	−0.143***	−0.051***	−0.084***
	(0.017)	(0.014)	(0.012)
Proportion of family members in in standard employment	−0.104***	−0.048***	−0.073***
	(0.018)	(0.012)	(0.011)
Family size	−0.019***	−0.012***	−0.014***
	(0.005)	(0.003)	(0.003)
Proportion of children in the family	0.019	0.040***	0.050***
	(0.025)	(0.014)	(0.015)
Proportion of family members over 64	0.014	−0.053***	−0.053***
	(0.022)	(0.012)	(0.012)
Years of education received by the head of household	−0.001	−0.003***	−0.003***
	(0.001)	(0.001)	(0.001)
Migrant family or not (yes = 1)	–	–	0.026***
	–	–	(0.007)
Age of the head of household	0.001***	−0.000	0.000**
	(0.000)	(0.000)	(0.000)
Wuhan	−0.015*	0.044**	0.014
	(0.009)	(0.019)	(0.010)
Shenyang	0.007	0.050***	0.036***
	(0.012)	(0.019)	(0.012)
Fuzhou	−0.011	0.041**	0.020**
	(0.008)	(0.016)	(0.009)
Xi'an	−0.012	0.016	0.008
	(0.008)	(0.014)	(0.009)
Guangzhou	−0.022**	0.011	−0.000
	(0.010)	(0.010)	(0.008)
Observed value	3610	4271	7881

Note: the observed values are weighted by the sampling ratio. Standard deviations are listed in brackets. *, **, and *** represent that result is significant at 10%, 5%, and 1%, respectively

By using data from China Urban Labor Survey, this paper thoroughly evaluates poverty among urban residents and migrant workers. Our results show that based on family income per capita, the total poverty incidence rate for urban is 4.15%, while for rural migrant workers, this number reaches 5.65%, 1.8 percentage points higher than local urban residents. Considering that the long-term unemployed rural migrant workers may choose to return home, the poverty of the migrant population that we fail to capture may be higher. This result shows that it is extremely necessary to unify the social assistance system of urban and rural areas in order to include the poor migrant population into the social security net.

Our analysis of micro data shows that although the proportion of rural migrant workers in informal jobs is declining, and they still constitute the main part of in standard employment in urban labor market. After Lewis turning point, the shortage

Table 3.8 Determinants of urban poverty: robustness test

	(1)	(2)	(3)
Explained variable: family poverty or not	Migrant	Local	All samples
USD 2 per day			
Proportion of family members in standard employment	−0.094***	−0.040***	−0.059***
	(0.015)	(0.011)	(0.010)
Proportion of family members in in standard employment	−0.080***	−0.039***	−0.059***
	(0.013)	(0.009)	(0.009)
USD 3 per day			
Proportion of family members in standard employment	−0.136***	−0.061***	−0.085***
	(0.018)	(0.014)	(0.012)
Proportion of family members in in standard employment	−0.120***	−0.052***	−0.082***
	(0.017)	(0.013)	(0.011)

Note: The observed values are weighted by the sampling ratio. Standard deviations are listed in brackets. *, **, and *** represent that result is significant at 10%, 5% and 1% respectively. Other variables are omitted

of low-skilled workers has led to the rapid rise of rural migrant workers' wages. Under this circumstance, in standard employment can still effectively help low-income families out of poverty. As the regression results in this paper show, both formal and in standard employments play a positive role in income growth. For families at the bottom of income distribution, income from the labor market, especially income from in standard employment, plays a significant role in poverty reduction. For policymakers, this implies that in standard employment should be fully utilized in urban anti-poverty process. Similarly, the simple normalization of the urban labor market, without considering the damage to the employment, will ultimately cause greater harm to the welfare of the poor.

We have observed that regulation of China's labor market has gradually strengthened in recent years. One of the goals is to formalize the labor market. However, with the development of economy and the growth of labor market, some inherent deficiencies of in standard employment may disappear spontaneously. After Lewis turning point, the improvement of low-income groups in the labor market is an example of such phenomenon. From this perspective, policymakers in developing countries may need to act more patiently when dealing with in standard employment.

References

Brandt, L., & Holz, C. (2004). *Spatial Deflators for China*. Working paper at University of Toronto.

Cai, F. (2010). Lewis turning point and economic development. *Economic Research, 1*.

Cai, F., & Du, Y. (2011). Wage increases, wage convergence and the lewis turning point in China. *China Economic Review, 22*(4), 601–610.

Cai, F., Du, Y., & Wang, M. (2005). *Transformation and development of China's labor market*. Commercial Press.

Cai, F., & Wang, M. (2004). Informal employment and labor market development: Explaining the growth of urban employment in China. *Economic Trends, 2*, 24–28.
Du, Y., & Park, A. (2007). Urban poverty in China: Social assistance and its effects. *Economic Research, 6*, 24–33.
Meng, X., Gregory, R., & Wang, Y. (2005). Poverty, inequality, and growth in urban China, 1986-2000. *Journal of Comparative Economics, 33*(4), 710–729.
OECD. (2009). In J. P. Jütting & J. R. de Laiglesia (Eds.), *Is informal normal? Towards more and better jobs in developing countries*. Development Center of OECD.
Ravallion, M. (1994). *Poverty comparisons*. Harwood Academic Publishers.

Yang Du, research fellow at Institute of Population and Labor Economy, Chinese Academy of Social Sciences.

Guanghua Wan, professor at Yunnan University of Finance and Economics.

Chapter 4
Education, Cities and Development of a Large Country: The Regional Development Strategy for China to Cross the Middle-Income Trap

Ming Lu

Abstract Whether China can cross the middle-income trap depends on its economic sustainability. Although upgrading education is important, as a large country, China should take the advantage of cities, especially large cities, to enjoy human capital externalities, and the complementarities among workers with different skills. Thus, the returns to human capital can be enhanced, which is beneficial for both the country and the people. Aiming at these goals, the central government should increase basic education investment, make the resources for basic education portable across regions, and increase educational resources through various channels. At the same time, basic public services should be equally provided within cities for migrants, and the institutional barriers against migration should be gradually removed.

Keywords Returns to education · Human capital externalities · Cities · Middle-income trap

4.1 Introduction

Although the concept of the "middle-income trap" is controversial, many countries did fall into the middle-income trap if we make judgements based on whether they ultimately narrow the development level gap between them and the United States Hu et al., 2012). Since the 1960s, among those middle-income countries or economies, only twelve have successfully "graduated" from "middle-come" to become high-income countries as of 2008, four of which are in East Asia (Rozelle, 2015). As for China, the question whether it can graduate successfully like its neighbors in

M. Lu (✉)
Shanghai Jiao Tong University, Shanghai, China
e-mail: lvqs@ssap.cn

F. Cai (ed.), *Income Inequality and Poverty Governance in China*, International Research on Poverty Reduction, https://doi.org/10.1007/978-981-95-5063-0_4

East Asia or be left behind like Latin American countries will be answered in the next decade.

To review the sustainability of China's economic growth, we should graft the "space" factor on to the economic growth theory. The theory of economic growth tells us that GDP per capita depends on two key factors: one is capital per capita and the other is total factor productivity (TFP). Capital per capita is easy to understand, while TFP is much more complex. Generally speaking, TFP mainly depends on the level of education, which is why Rozelle (2015) insisted that China should increase its investment in education, especially that of underdeveloped rural areas. Of course, it is important to increase investment to improve the level of education. Apart from that, in my opinion, for a large developing country like China, the efficiency of resource allocation between urban and rural areas and across regions is also an important determinant for TFP. If we look at China's education from the perspective of "space", education is no longer an issue about investment or level, but a question about where to invest and where to improve education returns.

From a global perspective, middle-income countries tend to have a middle urbanization rate; while among middle-income countries, China's urbanization level has already lagged behind those with a similar development level by about 10 percentage points (Lu & Wan, 2014). Therefore, there is no precedent worldwide to cross the middle-income trap without advancing the level of urbanization. Similarly, from the perspective of "space", China is a big country, and each of its provinces is as big as one or even several European countries. In terms of provinces, in 2014, nine provinces and cities, eight of which are in coastal areas, had GDP per capita of more than USD 10,000, and those are also regions with relatively high urbanization level. Therefore, from the perspective of the middle-income trap, the essence of China's development is to improve the GDP per capita and resident income of the central and western provinces. On this issue, a habitual misconception is that to increase the income of residents in the central and western provinces is to increase their income in hometown. From the perspective of national space, this is not the case. The places where residents in the central and western regions can raise their income can be their hometown or other places, that is, through moving to places with higher incomes. Breaking the barriers of population flow, taking full advantage of the limited resources to improve residents' education level, and letting everyone freely choose the work and residential place that can maximize their educational returns are the best ways to effectively improve the educational returns of residents in underdeveloped areas.

From the above mentioned "space" perspective, the key to China's success in crossing the middle-income trap is to achieve urbanization, and the reasonable flow of labor force in the process of regional economic development. In contrast, the existing discussions on China's human capital accumulation, on its sustained economic growth and the middle-income trap, have not paid enough attention on the spatial perspective. This article attempts to make up for such a deficiency, emphasizing the issue of where to educate and where to obtain educational returns. This article not only summarizes the existing relevant research, but also puts forward the topics for future research.

This paper is divided into five parts: Part II discusses the relationship between city and education return using the concept of human capital externality as its core. Part III provides a modern economic explanation for "People Always Strive to do Better" and discusses the impact of urban human capital on labor mobility. Part IV discusses the obstacles that hinder the spatial optimization of educational input and output. Part V consists of outlooks for the future and the policy implications.

4.2 Cities, Human Capital Externalities and Returns to Education

Within economic growth, the growth of labor input and capital input is the visible part, and the rest is classified as total factor productivity (TFP). But what is TFP? People attribute it to the quality and system of workforce. More specifically, in the process of development, the continuous improvement of education level is one thing, and whether the educational return can be improved is another. With a fixed level of education, the return to education may be very low, which will further reduce the enthusiasm to invest on education.

4.2.1 The Rise of Returns on Education: The Importance of Human Capital Externality

More than 30 years of development since China's reform and opening-up has confirmed the rising of returns to education. In the era of planned economy, individual's work was arranged by the state in a unified way, and the rate of return on education was seriously depressed (Cai et al., 2008). Different studies have shown that since the reform and opening up, the returns to education have been gradually increasing. In Fig. 4.1, we can see that the rate of return on education was only −0.642% in 1978, but increased to 3.707% in 1987 (Fleisher & Wang, 2005). During the 1990s, it increased from 2.43% in 1990 to 8.1% in 1999 (Li & Ding, 2003).[1] After 2000, it increased from 6.78% in 2001 to 8.6% in 2010 (Gao & Smyth, 2012). Using the micro data of the one-percent small-scale population census in 2005, after controlling age, square of age, gender, nationality and marital status, we found that the increase of education level in one year will increase the average wage by 13.2% (Liang & Lu, 2015a, 2015b).

The continuous rise of private education returns shows that education is indeed creating value. An intuitive understanding is that the reason for the rise of educational returns is because the suppression of educational returns in the planned

[1] Similarly, Zhang et al. (2005) found that the rate of return on education increased from 4.0 percent in 1988 to 10.2 percent in 2001.

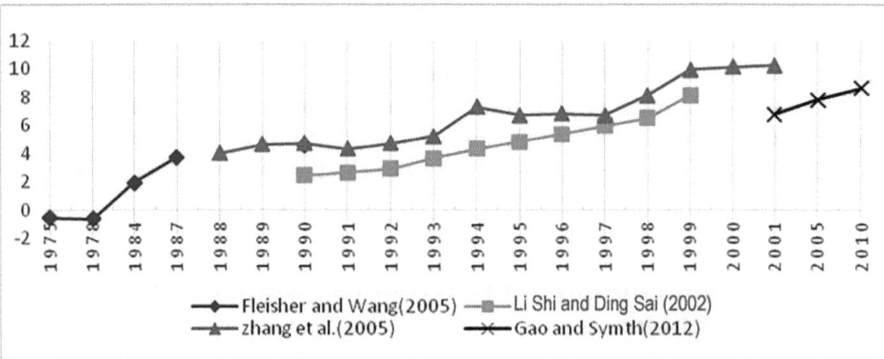

Fig. 4.1 Long-term trends in rate of return on education

economy period has been corrected under the market economy. Another natural explanation is that the quality of education has improved over time. One thing needs to be pointed out: our recent research finds that the role of human capital externalities in improving educational returns has been seriously ignored.

"Human capital externality" means that the improvement of one's education level not only improves one's own income, but also produces knowledge spillover in one's social interactions with other people, thus generating societal returns in the sense of aggregation. That is, one can obtain benefits from the improvement of other people's education level, and those benefits include the increase of income, the decrease of crime rate and the improvement of quality of life. If human capital externality is very large, then the labor force will earn higher income migrating from rural to urban area or from cities with low education level to cities with high education level. So, what is the impact of China's human capital externalities on income? I conducted a research with Glaeser of Harvard University, and by using CHIPS data in 2002 and 2007. We found out that if the average years of education in a city increases by 1 year, the average income of its residents will increase by about 21.9% (Glaeser & Lu, 2014). If we use the data from the one-percent small-scale population census in 2005, for every year of increase in the average years of education in a city, the average income of its residents will increase by about 19.6% to 22.7% (Liang & Lu, 2015a, 2015b). The estimated results of different data are very close, which means that even if we keep the level of education and all other personal characteristics constant, an individual's income can be increased by about 20% (the divisor of the estimated values of the above coefficients) simultaneously if we merely increase the average years of education in his residence city by 1 year. On the other hand, due to the externality of human capital, the previous estimate on private educational return is overrated, since it includes the social return of education.

So, in the process of urbanization, how much impact does the human capital externality have on income per capita at the aggregate level? Let us make a very rough estimate: at the end of 2014, there were about 260 million cross regional migrants in China. If we assume that all of them are rural migrants, that the average years of education in rural areas is about 3 years less than that in urban areas, and that their labor participation rate is about 80%, the income per capita of these 260 million people would increase by about 48% (= 20%×3 × 80%). If another 260 million people enter cities in the future, it would increase China's urbanization rate to 75% (= 55% +260 million/1.3 billion). Let us assume that there is still a three-year gap between the urban and rural education years, and even if we set the labor participation rate at 60% (considering that there are more old people and women in the existing rural population), the income per capita of these people would increase by 36% (= 20%×3 × 60%). These 260 million people account for 20% of the national population, and their income per capita increase can be transformed into about 7.2% (= 36%×20%) of the national average income growth. This migration effect is almost equivalent to the annual growth rate of China's GDP per capita. If the labor participation rate of this new urban population reaches 80%, and if they are relatively concentrated in the big cities with higher education level, then the average education level around them can be increased by 4 years, and their income per capita will be increased by 64% (= 20%×4 × 80%). Since they account for 20% of the national population, their income per capita increase can be transformed into around 14.4% (= 64%×20%) of the national average income growth, which is equivalent to two-year growth of income per capita. In other words, in the process of raising the level of urbanization to 75%, by merely utilizing the mechanism of human capital externality, we can make China leap over the middle-income level 1–2 years earlier. Of course, this estimate is very rough, and it can only provide a general perceptual understanding for readers.

As a large developing country undergoing economic transformation, the level of economic development in different regions of China is obviously different. Different regions have different factors affecting the return to education, including the economic proportion of private sector, different degrees of economic openness (the degree of attracting FDI), and different regional policies and so on. More importantly, there are huge differences in average education level between urban and rural areas and among different cities, which in turn will cause differences in educational returns between urban and rural areas and among different cities. Research by Xing (2015) shows that the return to education of cities is significantly higher than that of rural areas. At the city level, those big cities with higher education level have higher return to education.

Xing Chunbing's research (Xing, 2015) also demonstrates that in 1995, the annual return to education in different regions was about the same between 3 and 4%. In 2002, Guangdong Province ranked first in the country with 8.4% annual return to education, while Hubei and Yunnan had the lowest annual return to education (about 4.6–4.7%). From 2002 to 2007, the return to education in the central and western provinces stopped growing and started declining (for example, Anhui and Gansu). In contrast, the rate of return to education in coastal areas continued to rise, even with explosive growth in some areas. For example, the return to education in Beijing increased from 6 to 11%, as did the growth trend in Jiangsu Province. There are obvious regional differences in the national return on education. The return of higher education shows a similar trend. We see that the return on education mainly comes from the higher education stage. In particular, the return on higher education in coastal areas has become the main body of the return on education in these regions.

To further demonstrate the regional differences in educational returns, Xing Chunbing (Xing, 2015) estimated the educational returns at all city levels by using the one-percent small-scale population census in 2005, with the estimated results ranging from 5 to 15%, showing great urban differences. He found that, there was generally a positive correlation between the annual return on education and the urban population, and the larger the city, the higher the return on education. At the same time, the annual educational return is positively related to the proportion of university graduates in a city. The higher the proportion of university students is, the higher the educational return is.

4.2.2 Why Does the Agglomeration of High Skilled Labor Benefit Low Skilled Labor?

Readers may ask, isn't the human capital externality generated by highly skilled workers only obtained by the highly skilled workers themselves? In this way, cities would not need low skilled workers to achieve development. In other words, the improvement of urban education level would lead to the elimination of those low skilled workers. That is not the case. In fact, there are skill complementarities between high and low skilled workers, which make big cities with more college students needing even more low skilled workers. So why do big cities promote complementarity of skills? There are three possible reasons:

The first reason is labor division. When market capacity increases, it will promote a more detailed and specified labor division, and the labor force is more closely linked with one another. Workers with different skills are in different positions in the production process, and they work with each other, and in this way create complementarity. In fact, this is the "Smith's theorem", which states that market scale promotes labor division.

The second reason is human capital externality. The existence of human capital externality will improve the productivity of the labor force around highly skilled workers.

Combing the above two points, we see that when there is labor division, people with different skills will engage in occupations in line with their comparative advantages. When there is externality, the increase of high skilled workers will improve their own labor productivity, and at the same time improve the labor productivity of low skilled workers. As a result, big cities will promote complementary of different skill levels. Our research finds that the complementarity between high and low skilled labor force will appear in large enterprises, but the promotion effect of large cities is not significantly stronger than that of small and medium-sized cities (Liang & Lu, 2015a, 2015b), although large cities are indeed more likely to boost complementarities between high and low skills by promoting the externalities among different enterprises and among different industries (Liang & Lu, 2014).

The third reason lies in consumption externality. The increase of employment wage will increase the opportunity cost of housework. For high skilled workers, the high opportunity cost of housework will make them outsource their housework activities to low skilled workers engaged in household management, catering and other consumer services. At the same time, the increase of income level will also increase the demand for other services such as medical treatment, art, law, and employees in those fields are mainly high skilled workers. Through externality, sharing and matching mechanisms, large cities can increase the wages of high skilled workers, encourage high skilled workers to outsource more domestic activities, increase the demand for consumer services, which in turn will increase the employment on consumer services. It is estimated that for every new highly skilled position in a city, five new positions in the consumer service industry will be created, including two positions for high skilled workers in fields such as medical, art and law, and three positions for low skilled workers in catering, cashier and so on (Moretti, 2012).

The presence of skills complementarity mentioned here makes it possible that the improvement of urban education level drives the wages of low skilled workers to rise. We use the micro data of the one-percent small-scale population census in 2005 to investigate the impact that the proportion of urban high skilled workers plays on the wages of workers with different skills. The results show that when the proportion of urban high skilled workers (bachelor degree or above) increases by 1 percentage point, the hourly wages of high skilled people will increase by 6.11 percentage points; while the wages of low skilled people (below bachelor degree) will increase by 7.17 percentage points, which is slightly bigger than that for high skilled workers. In addition, if we further divide the low skilled labor force into the middle skilled workers with high school education and junior college education and the low skilled people with junior high school education and below, we also find that the increase of the proportion of urban high skilled workers has the greatest impact on the increase of wages for low skilled workers (Liang & Lu, 2015a, 2015b).

The process of high skilled people concentrating in big cities will also produce huge demand for low skilled workers, which shows the positive effect of city size on employment and income level. Using CHIP's personal data of 2002 and 2007, we found that people are more likely to find jobs in big cities. Both high skilled and low skilled workers benefit from the population size effect, and low skilled labor force gains more employment opportunities in large cities. In contrast, the employment situation of the middle skilled population is not significantly affected. Therefore, limiting urban population growth, especially the inflow of low skilled labor, has negative effects on efficiency and equity (Lu et al., 2012). In addition, studies also found that urban scale has a positive impact on labor income: after income inflation is eliminated, every 1 percentage point increase in urban population will increase the real personal income by about 0.082 to 0.143% (Gao, 2014).

4.3 People Always Strive to Do Better: Impact of Urban Human Capital on Labor Mobility

In modern economic, the old Chinese saying "People Always Strive to do Better" means that people will move to places with higher income and more employment opportunities. Therefore, people will move from rural areas to cities, from small cities to large cities.

4.3.1 Education Promotes Labor Migration from Rural to Urban Areas

The returns to education at industry and service sectors in urban area are higher than those in rural areas. Therefore, the transfer of labor force from rural to urban area is the way to improve educational returns. In a typical household, members with higher education level have relative advantages at industry and service sectors and will more likely be sent to work in the city. Empirical researches confirm this point. By using CHIPS' data of 2002, after controlling other variables such as individuals, households, and rural characteristics, different education levels have different positive effects on migrant workers entering cities. If we make illiterate rural migrant workers the reference group, the education level of middle school and primary school will increase the probability of rural labor migrating to work by 7.13% and 5.25%, respectively. The probability of people with higher education levels going out to work is lower (people with the education level of technical secondary school or junior college education increase the probability by 4.75%, and people with the level of high school education by 4.9%). Of course, one possible reason is that rural labor with education level above junior high school are more likely to obtain urban residence permits (*hukou*), and in that case they will not be counted as migrant workers (Chen et al., 2014).

4.3.2 High Skilled Workers Gather in Cities with Higher Education Level

The agglomeration of high skilled workers in cities with higher education level is the driving force that expands the scale of these cities. Due to the human capital externality, the higher the average levels of education in a city, the more learning opportunities the workers get, and the faster the growth of their labor productivity and wages (Xia & Lu, 2015). In general, cities with higher average education level attract more highly skilled workers. Specifically, several rounds of census data since the reform and opening-up period all show that cities with a higher proportion of college students in the early phase had faster growth rate of their proportion later.

We use the census data of 2000 and 2010 and the method that Berry and Glaeser (2005) proposed to investigate the impact of urban human capital in 2000 on the change of urban human capital during 2000–2010. Our results show that for every 1 percentage point increase in the proportion of high skilled people in 2000, the proportion of high skilled people between 2000 and 2010 would increase by 1.3 percentage points. Even after we control the urban population scale, GDP per capita and industrial structure in 2000, for every 1 percentage point increase in the proportion of urban high skilled workers in 2000, the proportion of high skilled workers in 2000–2010 will increase by 1.02 percentage points (Liang & Lu, 2015a, 2015b). It is worth mentioning that the same phenomenon also exists in the United States, which is that the current urban proportion of high skilled people affects the subsequent proportions of highly skilled people (Berry & Glaeser, 2005).

So far, we know that the existing proportion of highly skilled people in cities will affect the proportion of highly skilled people in the future, but is this the result of economic agglomeration, or the result of industrial transfer? Our research confirms that the difference in human capital level among Chinese cities mainly comes from the difference within the industry, not due to the different industries in different cities (Liang & Lu, 2015a, 2015b). Similarly, Berry and Glaeser (2005) found that the divergence of human capital among cities in the United States in 1970–2000 was not caused by the differences among industries, but mainly by the differences within the same industry.

4.3.3 Impact of Urban Human Capital on Labor Mobility

If there is skill complementarity between high and low skilled labor forces, then both high and low skilled workers will cluster to cities with higher human capital level at the same time. We use the census data of 2000 and 2010 to investigate the specific details. Our results show that the for every 1 percentage point increase in the proportion of high skilled workers in 2000, between 2000 and 2010, the proportion of high skilled people would increase by 1.129 percentage points, the proportion of medium skilled labor would decrease by 1.479 percentage points, while the proportion of low skilled labor would increase by 0.351 percentage point, which is not significant, but t value of the coefficient has exceeded 1 (Liang & Lu, 2015a, 2015b). A similar situation happened in the United States. From 1970 to 2000, cities with a high proportion of high skilled labor force in the early stage increased the proportion of high skilled labor force in the following 10 years, while the proportion of low skilled labor force also increased subsequently (Berry & Glaeser, 2005).

More intuitively, we can map the spatial distribution of cross regional population migration. Although generally more people migrate to the southeast coastal areas, it is the big cities and their surrounding areas, not eastern region, that attract more people.

The impact of urban human capital on labor mobility has a long history. In a recent research, Xia Yiran and I (Lu & Xia, 2015) used the number of successful candidates in the highest imperial examination in Ming and Qing Dynasties to construct the human capital of ancient Chinese cities. We found that in the history of China, different cities had very different human capitals. In 1952, China used administrative power to relocate some universities, which had a huge impact on the distribution of urban human capital. After the reform and opening-up, with time, the average years of education in a city is becoming more and more related to its historical human capital.

Income and employment opportunities are two main reasons to attract labor inflow. In addition, access to public services is also an attracting factor. Using the one-percent small-scale population census in 2005 and the characteristic data of 220 urban areas, we find that regions with higher income and more employment opportunities, as well as better basic education and medical services, attract labor inflow. However, the impact of public services on labor flow is less than that of wages and employment. Therefore, even if the policy of equalizing public services can moderately scatter the spatial distribution of population, it will not change the trend of labor agglomeration to large cities (Xia & Lu, 2015).

4.4 What Hinders the Spatial Optimization of Educational Input and Output?

The free flow of the labor force is the best way to maximize the return of individual human capital. So, how do we judge whether the individual human capital return is maximized? In theory, if this "optimization" is realized, then, among different regions, the real income of workers with the same characteristics should be similar or equalized, which is the basic idea of "spatial equilibrium". On the contrary, if there is a huge difference in the educational returns among different regions, it means that the cross regional flow of high skilled labor cannot fully respond to the demand differences among regions.

4.4.1 The "Spatial Equilibrium" of Labor Flow Is Hindered

In fact, China's cross regional "spatial equilibrium" has been greatly hindered. Xing (2015) found that in Beijing, Shanghai and Guangdong, migrant high skilled workers account for about one third of the total high skilled population, and there are more than 10% of migrant high skilled workers in 23 provinces. This proportion is far lower than the proportion of migrants among low skilled workers, especially in coastal areas, considering the gap between the number of high skilled workers and the number of low skilled workers, the absolute number of migrant high skilled workers is far lower than that of migrant low skilled workers. In terms of income gap, the income of university graduates in coastal provinces is much higher than that in central and western provinces, while for low skilled labor force, the wage gap in different regions is much smaller. Gao (2014) further studied the impact of city size on income at the individual level. He used the cost of living index and house price minus the nominal income, and both calculation methods showed that in cities with larger population size, the real income of their residents was higher. Moreover, in groups with higher income level, urban population size has a greater impact on individual real income. This result also shows that the "spatial equilibrium" of population flow among China's cities is far from being achieved, especially for the population with high education level and high-income level, such "spatial disequilibrium" is even more obvious.

Another perspective is to observe the distribution of labor force with different skill levels in different cities. If there is complementarity between the high and low skilled labor forces, then big cities will attract bot high and low skilled labor forces at the same time, but they will have limited attraction for the medium skilled labor force. In the United States, large cities have a higher proportion of high skilled labor force, but the average skill level of their labor force is almost the same as that of small cities (Bacolod et al., 2009), and skill levels among large cities show greater variances (Gautier & Teulings, 2009). Eeckhout et al. (2014) found that large cities in the United States have a higher proportion of both high skilled and low skilled workers, yet a lower proportion of medium skilled labor, which fully demonstrates that large cities can promote skill complementarity.

We use the micro data of the 2005 census to compare the skill distribution among different cities in order to investigate the complementarity between high and low skilled workers. We define workers with a bachelor's degree or above as high skilled, those with an associate's or high school degree as medium skilled, and those with a junior high school degree or below as low skilled. We then directly compare the numbers of these three types of skilled labor force among cities of different scales. Table 4.1 shows the details. We see that the average years of education in big cities is 9.785, while in small cities it is 8.465. The difference between the two is 1.32, which is significant under 1%. In addition, we can see that large cities have a higher proportion of high skilled and medium skilled workers, but lower proportion of low skilled workers. Contrary to Table 4.1, major cities in the United States have higher proportions of both high skilled and low skilled workers.

If all the above findings are accurate, then in terms of regional income gaps, the flow of high skilled labor seems to be more hindered. While in terms of proportion of labor force with different skills, it seems that the flow of low skilled workers is

Table 4.1 Quantitative comparison of different skills in large and small cities

City scale	High skilled	Medium skilled	Low skilled	Average years of education
Small Cities (173)	0.0187	0.179	0.803	8.465
Large Cities (24)	0.0597	0.276	0.664	9.785
Difference	0.041***	0.097***	- 0.139***	1.32***

Note: Small cities in the Table are defined as cities with a population of less than one million, while large cities are defined as cities with a population of more than 2.5 million, * * * p <. 01

hindered instead. How can these two seemingly contradictory results appear at the same time? In the absence of further research, I think the following explanation is logically and institutionally feasible: the flow of low skilled labor is more seriously hindered by institutional barriers; meanwhile, for high skilled workers, they are so heterogeneous that we cannot judge whether they have reached the spatial equilibrium of labor flow merely by the regional differences of their real income. In other words, compared with those college graduates in underdeveloped areas and small and medium-sized cities, the industries, occupations and other characteristics of the college graduates in developed areas and large cities bring them higher income.

So, why has the labor mobility barrier represented by household registration system not been eliminated after such a long time? Why do big cities always believe that it is necessary to control the scale of migrant population, especially the scale of low skilled labor force? In my opinion, the first obstacle comes from knowledge and cognition, which I often call as "not understanding". Specifically, if people do not realize that the city scale will have a positive impact on income and employment through human capital externalities, and if people fail to understand that the migration of low skilled workers to large cities is due to the demand of "skill complementarities", while at the same time, they simply attribute the occurrence of urban problems to population overflow,[2] not understanding that controlling population flow will do more harm than good to the local area, then it's not surprising that the policy of controlling population flow is advocated. The other reason is that the local government pursues short-term local interests and sets up manmade barriers to population flow. This reason is in the sense of "political economics" and reflects the contradiction between local short-term interests and long-term public interests. Basically, it is not due to "not understanding", but to "pretending not understand", which needs to be solved through system design.

4.4.2 Negative Impact of Labor Mobility Barriers on Human Capital Investment

Local governments are willing to implement policies to attract high skilled talent, but they are usually reluctant to invest directly in education, especially in basic education. The reason is that the spatial agglomeration of high skilled workers benefits the development of the local economy: if local governments invest in education directly, then in the process of frequent labor flow, the human capital created by local education investment may produce educational returns in other places. This will result in the cross regional return of human capital investment and reduces the incentive of local governments to invest in human capital. Currently, China's basic

[2] In fact, we cannot establish a causal relationship between urban disease and urban population size. Urban diseases are mainly caused by problems in planning, management and technology. The policy of population control based on urban disease lacks theoretical and empirical basis (Lu, 2015).

education is mainly funded by the county and township governments, and the proportion of financial funding at the central and provincial levels is too low. Local governments in the cities (especially in the megacities) where labor force flows into are not willing to increase the education investment for the low skilled workers. Instead, they regard the educational discrimination against their children who migrate with them as the policy to prevent them from flowing in. Therefore, China should change its current policy that the primary education is mainly undertaken by the local governments and the central government's financial funding is too low.

It is particularly worth mentioning the education of left behind and migrating children in the process of urbanization. China's rapid urbanization has increased the accumulation of human capital. However, under the current household registration system and education financial system, urbanization is accompanied by some problems, which bring harm to the long-term development of human capital. Due to the restriction of China's household registration system, most migrant workers cannot enjoy social welfare such as pension, medical services or public education in their places of work. Although the scale of cross regional population flow is huge, the primary education funds are mainly determined by the number of children with local household registration, and the funds cannot be transferred or carried across different administrative regions. Therefore, local governments lack incentives and financial resources to solve the enrollment problem for children of migrant workers. Facing the challenge of difficult enrollment for their children, migrant parents rely on one of the following three ways: one is to pay school selection fees to let their children go to local public schools, the other is to have their children go to private schools, and the third is to leave their children in their hometown to be cared for by their own parents or other relatives. In fact, due to the high cost of the first two ways, many parents choose to leave their children behind in their hometown, resulting in a huge number of left-behind children.

According to the *National Monitoring and Investigation Report of Rural Migrant Workers* provided by the National Bureau of Statistics, only 20% of the total migrant population moved with the whole family, while the "seasonal migration like the migratory bird" is still the main form of employment for migrant workers. Because children of migrant workers do not have equal access to education in urban areas, the family migration rate has always been very low, accompanied by many left-behind children. According to the data of the sixth national census, there are about 61 million left-behind children in the country. These children do not follow their parents to urban cities but stay in rural areas for schooling. Jia et al. (2010) found that the living and health status of left-behind children were worse than that of non-left behind children, and psychological problems rather than physical problems were the main reasons for this situation. Chang et al. (2011) pointed out that the absence of parents increased the agricultural tasks and domestic work for the elderly and children left behind, especially for the elderly women and girls. Gao et al. (2010) found that left-behind boys are prone to not eating breakfast, lack of exercise, Internet addiction, smoking, suicide fantasy, obesity and other problems, while left-behind girls are prone to excessive intake of sugary drinks, indulgence in television, smoking and drinking. In 2014, the China Youth & Children Research Center (under the Central Committee of the Communist Youth League of China) investigated the population of left-behind children in China and found that when growing up, left-behind children face many social and psychological problems, especially in academic performance, physical condition, mental health, life satisfaction, manners and behaviors. This study causes deep concern and worry in the whole society for the living conditions and growth environment of left-behind children.

Many people intuitively believe that the problem of left-behind children is caused by the fact that working parents do not care enough for their children, so we should encourage them to return home, and we should increase investment in rural education. Given the current state of labor mobility, by increasing the financial investment in rural education, and strengthening the care of the government and society for left-behind children can certainly solve part of the problem, but this method cannot resolve the fundamental problem. Encouraging working parents to return to their hometown is not a solution, because it means that they must give up their urban income and such action deviates from the direction of urbanization. At the same time, the scale economy effect of urban education input (the same input produces more output) means that the quality of urban education is higher, and there are knowledge and skills needed by modern society outside the urban school walls, so reuniting left-behind children with their parents in cities, and letting them receive urban education is far better than making their parents return home, where their children can only receive rural education.

Unfortunately, if we do not change the current system, the education of migrant children in urban areas is equally worrisome. According to the data of the sixth population census, the number of migrant children ages 0 to 17 reached 35.81 million. Although these children live in cities, they do not receive the same education as urban children (Research Group of All-China Women's Federation, 2013). The probability of temporary migrant children being admitted to urban schools is far lower than that of local children, especially for children who migrated to cities with their family less than a year ago (Liang & Chen, 2006). The difficulty to enroll in urban schools is more serious for children of migrant workers in big cities. For some time, under the policy principle of controlling the population of megacities, Beijing and Shanghai's household registration policy and migrant population policy has been particularly strict, and the enrollment of migrant children shows an even more serious situation. Chen and Feng (2013) found that migrant children who cannot enter urban public schools have significantly lower developmental levels of Chinese and mathematics than those of local children. In recent years, the population of many cities (especially some big cities) has been growing rapidly. Because of the rigid and limited housing supply in downtown areas, many new migrants can only live in suburbs or some areas recently changed to urban areas from suburbs. Because each district and county provides the education funds for big cities and megacities, and the center of a city is often an area with more developed economy and rich high-quality education resources, there is abundant education resources in downtown areas, while the teaching quality of public schools and newly-built schools for migrant children in remote areas of a city are relatively poor. Therefore, the uneven distribution of educational resources is reflected in the worse educational conditions of migrant children.

After children's education, let us talk about adult training. Because migrant workers are usually not regarded as "local residents" by local governments, and as a group they are in constant migration, enterprises are not willing to pay for their training costs. At the same time, there are regional differences in the supply of training in China. As shown in Table 4.2, in terms of the number of private vocational training institutions and the number of public employment training centers, the average value of all provinces in the central region is higher than that in the eastern region. The number of public employment training centers in the central region is 1.5 times that in the eastern region. The training funds of private vocational training institutions in the eastern region are higher than the central region, but the funds of public employment training centers are lower than the central region. In terms of the number of trainees, the number of trainees from private vocational training institutions in the eastern region is higher than that in the central region, but the number of trainees from public employment training centers in the central region is higher than that in the eastern region. In terms of the total number, the total number of trainees from those two types of training institutions in the central region is greater than that in the eastern region. In summary, the supply of training in the central region is greater than that in the eastern region, while the western region has the least training supply. The training demands mainly come from the economically active people who have completed formal education and the rural migrating labor force. According to the 2010 census, the number of both economically active population and migrant population is the largest in the eastern region, and the number of migrant population in the eastern region is almost twice that in the central region. We can conclude that there is a regional dislocation in the supply and demand of training in China, and such a mismatch is mainly reflected in the government dominated training supply structure.

Sources: The training data comes from *China Labor Statistics Yearbook in 2011*, while the number of economically active population and migrant population comes

Table 4.2 Regional differences of training input and employment population in 2010

	Eastern region	Central region	Western region
Private vocational training institutions			
Number	736.92	779.33	428.70
Funds (RMB 100 million)	4.92	1.91	1.73
Number of trainees	441,474.5	373,821.4	289,486.4
Public employment training centers			
Number	100.91	150.56	72.70
Funds (RMB 100 million)	0.75	0.87	0.31
Number of trainees	310,718.5	396,461.3	119,321.1
Economically active population	31,420,764	22,268,284	19,977,253
Migrant population	13,949,658	5,142,117	3,786,410

Note: The values in the table are the average values of each province within each region from *China 2010 census data*. The number of economically active population and migrant population is the sample number of long table sampling survey, which is different from the total number of national samples, but such difference does not affect our regional comparison.

4.4.3 Negative Impact of Labor Mobility Barriers on Human Capital Returns

As we mentioned before, urban development requires not only high skilled labor, but also low skilled labor. There is skill complementary between labors of different skilled levels, and employment increase of high skilled labor will increase at the same time the employment of low skilled labor force. In terms of productivity and wages, the increase in the number of highly skilled workers will increase the productivity and wages of low skilled workers.

However, China's household registration system is very strict, especially in big cities. In particular, in megacities such as Beijing, Shanghai and Guangzhou, only graduates with a bachelor's degree or above are likely to get permanent residence. This strict household registration system hinders the free flow of low skill labor to places with more demand and higher income levels. Our research confirms that indeed more high skilled and less low skill labor force are concentrated in cities with higher household registration threshold where becoming permanent residents is more difficult (Liang & Lu, 2015a, 2015b). When there are relatively more high skilled workers and less low skilled workers in big cities, it will hinder the complementarity between the high skilled and the low skilled workers there, which is harmful to the development of big cities themselves (Liang & Lu, 2015a, 2015b).

The household registration system also affects the educational returns of immigrant groups. It is difficult for those without local urban household registration to enter high-end service industries (Chen et al., 2013). Using data from city of Shanghai, Yan (2007) found that from 1995 to 2003, the growth rate of educational returns of local labor force and migrant labor force in Shanghai was different, and the educational returns of migrants were undercut. Using the same data, Yan (2011) also discovered that the share of migrant population in the employment market has gradually risen, and at the same time, their educational returns have also steadily increased. The reduction of the educational return gap between local and migrant labor indicates that the urban employment market has improved at integrating these two types of labor force. At present, the employment discrimination toward migrant labor force mainly is reflected in the system discrimination in job hunting and social security. Unfortunately, in recent years, the institutional exclusion of migrant workers in Beijing and Shanghai has aggravated the situation.

Now let us examine the return of training. Because a large proportion of the labor force is employed across regions, their training and employment places are different. Chen and Feng (2015) found that on average, people who received vocational training in eastern region performed better in the labor market than those who received it inland. This result indicates that the spatial distribution of vocational training resources still has room for improvement, that is, more investment in the eastern region can improve the overall efficiency of vocational training.

4.5 Outlook and Policy Implications

All around the world, urbanization is the only way to realize national modernization. If China wants to realize modernization, the continuous improvement of urbanization level will be an inevitable trend. For a big country like China, establishing an efficient urban system and urban spatial layout is more important than the continuous improvement of urbanization level, which requires correct urban development planning in order to achieve a regional development model that take both efficiency and equality into account. The key to achieve this goal is to form a regional economic growth pattern driven by big cities and metropolitan, and based on free flow of production factors between rural and urban areas and cross different regions, to realize the clustering economic development and effective labor division in regional economy, and eventually to move towards the balanced development of income per capita level, especially the balanced development of the quality of life between urban and rural areas and among different regions.

As shown in discussions here, the total amount and structure of human capital investment in China is far from meeting the needs of the scale or direction of population mobility. Therefore, this article proposes that China should carry out comprehensive policy adjustments and reform in education investment, labor market and household registration system, among others.

4.5.1 Central Government Should Increase Investments in Basic Education, Make Sure that Basic Education Resources Can Be Carried with Population Flow, and Promote the Equalization of Basic Public Services in Population Inflow Areas

The central government should allocate funds for basic education to all regions in a unified way. Local educational resources such as funds for basic education, school buildings and number of teachers should be allocated according to the number of school-age children in the permanent population. And in view of the scale economic effect of education, the expenditure per capita in areas with low population density should be increased appropriately.

In view of the fact that a large number of labor force has moved across regions and there are a large number of left behind children in rural areas, the central government should increase the education transfer payment to the population outflow areas, so that the education resources can be carried across regions as soon as possible. In population inflow areas, central government should take the Constitution and compulsory education law as the basis to allow children of migrant population enjoy the local educational resources in urban areas where their parents work. In megacities, due to the different economic scale and financial situation of each district and county, municipal governments should strengthen the overall allocation of educational resources of each district and county in order to achieve the balanced distribution of educational resources in downtown areas and suburban areas.

4.5.2 Increase the Total Amount of Educational Resources through Multiple Channels, so that Children of Migrant Population Can Attend School Equally at Places where their Parents Work

The right way to reduce the mismatch between the supply and demand of educational resources is to increase the supply, not to reduce the demand. First, in terms of fund-raising, we should increase the total amount of educational resources by means of self-payment from migrant workers, central financial transfer as well as more local financial investment, and funds from other social channels. The education financial transfer payment from the central government should be linked with the number of migrant population absorbed by each city. In terms of the allocation of education resources, it should tilt toward large-scale residential areas and migrant population concentrated areas. Second, in terms of the supply model, we should lower the entry threshold of running a school, set reasonable standards for running a school, make all kinds of funds and investors provide differentiated and multi-level education services, and meet the needs of different children with the help of market forces. Third, as long as the capacity of school allows, no other restrictive conditions shall be set for any child who has educational needs, except for the residence permit, social security payment and entering the school close to their residence.

4.5.3 Promote the Reform of Household Registration System, Accelerate the Steps so that Migrants Could Live a Prosperous and Contented Life, and Increase their Human Capital Investment

The current household registration system is unable to meet the needs of the population agglomerated in large cities and megacities, so we need to speed up the reform of household registration system, reduce the threshold, and take big cities and megacities as breakthrough points. Therefore, for those migrant residents who have been working in large cities for a long time, except for employment requirements and social security payments, other restrictions on urban settlement should be removed. For college graduates who have already worked in big cities and megacities, we should shorten the requirement of employment years before they can apply for urban residency. The education level and the threshold of professional titles should cease to be the residency criteria in order to facilitate the settlement and social integration of low skilled labor force in their employment places.

In the process of the reform of household registration system, local governments should equalize basic public services for all permanent residents. In terms of basic education, local governments should allow children of migrant workers to enter public schools after the payment of a certain fee (with help of the portable central education input). The local government's investment in vocational education and training should cover all permanent residents and lay the foundation of human capital for future urban developments. At the same time, in the labor market, we should promote fair employment, increase migrant workers' expectations of their human capital investment returns, and strengthen their willingness to invest in human capital.

References

Bacolod, M., Blum, B. S., & Strange, W. C. (2009). Skills in the city. *Journal of Urban Economics, 65*(2), 136–153.

Berry, C. R., & Glaeser, E. L. (2005). The divergence of human capital levels across cities. *Regional Studies, 84*(3), 407–444.

Cai, F., Park, A., & Zhao, Y. (2008). The Chinese labor market in the reform era. In L. Brandt & T. G. Rawski (Eds.), *China's Great Economic Transformation* (pp. 167–214). Cambridge University Press.

Chang, H., Dong, X., & MacPhail, F. (2011). Labor migration and time use patterns of the left-behind children and elderly in rural China. *World Development, 39*(12), 2199–2210.

Chen, B., Chen, Z., Freeman, R. & Lu, M. (2013). *Language as a bridge: The effects of dialect on labor market performance in urban China*. Paper Presented at the International Conference on Chinese Labor Market. Zhejiang University

Chen, Y., & Feng, S. (2013). Access to public schools and the education of migrant children in China. *China Economic Review, 26*(1), 75–88.

Chen, Z., Feng, J. (2015). Spatial Differences in Vocational Education Returns. *World Economy* forthcoming

Chen, Z., Jiang, S., Lu, M., & Sato, H. (2014). Escaping low-level equilibrium of urbanization: Institutional promotion, social interaction and labor migration. *China Economics, 9*(1), 68–85.

Eeckhout, J., Pinheiro, R., & Schmidheiny, K. (2014). Spatial sorting. *Journal of Political Economy, 122*(3), 554–620.

Fleisher, B. M., & Wang, X. (2005). Returns to schooling in China under planning and reform. *Journal of Comparative Economics, 33*(2), 265–277.

Gao, H. (2014). Urban population scale and labor income. *World Economy, 10*, 145–164.

Gao, Y., Li, L., Kim, J. H., Congdon, N., Lau, J., & Griffiths, S. (2010). The impact of parental migration on health status and health Behaviours among left behind adolescent school children in China. *BMC Public Health, 10*(56), 1–10.

Gao, W. S. & Smyth, R. (2012). *Returns to schooling in urban China, 2001-2010: Evidence from three waves of the China urban labor survey*. Monash University, Department of Economics, discussion paper, 12(50)

Gautier, P. A., & Teulings, C. N. (2009). Search and the city. *Regional Science and Urban Economics, 39*(3), 251–265.

Glaeser, E. L., & Lu, M. (2014). *Human Capital Externalities in China*. Harvard University and Shanghai Jiaotong University Working Paper.

Hu, Y., Lu, M., Sachs, J., & Chen, Z. (Eds.). (2012). *Crossing the "middle-income trap": Outlook on the sustainability of China's economic growth*. Gezhi Publishing House and Shanghai People's Publishing House.

Jia, Z., Shi, L., Cao, Y., James, D., & Tian, W. (2010). Health-related quality of life of left-behind children: A cross-sectional survey in rural China. *Quality of Life Research, 19*(6), 775–780.

Li, S., & Ding, S. (2003). The long-term changing trend of returns to education in urban China. *Chinese Social Sciences, 6*, 58–72.

Liang, Z., & Chen, Y. (2006). The impact of rural-urban migration on the education of migrant children. *World Economic Papers, 1*, 1–17.

Liang, W., & Lu, M. (2014). *Cities in post-industrial era: Micro evidence of the impact of urban scale on externality of human capital in service industry*. Working papers of Fudan University and Shanghai Jiaotong University.

Liang, W., & Lu, M. (2015a). *Skill Complementarities within Firms*". Working Paper,. Shanghai Jiaotong University.

Liang, W., & Lu, M. (2015b). Differentiation of urban human capital: Exploring the complementarity and spatial agglomeration of different skilled workers. *Comparison of Economic and Social Systems, 3*, 185–197.

Lu, M. (2015). Urban disease treatment: Great potentials in planning, management and technology. *Wenhui Scholar, Wenhui Daily*

Lu, M., Gao, H., & Sato, H. (2012). Urban scale and inclusive employment. *China Social Sciences, 10*, 47–66.

Lu, M., & Wan, G. (2014). Urbanization and urban system in China: Research findings and policy recommendations. *Journal of Economic Survey, 28*, 671–685.

Lu, M., & Xia, Y. (2015). *The footprint of human capital: A 700-Year historical perspective of cross-city migration in China*. Shanghai Jiaotong University and Wenzhou University, Working Paper.

Moretti, E. (2012). *The new geography of jobs*. Houghton Mifflin Harcourt.

Research group of all-China Women's Federation (2013). *Research Report on Left behind Children and Migrant Children in China's Rural Areas*, http://www.docin.com/p-659569964.html

Rozelle, S. (2015). China's high school education crisis and the challenge of crossing the middle-income trap. *Report of international academic seminar on human capital and the challenge of China's economic development*.

Xia, Y., & Lu, M. (2015). Resettlement competition among cities: Empirical study on the impact of public services on the flow of labor force. *Management World, 10*, 78–90.

Xing, C. (2015). *Human capital and urbanization in China*. Asian Development Bank Working Paper.

Yan, S. (2007). Human capital, system and wage difference: An empirical analysis of the dual labor market in big cities. *Management World, 6*, 4–13. 171–172.

Yan, S. (2011). Structural transformation of labor market in China's big cities: An empirical analysis of Shanghai employment survey in 2003 and 2009. *Management World, 9*, 53–62.

Zhang, J., Zhao, Y., Part, A., & Song, X. (2005). Economic returns to schooling in urban China. *Journal of Comparative Economics, 33*(4), 730–752.

Ming Lu, professor at Shanghai Jiao Tong University.

Chapter 5
Poverty of Migrant Workers and Determining Factors: A Comparison with Urban Residents

Meiyan Wang

Abstract The number of migrant workers from the countryside to cities has kept increasing in the course of urbanization, and they have become a component of urban poverty. Using data from the 2010 China Urban Labor Survey (CULS), this paper discusses the poverty of migrant workers on a wide range of dimensions, including income, living consumption, housing, social insurance and children's education. It analyzes the determining factors of poverty and makes a comparison with urban residents, and finds that poverty incidence calculated based on permanent population is slightly lower of migrant workers than that of urban residents, but it may be underestimated. Labor income takes a lion's share (more than 95%) in migrant workers' total income, and they may easily fall into poverty after losing their job and income. Their level of education, employment or unemployment have a significant impact on their poverty status, which is unsettling in terms of living consumption, housing, social insurance and children's education. As migrant workers are consistently excluded from the scope of minimum living allowance, how to incorporate them in that system and make the allowance more targeted and efficient is a key challenge for the government.

Keywords Migrant workers · Income poverty · Multi-dimensional poverty · Minimum living allowance

M. Wang (✉)
Institute of Population and Labor Economics, Chinese Academy of Social Sciences, Beijing, China
e-mail: lvqs@ssap.cn

F. Cai (ed.), *Income Inequality and Poverty Governance in China*, International Research on Poverty Reduction, https://doi.org/10.1007/978-981-95-5063-0_5

5.1 Introduction

The employment policy implemented in cities before the reform and opening-up ensured jobs, salary and income for urban residents. At that time the poor group mainly referred to a limited number of "people of three withouts"[1] (Cai et al., 2005). The World Bank estimated about 1.3 million urban poor people in 1990 (World Bank, 1992), a group that was concentrated in the countryside before the 1990s. An estimate based on a comparable definition of poverty shows that the rural and urban poverty rate was 12.7 and 2.7% in 1988 and 12.4 and 4.1% in 1995 (Riskin & Li, 2001; Khan et al., 2001). The relative poverty in rural and urban areas has not changed much in recent years, and the countryside and the cities contributed 75.5 and 24.2% to the multi-dimensional poverty incidence in 2009 (Wang, 2012).

With the reform of state-owned enterprises (SOE) and with the growing number of migrant workers in cities since the late 1990s, urban poverty has seen marked changes and drew close attention.

First of all, the laid-off and the jobless became an important part of urban poor population. The SOE reform since 1998 caused huge amounts of workers to be laid off or lose jobs from state-owned or collective enterprises, many of whom failed to find new jobs due to low human capital or old age. For those who were re-employed, their jobs were mostly characterized by instability and lower wages (Knight & Song, 2005). This group of people, the majority of which were married and had a family to support, was easily left in poverty.

Second, migrant workers and their families made part of the poor population in cities. Since the 1990s, old institutional restrictions on the flow of rural laborers were lifted gradually, giving them the freedom to find jobs in cities. They generally worked in informal sectors or on their own (e.g. providing housekeeping services or doing business), with relatively low income (Cai et al., 2005). Although their income has increased considerably in recent years, the absolute amount remains low, averaging only RMB 2290 per month in 2012 (National Bureau of Statistics, 2013). This money has to sustain the life of the migrant workers and their families, which easily reduces them to poverty.

Besides, labor income is the main source of income for migrant workers, who have barely any income from properties or transfer, so they easily become poor when they lose their jobs and then income. Another reason is their non-participation in social insurance programs such as endowment insurance and medical insurance. For example, if a migrant worker does not join the endowment insurance program, he will not be able to receive pension in old age when he is unable to work anymore, and those do not join the medical insurance program may fall into or slip back into poverty because of illness. Furthermore, migrant workers do not have equal access to the social benefits and public services enjoyed by urban residents, including housing and children's education.

---

[1] "People of three withouts" refer to those without source of income, labor capacity or eligible supporter.

The number of migrant workers has kept rising in the course of urbanization[2] and reached 163 million in 2012 (NBS, 2013). Close attention must be drawn to them and their families as they have become a part of urban poverty. But a common problem of most studies is that the survey samples and data they used did not include migrant workers. Only a few (e.g. ADB, 2004; Du et al., 2006; Park & Wang, 2010) included both migrant workers and urban residents and compared the poverty of the two groups. Yet their data had their own problems[3] and were collected many years ago.

This paper uses data of the 2010 China Urban Labor Survey (CULS)[4] to study the poverty of migrant workers. The greatest advantage of CULS data is that it covers both migrant and urban households in each city, thus ensuring its representation of both groups to the largest extent possible. The paper compares the poverty of migrant workers with that of urban residents to reveal poverty status of the former and latest situation in the city more clearly, as the survey data are quite recent.

It is worth noting that, unlike other studies that only focus on income, this paper conducts a multi-dimensional analysis of migrant workers' poverty. A high-quality life entails high income and good educational, medical and living conditions (Sen, 1985, 1999). Apart from low income, migrant workers are also troubled by living consumption, low coverage rate in social insurance, poor living condition and limited access to good education for children, and this paper will encompass all those aspects. On that basis, it will offer suggestions on how to keep migrant workers from becoming poor and how to help the poor.

Part II of this paper is a summary and review of literature. Part III introduces the data used in the paper, analyzes migrant workers' income poverty incidence in comparison to urban residents, and discusses their income composition. Part IV studies the determining factors for migrant workers' income poverty with a comparison to those for urban residents. Part V discusses migrant workers' poverty on such dimensions as living consumption, living conditions, participation in social insurance and children's education. Part VI summarizes the paper and offers suggestions.

5.2 Literature Review

Some studies of migrant workers' poverty are limited to general discussions without concrete data. Fan (2007) pointed out that the poverty of migrant workers, who are vulnerable groups in cities, stems from their rural household registration (*hukou*) that restricts them to get jobs, which makes them unable to earn enough money to eradicate poverty. Han and Ma (2007) said the migrant population is neglected in

---

[2] Migrant workers refer to rural laborers who have worked for six months or longer in a place other than their local township in the year of survey.

[3] Part II of this paper analyzes the problems with data used in those studies.

[4] Part III of this paper elaborates on the data.

hukou-based poverty surveys. Han and Zhang (2011) held that the poverty of migrant population is a compound issue involving low income, lack of job skills, weak social support and unprotected rights and interests.

A few studies discuss the poverty of urban migrant population with data from micro-level survey. Yang and Ma (2012), based on a survey in Chengdu, described the income, assets, housing and social security of migrant population, but did not calculate its poverty incidence. Yin and Huang (2010) analyzed the living status and poverty features of urban migrant population based on a micro-level survey in Harbin, but the representation of the data and the accuracy of the conclusion is questionable given the small number of samples (only 156 people participated).

After migrant workers move to live and work in cities, their reference group becomes urban residents, and it is meaningful to compare them when discussing poverty of the former. ADB (2004), together with Du et al. (2006) studied the poverty of both groups using detailed micro data, but they arrived at different poverty rates as they set different poverty lines. Based on the poverty line it set, ADB (2004) calculated the poverty incidence of migrant population to be 15.2% and that of urban residents to be 10.3%. Du et al. (2006), on the other hand, set two poverty lines, and calculated the two groups' poverty incidence to be 10 and 3% respectively according to the lower one and 16 and 6% according to the higher one.

The data about migrant workers used by ADB (2004) were collected from a survey in 1999 and those used by Du et al. (2006) were from a survey in 2002, both being a one-time activity, but their data about urban residents both came from NBS urban household survey of the current year, in which income information was collected in the form of a journal. Compared with urban household survey, one-time survey tends to record lower-than-actual income, which leads to over-estimated poverty incidence. In this case, the two groups are less comparable in poverty.

Park and Wang (2010) discussed the poverty of migrant population and urban residents by matching the micro data of 2004 and 2005. They found a tiny difference in the poverty incidence of the two groups, which differed widely from the conclusion that poverty incidence of the former is much higher than that of the latter, which was drawn by most studies (ADB, 2004; Du et al., 2006). The paper holds that although migrant workers have a much lower hourly wage than urban residents, they work longer with a higher labor participation rate. Park and Wang used the same sampling method to collect data about the two groups, but the data were the result of matching those of two years, which affects their comparability.

There is little analysis of poverty relief for migrant workers. Only few studies have mentioned this topic. According to Fan (2007), migrant workers are not entitled to relief provided by the urban minimum living allowance system because of their rural *hukou*. Han and Ma (2007) pointed out that the urban poverty monitoring system should have no *hukou* restriction, and should encompass everyone living in the city during a certain period, and poverty relief measures should be formulated and adopted and a comprehensive social security system established.

Studies of migrant workers' poverty should go beyond income to include more dimensions as well, but most current studies merely make such a suggestion. For instance, Fan (2007) said that other than income, housing, working status, consumption level and public services should also be considered when analyzing migrant workers' poverty, but hardly any study has conducted an in-depth analysis of all these dimensions.

5.3 Income Poverty of Migrant Workers

As pointed out earlier, migrant workers' income remains low in terms of absolute amount despite a rapid increase in recent years, so some migrant workers and their families are still below the poverty line. Besides, as labor income makes up the majority of their income, with little property and transfer income, migrant workers will have drastically reduced income and probably become poor if they lose their jobs for various reasons. This part analyzes their poverty from the income perspective, calculate their poverty incidence and study their income composition with a comparison with urban residents.

5.3.1 Introduction to Research Data

This paper will use data of the labor force survey (hereinafter referred to as "2010 CULS") conducted by the Institute of Population and Labor Economics, the Chinese Academy of Social Sciences, in six cities (Shanghai, Wuhan, Shenyang, Fuzhou, Xi'an and Guangzhou) from the end of 2009 to early 2010. The survey conducted phased random sampling of 700 urban households in each city and asked them to fill in the questionnaires on the family and its members. It also sampled 600 migrant households in the same way with the questionnaires. Some of the migrant population surveyed in 2010 had rural *hukou* and some non-rural *hukou.* This paper only analyzes the first group, commonly known as migrant workers.

The information collected in this survey can be divided into two categories. The first category is the personal information on every family member, including basic information, human capital features, employment, income and social security status. The other is household information, including housing and its income and consumption level.

5.3.2 Income Poverty of Migrant Workers

The general definition is that if a family's income per capita is below the poverty line, it is considered as a poor family and its members as poor population. There are two methods to determine poverty, by absolute standard or by relative standard, each with its pros and cons. With the absolute standard method, resident's spending on daily necessities like clothing, food, housing and travel is calculated in a certain method and the result is taken as the poverty line to estimate poor population. With the relative standard method, resident's income is ranked and a fixed percentage of those at the bottom is considered poor population, or half of the median income (or average income) is taken as the poverty line to estimate poor population (Wang, 2003).

With the absolute standard method, the daily income of USD 1 or 1.5 is a typical poverty line (Ravallion et al., 1991), and it is common to estimate poor population on that basis in developing countries. But using this line has many problems. First, it neglects the price change in different regions and periods in a country; second, using purchasing power parity (PPP) exchange rate as the proxy of local living cost is questionable (Ravallion & Chen, 1997). Some studies use the official poverty line to estimate poverty incidence (Newman & Struyk, 1983), which is typical absolute standard method, but many others adopt the relative standard method, such as Casper et al. (1994), who set the poverty line at half of the median income per capita.

China has set a uniform rural poverty line across the nation[5] but never set a uniform poverty line for cities. As stated before, various studies usually posit a reasonable poverty line when estimating urban poverty. This paper discusses the poverty of migrant workers. Since they live in the city, urban residents make the most important reference group, so a poverty line is drawn in reference to their minimal minimum living standard.[6] But since this standard is generally low in the cities,[7] this paper posits two poverty lines, one being 1.5 times of the minimum living standard and the other 2 times, and the poverty incidence calculated against them is denoted with Poverty Incidence I and II respectively.

The calculations show that both poverty incidence I and II of migrant workers is slightly lower than that of urban residents (Table 5.1), I being 0.38 percentage point lower and II 0.2 percentage point, but the situation differs from city to city. In Shanghai, Fuzhou and Xi'an, poverty incidence I and II of migrant workers is higher than that of urban residents; in Wuhan and Guangzhou, the situation is the opposite; in Shenyang, migrant workers have a higher poverty incidence I but lower II than that of urban residents.

People generally think that migrant workers must have a higher poverty incidence than urban residents as they have a lower average income, but the results in Table 5.1 say otherwise. This seems baffling, but is actually reasonable if we take a closer look at the total income and family size of the two groups and compare their income per capita. On average of these cities surveyed, the family income of migrant workers is only 73% that of urban residents, but their income per capita reaches

[5] NBS announced a rural poverty line every year before 2010 and a rural low-income line after that.

[6] According to *Regulations on Minimum living allowance for Urban Residents,* the allowance standard takes into account the cost for meeting the local urban residents' basic needs (including clothing, food and accommodation), the cost of water, electricity and coal or piped gas, as well as the compulsory education fee for minors.

[7] For instance, the disposable income per capita in Shanghai was RMB 31,838 in 2010, and the annual minimum living allowance standard calculated based on the Q1 standard was RMB 5100, less than one sixth of the disposal income per capita. The situation is basically the same in other cities.

Table 5.1 Poverty of migrant workers and urban residents

City	1.5 times the minimum living standard (RMB/year)	2 times the minimum living standard (RMB/year)	Poverty incidence I (%)		Poverty incidence II (%)	
			Migrant workers	Urban residents	Migrant workers	Urban residents
Shanghai	7650	10,200	7.34	4.56	16.72	10.42
Wuhan	4932	6576	2.96	6.33	7.39	10.28
Shenyang	5904	7872	11.21	10.89	17.83	20.88
Fuzhou	4050	5400	10.49	7.53	13.11	9.93
Xi'an	4140	5520	8.64	7.61	15.20	12.72
Guangzhou	7182	9576	4.04	7.94	8.75	14.21
Total	–	–	7.07	7.45	12.76	12.96

Note: Bureaus of civil services usually publicize the monthly minimum living standard on their websites, but the figure in the table is the annual standard, which is the product of the average monthly minimum living standard in 2010 Q1 times twelve. Family income is calculated according to the income indicator in the urban household survey of NBS. Since this paper focuses on poverty, transfer income does not include income from urban minimum living allowance and other subsidies
Source: The urban minimum living standard is from the website of bureaus of civil service of each city; the poverty incidence is calculated based on 2010 CULS

93% that of the latter due to a smaller family size. There are usually 2.27 members in a family of migrant workers and 2.89 members in a family of urban residents (Table 5.2). When it comes to each specific city, migrant workers have less family income than urban residents in all cities surveyed, but their income per capita is relatively high given the small family size. In Shenyang and Guangzhou, income per capita of migrant families is higher than that of urban ones, but it is on a par in Fuzhou.

It must be pointed out that family size in this paper refers to the number of permanent residents, and it may be underestimated for migrant workers as some of their family members have not come along to the city but stay in the rural areas or work and live in other cities. According to 2010 CULS, 11% of the married migrant workers live in the city without their spouses and one third of migrant families have not brought along their children. If these spouses and children are all counted, the average family size of migrant workers would be bigger, their income per capita smaller, and poverty incidence higher. Therefore, Table 5.1 that only counts the permanent residents in migrant worker families is likely to underestimate their poverty incidence.

It must be also noted that a look at the income composition of migrant workers and urban residents shows that when they lose their jobs and consequently their income due to illness, loss of work capacity or for other reasons, the former is more likely to fall into poverty than the latter. The reason is that labor income takes a lion's share (more than 95%) in migrant worker's total income, with little property and transfer income, so they will almost definitely become poor once they lose their labor income. On the contrary, labor income only takes up 65% of urban resident's

Table 5.2 Income and its composition for migrant worker households and urban households

	Income			Income per capita		
	Migrant workers (RMB) (MT)	Urban residents (RMB) (UT)	MT/UT	Migrant workers (RMB) (MA)	Urban residents (RMB) (UA)	MA/UA
Shanghai	54,041	67,685	0.80	22,654	24,819	0.91
Wuhan	37,616	65,847	0.57	16,334	20,252	0.81
Shenyang	33,380	40,778	0.82	16,286	15,359	1.06
Fuzhou	35,842	52,279	0.69	18,257	18,254	1.00
Xi'an	33,735	46,028	0.73	13,905	16,802	0.83
Guangzhou	76,336	88,073	0.87	30,414	28,450	1.07
Total	43,840	59,895	0.73	19,288	20,749	0.93

Source: Calculated based on 2010 CULS

total income, so even if they lose it, their transfer and property income can sustain their living to some extent (Fig. 5.1).

5.4 Determining Factors of Poverty of Migrant Workers

Understanding the poverty of migrant workers is only the first step to study it. Other than that, we also hope to ascertain the determining factors of their poverty and compare them with the situation with urban residents. The Probit model will be used to analyze which factors contribute to the poverty of migrant workers or urban residents. As most studies have explained, whether a family is in poverty is determined by a number of factors, including the human capital of family members, employment and family structure. The model to analyze those determining factors is below:

$p = X'\beta + \varepsilon$Here P indicates whether the family is in poverty. X' is an explained variable vector, covering the family members' human capital features (gender, age, level of education, health status, membership in the Communist Party of China and marital status of the head of household), employment features (ratio of employed and unemployed family members to adult members), and family structure features (size, ratio of members aged 0–14 and those aged 65 and above). There is also a dummy variable of the city: ε as a stochastic error term. Table 5.3 lists the dependent and independent variables of the model.

The dependent variable, "whether a family is in poverty", is a dichotomous one. It is 1 if the family is poor and 0 if not. The first independent variable is the head of household's human capital features. The family members' human capital level is an important reflection of the family's earning power. As an important member, the head of household's human capital level is critical for whether the family is in poverty or not, so we choose his/her human capital features to serve as proxy variable of the whole family's human capital features. To be more specific, the variables that

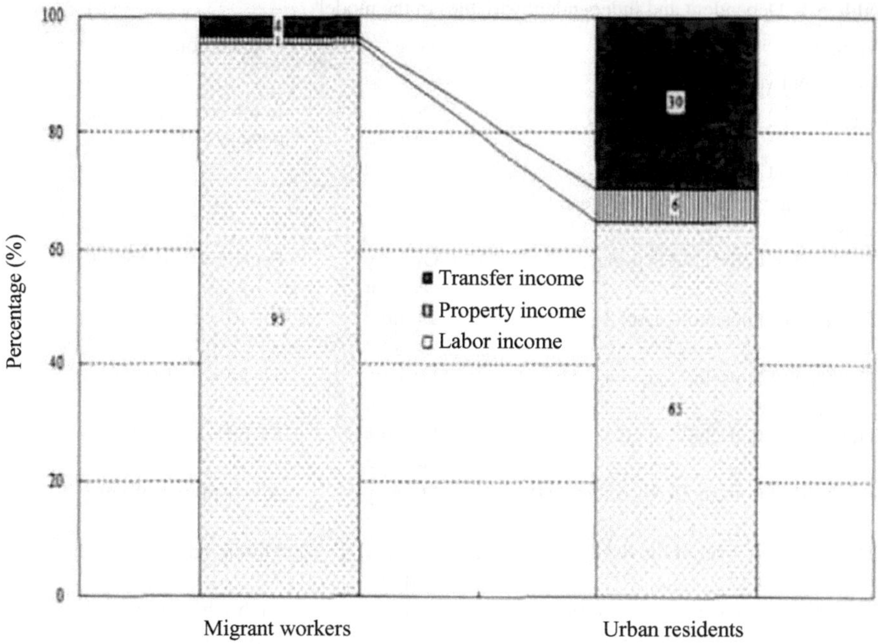

Fig. 5.1 Income composition of migrant workers and urban residents. Source: Calculated based on 2010 CULS

reflect the household head's human capital features include gender, age, level of education, health status, CPC membership and marital status.

The determination of the head of household is quite random in China, so we could not decide how their gender affects the family's poverty status before the model is established. The impact of the age of the head of household on whether the family falls into poverty should be seen from two aspects. On the one hand, the older the household heads, the more experienced they are and the higher their income, which reduces the possibility of poverty. On the other hand, the household head's income may drop after they reach a certain age, which increases the possibility of poverty. It is hard to decide how their age affects family poverty as a whole.

As an important indicator of human capital, the level of education has obvious impact on poverty. The higher education one receives, the more capable he is to make money and the less possible for the family to become poor. With those whose educational level is elementary school and below as the reference group, we posit three dummy variables: middle school; high school or technical secondary school; and junior college and above. Of the migrant worker samples, the percentage of household heads who have received the above four levels of education is 13.6, 50.9, 25.8 and 9.7% respectively, and the percentage is 11.4, 28, 34.6 and 26% among urban resident samples.

Health status is another important indicator of human capital. Self-assessed health status is used here. We expect to see a lower probability of poverty for better

Table 5.3 Dependent and independent variables in the model

Variable	Type	Explanation
Dependent variable		
Whether the family is in poverty	Dummy variable	In poverty = 1, not in poverty = 0
Independent variables		
Human capital features of the head of household		
The head of household is female	Dummy variable	Female = 1, if not = 0
The head of household aged 31–40	Dummy variable	31–40 = 1, if not = 0
The head of household aged 41–50	Dummy variable	41–50 = 1, if not = 0
The head of household aged 51–60	Dummy variable	51–60 = 1, if not = 0
The head of household aged above 60	Dummy variable	Above 60 = 1, if not = 0
The education level of the head of household is middle school	Dummy variable	Middle school = 1, if not = 0
The education level of the head of household is high school or technical secondary school	Dummy variable	High school or technical secondary school = 1, if not = 0
The education level of the head of household is junior college and above	Dummy variable	Junior college and above = 1, if not = 0
The head of household is in mediocre health	Dummy variable	Mediocre health = 1, if not = 0
The head of household is in good health	Dummy variable	Good health = 1, if not = 0
The head of household is a CPC member	Dummy variable	CPC member = 1, if not = 0
The head of household is married	Dummy variable	Married = 1, if not = 0
Employment features of family members		
Percentage of employed members in adult members	Continuous variable	Percentage of employed members in adult members
Percentage of unemployed members in adult members	Continuous variable	Percentage of unemployed members in adult members
Family structure features		
Family size	Continuous variable	Number of family members
Percentage of family members aged 0–14	Continuous variable	Percentage of family members aged 0–14
Percentage of family members aged 65 and above	Continuous variable	Percentage of family members aged 65 and above
A set of dummy variables of the city	Dummy variable	–

health. With those in poor health as the reference group, we add two dummy variables: mediocre health and good health. The percentage of household heads in those three health status is 0.6, 7 and 92.4% among migrant worker samples, and that among urban resident samples is 7.3, 20.4 and 72.3%.

The dummy variable of CPC membership is also put in the model as a proxy for the household heads' political capital, and those who are not CPC members serve as the reference group. 2.4% of the heads of migrant worker households are CPC members as opposed to 19.4% among urban households. Studies show that while other conditions are the same, CPC members have higher income than non-CPC members (Wang, 2004), which leads to the conclusion that households whose heads are CPC members are less likely to become poor. There is also the dummy variable that the household head is married, with unmarried ones being the reference group. Generally, marriage means the spouse can make economic contributions, thus reducing the possibility of poverty.

The employment status of family members reflects the family's earning power. When employed members take a higher percentage in the family, there is more income and a smaller possibility of poverty. When unemployed members take a higher percentage, there is less income and a larger possibility of poverty. Both the percentage of employed and unemployed members in adult members are variables that reflect the employment status of family members, which is 89 and 0.7% among migrant worker samples and 50.5 and 2.3% among urban resident samples.

The model also includes variables that reflect the family structure features: family size and the percentage of family members aged 0–14 and aged 65 and above. The larger the family, the heavier its economic burden, so size has positive impact on family poverty. The percentage of family members aged 0–14 indicates the family's dependency burden as that age group has to be supported without making any money. The higher this percentage is, the more possible the family may become poor.

People aged 65 and above can be divided into two groups. Some are retirees with pension and can help the family stay out of poverty, but some have no pension and have to depend on their children. For migrant worker families, only 23% of those aged 65 and above have endowment insurance, but the percentage is 73% for urban families. This means most migrant workers in this age group do not have pension and need economic help from their children, which may cause the family to become poor. Quite on the contrary, most urban residents aged 65 and above have pension and can increase family income and therefore reduce the possibility of poverty.

Since the samples are collected from six cities, a set of dummy city variables of Wuhan, Shenyang, Fuzhou, Xi'an and Guangzhou are used, with Shanghai being the reference group. Setting the poverty line at 1.5 times and 2 times of the minimum living standard, we studied the independent variables' impact on whether a family is in poverty, and established a Probit model, Model I and Model II, for migrant workers and urban residents separately. Table 5.4 lists the marginal effects of various independent variables. The Pseudo R^2 of both models is above 0.17 for migrant workers and above 0.21 for urban residents. All in all, the poverty model has a high fitting degree.

Table 5.4 Estimation of determining factors for poverty in migrant worker households and urban households based on the Probit model (marginal effect)

Variable	Migrant worker households		Urban households	
	1.5 times the minimum living standard	2 times the minimum living standard	1.5 times the minimum living standard	2 times the minimum living standard
	Model I	Model II	Model I	Model II
Human capital features of household head				
The head of household is male				
The head of household is female	−0.0174**	−0.0160	−0.0049	−0.0053
The head of household aged under 30				
The head of household aged 31–40	−0.0093	0.0127	−0.0077	0.0038
The head of household aged 41–50	−0.0057	0.0259	0.0122	0.0429*
The head of household aged 51–60	−0.0061	0.0008	−0.0313***	−0.0489**
The head of household aged over 60	0.0173	0.0990	−0.0581***	−0.0930***
The education level of the head of household is primary school and below				
The education level of the head of household is middle school	−0.0209**	−0.0284*	−0.0173*	−0.0487***
The education level of the head of household is high school or technical secondary school	−0.0299***	−0.0512***	−0.0267***	−0.0669***
The education level of the head of household is junior college and above	−0.0245**	−0.0420**	−0.0476***	−0.1030***
The head of household is in poor health				
The head of household is in mediocre health	0.0780	−0.0065	−0.0272***	−0.0543***
The head of household is in good health	0.0322	−0.0129	−0.0797***	−0.1354***
The head of household is non-CPC member				
The head of household is CPC member	−0.0363***	−0.0081	−0.0316***	−0.0485***

(continued)

Table 5.4 (continued)

Variable	Migrant worker households		Urban households	
	1.5 times the minimum living standard	2 times the minimum living standard	1.5 times the minimum living standard	2 times the minimum living standard
The head of household is single				
The head of household is married	−0.0261**	−0.0373**	−0.0156*	−0.0263*
Employment features of family members				
Percentage of employed members in adult members	−0.0877***	−0.1666***	−0.1026***	−0.1889***
Percentage of unemployed members in adult members	0.0882***	0.1368**	0.1196***	0.2658***
Family structure features				
Family size	0.0091**	0.0149**	0.0025	0.0102**
Percentage of family members aged 0–14	0.0669**	0.1574***	0.0431*	0.1122***
Percentage of family members aged 65 and above	0.1778***	0.2066**	−0.0583***	−0.1135***
Dummy variables of the city	–	–	–	–
Constant term	–	–	–	–
Number of observed values				
Log-likelihood	−462.4869	−684.2964	−869.6630	−1237.4620
Prob > chi2	0.0000	0.0000	0.0000	0.0000
Pseudo R^2	0.1775	0.1720	0.2127	0.2227

Note: The signs "***", "**" and "*" mean the variable is significant at 10, 5 and 1%; marginal effect means the impact probability of a changed independent variable on family poverty while other factors are controlled; we use robust standard errors to eliminate the effect of heteroscedasticity

Source: Calculated based on 2010 CULS

Whether the poverty line is 1.5 times or 2 times the minimum living standard, most independent variables' impacts on the family's poverty status are similar for migrant workers and urban residents, but there are certain exceptions. Overall the estimation consists with our expectation. Next we will explain the impacts of each independent variable in the model.

Of all variables of the household head's human capital features, gender and age are only significant in few models for both migrant workers and urban residents. The three dummy variables of the level of education are negatively significant in all models, meaning if the household head's educational level is middle school, high school or technical secondary school, or junior college and above, the family has a lower probability of becoming poor than when the educational level is only primary school or below. This paper has corroborated a conclusion drawn by many studies that human capital plays a critical role in reducing poverty (Li, 2004; Gregory et al., 2005).

As far as the marginal effect of educational level, a dummy variable, is concerned, the probability of poverty is lowest for migrant worker families if the household head has finished high school or technical secondary school, followed by junior college and higher education, and then middle school, whereas the probability is highest if the head has only received primary school education or less. In Model II, compared with families in which the household head's educational level is primary school and below, the probability of family poverty is 5.12% lower if the educational level is high school or technical secondary school, 4.2% lower if it is junior college and above, and 2.84% lower if it is middle school.

For urban resident families, the better educated the household head is, the less probable the family will become poor. Still in Model II, compared with families in which the household head's educational level is primary school and below, the probability of family poverty is 4.87% lower if the educational level is middle school, 6.69% lower if it is high school or technical secondary school, and 10.3% lower if it is junior college and above.

The household head's health status has no impact on whether a migrant worker family is in poverty, but it does for urban families, probably because migrant workers keep working to make money even when they are in bad health. For urban families, the healthier the household head is, the less likely the family will become poor. In Model II, compared with households with an unhealthy head, the probability of family poverty is 5.43% lower if the household head is in mediocre health and 13.54% lower if in good health. Many urban residents choose to work less or not at all when they are in bad health, which results in the decrease or loss of labor income and affects family poverty.

The variable of CPC membership is significant in Model I for migrant workers and significant in both models for urban residents, which means CPC membership, as the proxy variable of the household head's political capital, has significant negative impact on family poverty in most models. Although China is in the transition period from planned economy to market economy, political capital is still vital for family income and poverty. This is consistent with Li Shi's research findings (2004). The variable that the household head is married is significantly negative for both groups in Model I and II, meaning families where the household head is married is much less likely to become poor than if unmarried.

As we expected, the two variables that reflect the family member's employment status, percentage of employed and unemployed family members in adult members, have significant negative and positive impacts on family poverty. In other words, if employed members take a larger percentage, the family is less likely to become poor; if unemployed members take a larger percentage, the family is more likely to become poor.

According to Li Shi's study (2004), unemployment and layoff are important reasons for urban poverty. The data used by Gregory et al. (2005) lacked information on unemployment and their model only had the percentage of employed family members, which was found to have significant negative impact on family poverty. They therefore inferred unemployment to be positive on poverty. Xue and Wei (2004) compared the poverty rate of households with and without unemployed members and found it higher in the first group, and the more unemployed members there are, the higher the poverty rate. This paper comes to a conclusion consistent with those mentioned above.

Variables that reflect family structure features are significant in most models. Family size is significantly positive in Model I for migrant workers and in both models for urban residents. This means a larger family size leads to a higher probability of poverty, which corroborates the conclusion drawn by Gregory et al. (2005). The percentage of family members aged 0–14 is significantly positive on family poverty for both groups, indicating that the higher this percentage, the more likely the family will become poor, which consists with our expectation.

The percentage of family members aged 65 and above has significant impacts on poverty, but in opposite directions on the two groups, namely positive for migrant workers and negative for urban residents, which also fits our expectation. Most migrant workers aged 65 and above do not have pension and are supported by their children, leading to family poverty, whereas most urban residents in this age group have pension and can help reduce the possibility of family poverty.

5.5 Multi-Dimensional Poverty among Migrant Workers

Apart from income poverty, migrant workers also have difficulties in living consumption, living conditions, participation in social insurance and children's education. Not joining social insurance not only exposes migrant workers to a higher risk of poverty, but also makes them feel insecure about the future and therefore affects their consumption. Furthermore, there is much room for improvement regarding their living conditions, children's education, among others. This part will study the poverty status of migrant workers on these dimensions.

Consumption poverty is an important reflection of migrant worker poverty. According to 2010 CULS, the annual living consumption per capita of migrant worker families is RMB 12,530 and that of urban families is RMB 12,683, basically on a par in terms of the sum (Table 5.5). But looking at the consumption items reveals that although migrant workers spend much more on housing than urban residents, they spend less on other items, especially much less on certain ones. For instance, migrant worker families spend RMB 150 per year on household appliances and services on average, only 38% of urban resident families' RMB 399, and the former's spending on medical services and cultural and entertaining products and services is only 43 and 42% of the latter's.

Table 5.5 Annual living consumption per capita of migrant workers and urban residents (RMB)

Items of living consumption	Migrant workers (I)	Urban residents (II)	(I) - (II)	(I) / (II)
Food	4626	5401	−775	0.86
Clothing	910	1048	−138	0.87
Housing	3605	1245	2360	2.90
Household appliances and services	150	399	−249	0.38
Medical services	347	808	−461	0.43
Traffic & communication	1559	1715	−156	0.91
Education	673	956	−283	0.70
Cultural & entertaining products and services	261	620	−359	0.42
Other goods & services	399	491	−92	0.81
Total	12,530	12,683	−153	0.99

Note: The categorization of living consumption is based on the statistical items in NBS urban household survey
Source: Calculated based on 2010 CULS

Migrant workers spend RMB 3605 on housing per year on average, 2.9 times that of urban residents. This looks elusive but it is easy to understand if we know what housing consumption consists of: rent, electricity, water, gas and heating. According to 2010 CULS, 67% of migrant workers live in rental housing, 20% at the workplace, and others in dorms, purchased housing or other places. In comparison, 82% of urban residents have their own housing and only a very small percentage has to rent a place. Rent accounts for nearly 80% of migrant workers' housing consumption and about one fourth of their living consumption, whereas urban residents only spend RMB 265 on rent, just a little more than 20% of their housing consumption. If we remove housing, the annual average living consumption of migrant workers is only RMB 8925, 78% of urban residents' RMB 11,438.

Migrant workers live in poor conditions and environment. The 2010 CULS shows that 93% of migrant workers' living places have running water and 79% have bathroom, while almost all of urban residents' living places have them; 37% of migrant workers' living places have piped gas or natural gas, but more than 60% for urban residents (Fig. 5.2).

Only a small percentage of migrant workers have joined social insurance programs, which is an indication of their poverty. The 2010 CULS shows, the percentage of migrant workers joining the basic urban endowment insurance, basic urban medical insurance, unemployment insurance and work-related injury insurance is all less than 10%, much lower than that of urban residents (Fig. 5.3). Studies show that social security can boost consumption (Feldstein, 1974; Zhang, 2008), and the lack of it makes migrant workers feel insecure about the future and therefore affects their consumption, as shown in Table 5.5.

The education of migrant workers' children has always been on the spotlight. A person's educational level has a direct bearing on his/her future employment and income. There may be intergenerational transmission of poverty if migrant workers'

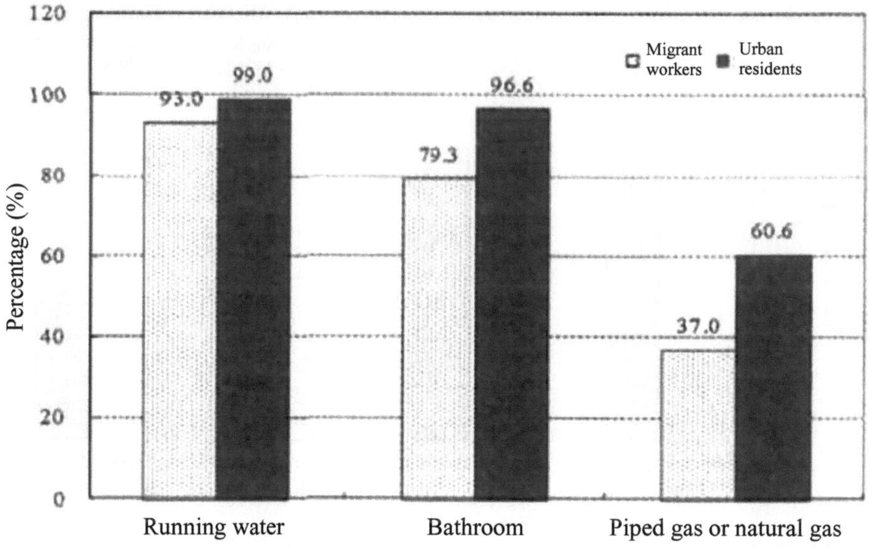

Fig. 5.2 Living standards of migrant workers and urban residents. Source: Calculated based on 2010 CULS

children do not receive good education. As is known to all, some migrant workers bring their children to the city while others have to leave them in the countryside due to low income, limited living space and other restrictions. But wherever they are, these children's education is far from satisfactory. Current rules provide that children of migrant workers can go to public schools in cities for free, but in reality they have to pay extra money in most cases. For those who live in the city, their school retention rate falls behind that of urban children, especially after finishing the compulsory education (Gao, 2009). For those children who stay in rural areas, the education they receive is generally not as good as that in cities.

5.6 Conclusions and Policy Recommendations

Using the 2010 CULS data, this paper discusses migrant workers' poverty on a wide range of dimensions, including income, consumption, housing, social insurance and children's education, analyzes the determining factors, and makes comparisons against urban residents as reference. This part will come to main conclusions and provide policy suggestions on poverty reduction and prevention for migrant workers.

First of all, the paper finds that migrant workers have a slightly lower poverty incidence than urban residents based on permanent residents of a family. Park and Wang (2010) also found that migrant population and urban residents only have a tiny disparity in poverty incidence. If we are not careful and take these findings on

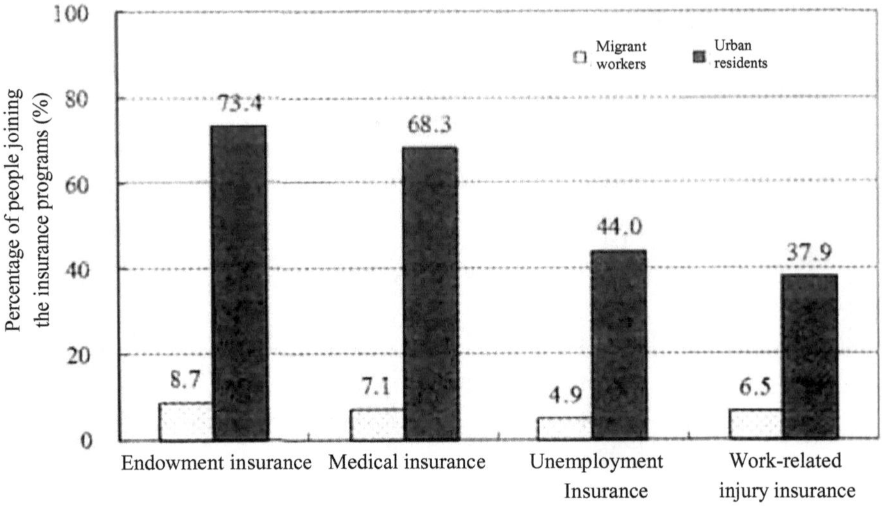

Fig. 5.3 Social insurance coverage for migrant workers and urban residents. Source: Calculated based on 2010 CULS

face value, we may overlook the issue of migrant worker poverty. A closer look would show that poverty incidence calculated on the permanent resident basis is underestimated as some migrant workers have not brought their spouses and children to the city, and their poverty incidence will probably be higher if those family members are all taken into account. More attention should be paid to this issue.

Second, labor income takes a lion's share (more than 95%) in migrant workers' total income, with little property and transfer income, so they will easily fall into poverty if they lose their jobs and consequently the income due to illness, loss of work capacity or for other reasons. In comparison, labor income only takes up 65% of urban residents' total income, and their transfer and property income can sustain their lives even if they lose their jobs.

This tells us that having work capacity and work opportunity is extremely important for migrant workers, and there is much the government can do here. For example, the health of many migrant workers is damaged because they work in poor conditions for a long time (Lu & Li, 2009). Degraded health undermines their ability to make labor income or even costs them the income altogether, reducing some to poverty. The government should formulate working environment standards and supervise their strict execution to improve the working conditions for migrant workers and protect their health. The government has done a lot in this aspect during recent years, but with limited progress.

Third, migrant worker poverty is worrisome if we take a comprehensive perspective of their consumption, housing, social insurance participation and children's education. Migrant workers spend less on almost all living items than urban residents except housing because most of them have to live in rented places. Meanwhile, their living conditions and environment are poor. Some places have no running water and bathroom, and more without piped gas or natural gas. The percentage of migrant workers joining the basic urban endowment insurance, basic urban medical insurance, unemployment insurance and work-related injury insurance is all less than 10%. Their children's education is far from satisfactory whether they live in the city or stay in the countryside.

Fourth, empirical analysis of the paper shows that migrant workers' educational level and employment/unemployment have significant impact on their poverty. For migrant worker families, the probability of poverty is lowest if the household head has finished high school or technical secondary school, followed by junior college and higher education, and then middle school, whereas the probability is highest if the head has only received primary school education or less. When employed members take a larger percentage in the family's adult members, the family is less likely to become poor; when unemployed members take a larger percentage, the more likely. These results all tell us that raising the educational level and creating more jobs for migrant workers are effective ways to keep them from poverty.

It is almost impossible to raise the educational level of adult migrant workers, but the conclusion still sheds light on how to reduce poverty for them, which is to offer better education for their children. Their children will be a main part of future migrant workers, and providing more and better education for them to increase their human capital can improve their employment and income prospects and reduce or avoid the intergenerational transmission of poverty. To improve the education of those children who study in the city, we should overhaul the *hukou* system and ensure them access to the same education opportunities and conditions as those for their city-born peers. To improve the education of those children who stay in their rural home, we need to keep increasing educational investment to improve the quality of education in rural areas.

A phenomenon that is worth special attention is that the labor market has seen rapid salary increase in recent years, so some migrant workers ask their children to drop out of school at an early age and join the labor force (Su, 2013). As China's economic structure is shifting from labor-intensive to capital- and technology-intensive, industries will have ever higher requirements on the workers' educational level. Early dropouts are deprived of the opportunity to receive education that will adapt them to the future labor market, but migrant workers are usually focused on immediate interests without any foresight. That is where the government and society should step in and provide guidance.

Fifth, the empirical analysis also shows that the percentage of family members aged 65 and above has significant positive impact on the poverty of migrant worker families but negative impact on that of urban resident families. This is because most migrant workers are not covered by endowment insurance and have no pension when they get old, so they have to rely on their children and that may lead to poverty. Expanding the endowment insurance coverage of migrant workers is an important task for the government, which should continue to energetically urge migrant workers to join the endowment insurance for urban employees, and perfect that for migrant workers as well as the new-type rural endowment insurance system.

If migrant workers are already in poverty, the government should think about how to provide effective relief for them. The minimum living allowance system, the major poverty relief system in China, covers both the urban and rural areas. According to relevant rules, eligible urban and rural residents have the right to apply for minimum living allowance to the township government (sub-district office) where their *hukou* is registered, and the government will then visit every applicant and check the verity and integrity of the application materials. After that, villager (resident) representatives or a community panel will review the applications, the county-level civil affairs authority will review and approve them, and a public notice will be made where the applicants live, before the final approval is granted. Since migrant workers usually have rural *hukou* but live in cities, they cannot apply for rural minimum living allowance, and they are not qualified to apply for urban minimum living allowance in the city of residence either. They are excluded from this relief system.

As there are more migrant workers in cities, it is not fair to keep them out of the minimum living allowance system and that will bring about a string of social problems. It is important for the government to include them in the scope of relief. Besides, the allowance standard is rather low and the system is not targeted enough (Wang, 2007). How to continuously increase the input of minimum living allowance, expand its coverage and make it more effective and targeted is another challenge faced by the government.

References

ADB (2004). "Poverty Profile of the People's Republic of China". Asian Development Bank

Cai, F., Du, Y., & Wang, M. (2005). *Transformation and development of Chinese labor market*. The Commercial Press.

Casper, L. M., McLanahan, S., & Garfinkel, I. (1994). The gender-poverty gap: What we can learn from other countries. *American Sociological Review, 59*(4), 594–605.

Du, Y., Gregory, R., & Meng, X. (2006). The impact of the guest-worker system on poverty and the Well-being of migrant workers in Urban China. In R. Garnaut & L. Song (Eds.), *The turning point in China's economic development*. Asia Pacific Press at the Australian National University.

Fan, J. (2007). On migrant worker poverty in the course of urbanization. *Journal of Yunnan Minzu University (Social Sciences), 1*, 17–21.

Feldstein, M. (1974). Social security, induced retirement and aggregate capital accumulation. *J. Polit. Econ., 82*(5), 905–926.

Gao, W. (2009). On education of left-behind and migrant children. In F. Cai (Ed.), *Report on China's population and labor (No. 10): Reforming the education system to promote human capital*. Social Sciences Academic Press.

Gregory, R., Meng, X. & Wan, G. (2005). China urban poverty and its contributing factors, 1986-2000. Paper Presented on the Project Conference "Inequality and Poverty in China, Helsinki, Finland"

Han, J., & Ma, Z. L. (2007). On the evolution of urban poor groups in the new era. *Ningxia Social Sciences, 4*, 58–61.

Han, J., & Zhang, Y. (2011). Poverty of migrant population: A multi-dimensional perspective. *Guizhou Social Sciences, 12*, 58–63.

Khan, A., Griffin, K., & Riskin, C. (2001). Income distribution in urban China during the period of economic reform and globalisation. In C. Riskin, R. Zhao, & S. Li (Eds.), *China's retreat from equality: Income distribution and economic transition*. M.E. Sharpe.

Knight, J., & Song, L. (2005). *Towards a labour market in China*. Oxford University Press.

Li, S. (2004). Deterioration of urban poverty in China in late 1990s and its reasons. In S. Li & H. Sato (Eds.), *Price of economic transformation: Empirical analysis of unemployment, poverty and income gap in Chinese cities*. China Financial & Economic Publishing House.

Lu, W., & Li, Y. (2009). Theoretical analysis of migrant workers' health rights and interests: From the perspective of environmental equity. *Chinese Journal of Population Science, 3*, 13–20.

National Bureau of Statistics. (2013). *China Yearbook of Rural Household Survey (2013)*. China Statistics Press.

Newman, J. S., & Struyk, R. (1983). Housing and poverty. *Review of Economics and Statistics, 65*(2), 243–253.

Park, A., & Wang, D. (2010). Migration and urban poverty and inequality in China. *IZA Discussion Paper, 4877*, 49–67.

Ravallion, M., & Chen, S. (1997). What can new survey data tell us about recent changes in distribution and poverty? *World Bank Economic Review, 11*(2), 357–382.

Ravallion, M., Datt, G., & Van de Walle, D. (1991). Quantifying absolute poverty in the developing world. *Review of Income and Wealth, 37*(4), 345–361.

Riskin, C., & Li, S. (2001). Chinese rural poverty inside and outside the poor regions. In C. Riskin, R. Zhao, & S. Li (Eds.), *China's retreat from equality: Income distribution and economic transition*. M. E. Sharpe.

Sen, A. (1985). *Commodities and Capabilities*. Oxford University Press.

Sen, A. (1999). *Development as Freedom*. Oxford University Press.

Su, G. (2013). Drop-out from middle School in Rural Areas and Analysis of solutions. *Journal of Educational Development, 8*, 22–26.

Wang, Y. (2003). Measuring urban poverty in China. In F. Cai (Ed.), *Report on China's population and labor (No. 4): Urban poverty in the transition period*. Social Sciences Academic Press.

Wang, M. (2004). Economic transformation, social stratification and social migrant: A bi-department inspection. *China Labor Economics, 2*, 45–60.

Wang, M. (2007). Emerging urban poverty and effects of the Dibao program on alleviating poverty in China. *China World Economy, 15*(2), 74–88.

Wang, X. (2012). *Measuring poverty: Theories and methods*. Social Sciences Academic Press.

World Bank. (1992). *China: Strategies for reducing poverty in the 1990s*. World Bank Report, No. 10409-CHA

Xue, J., & Wei, Z. (2004). Unemployment, poverty and income gap in Chinese cities. In S. Li & H. Sato (Eds.), *Price of economic transformation: Empirical analysis of unemployment, poverty and income gap in Chinese cities*. China Financial & Economic Publishing House.

Yang, Y., & Ma, X. (2012). Empirical study of migrant population and relative poverty in cities. *Guizhou Social Sciences, 10*, 125–128.

Yin, H., & Huang, W. (2010). Living status and poverty features of migrant population in cities. *Journal of Harbin Institute of Technology (Social Sciences Edition), 1*, 51–64.

Zhang, J. (2008). How social security affects urban residents' consumption and saving behavior in China.: China Social Sciences Press

Meiyan Wang, research fellow at the Institute of Population and Labor Economics, Chinese Academy of Social Sciences.

Chapter 6
Development of the Middle-Income Group and Determining Factors

Xiaolu Wang

6.1 Review of China's Economic Development and Income Distribution

To find out the development of China's middle-income group, we need to first have a brief overview of China's economic development and income distribution in the past few decades.

6.1.1 Residents' Income before Economic Reform

Chinese residents generally had a low income before the economic reform began. Based on the standard in developed countries or middle-income ones, China did not have a middle-income group at that time because they would be put in the low-income category. But the urban-rural income gap was wide and urban residents had an average income 2.6 times that of rural ones, being the high-income group in relative terms.

In 1978, the year when the reform and opening-up was launched, China's urban population only accounted for 18%, whose annual income per capita was only RMB 343, about USD 200 according to exchange rate at the time, whereas that in rural areas was only RMB 134. Besides, the income level was relatively even for urban residents, but that in rural areas, low as it was, varied markedly among different regions.

X. Wang (✉)
China Reform Foundation, Beijing, China
e-mail: lvqs@ssap.cn

F. Cai (ed.), *Income Inequality and Poverty Governance in China*, International Research on Poverty Reduction, https://doi.org/10.1007/978-981-95-5063-0_6

6.1.2 *Economic Development since the Reform and Opening-up (1978–2015)*

6.1.2.1 GDP Per Capita

GDP per capita in China has soared from RMB 385 to RMB 49,992 since the reform and opening-up began (1978–2015), or from USD 229 to USD 8031. Fig. 6.1 shows changes in GDP per capita in this period. The blue curve means GDP per capita calculated in RMB at constant price in 1978, while the red one means GDP per capita calculated in USD at current price that year.

6.1.2.2 Urbanization Rate

China's urbanization rate rose from 17.9 to 56.1% in 1978–2015, as shown in Fig. 6.2. Its rapid rise is an important contributor to the expansion of the middle-income group.

6.1.2.3 Income Gap

In the same period, the income gap among Chinese residents has widened drastically, which is detrimental to enlarging the middle-income group. Data show that the Gini coefficient of the nation increased from 0.317 in 1978 to 0.462 in 2015. Fig. 6.3 shows that the income gap quickly narrowed from about 0.3 to 0.25 in the early period of the reform. The reason is that the reform was first implemented in

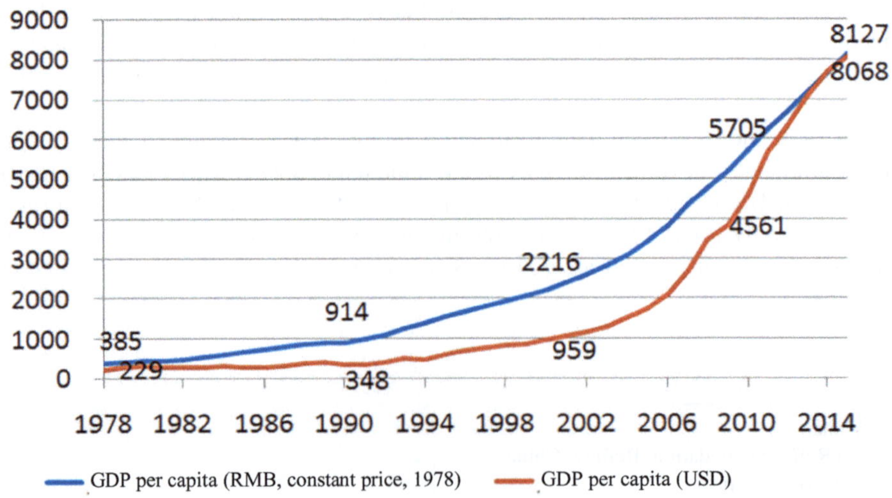

Fig. 6.1 GDP per capita in China, 1978–2015

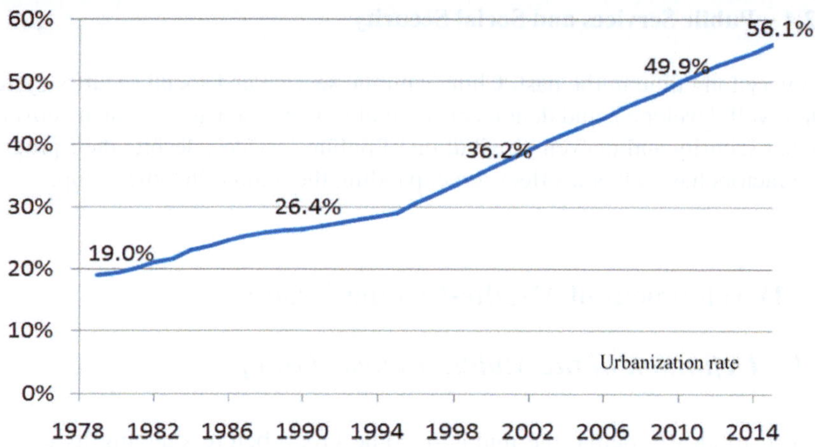

Fig. 6.2 Urbanization rate in China since the reform and opening-up

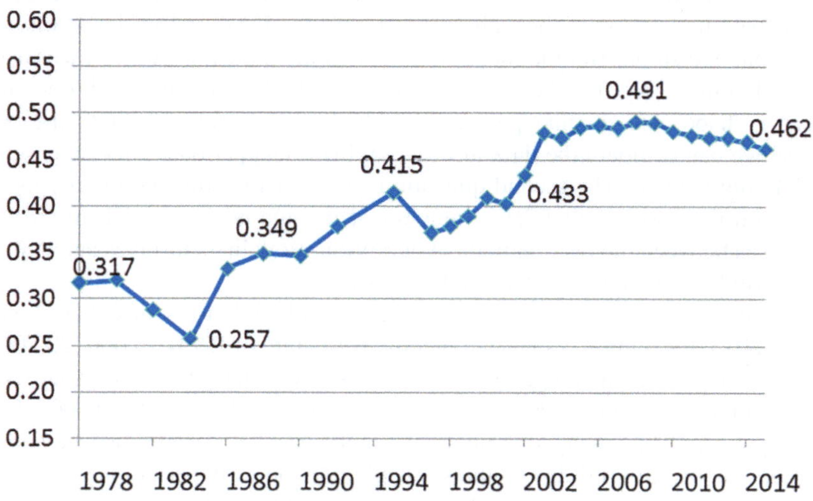

Fig. 6.3 Gini coefficient since the reform and opening-up

rural areas, so farmers had more income and the urban-rural income gap narrowed. But further reform accelerated the economic development in cities, especially coastal areas in the east. As a result, the gap between urban and rural areas and among different regions kept widening, so did the income gap between people of different strata. The Gini coefficient approached 0.5 (2009–2010) when the gap was widest, which fell a little in recent years but was still as high as 0.46 in 2015.

6.1.2.4 Public Services and Social Security

For a very long time in the past, China's public service and social security systems are not well developed, and deficiencies remain today, such as inadequate coverage of social security and uneven distribution of public services, despite their progress. These factors have adverse effects on expanding the middle-income group.

6.2 Development of Middle-Income Group

6.2.1 Definition of the Middle-Income Group

We need to clearly define the middle-income group before studying its development. There are many standards and methods to gauge this group, usually called the middle class, and they all involve two basic questions. The first is what indicators to use. The indicators commonly used by different researchers in different countries include income per capita, household assets, professional and social status, self-perception, and so on. But the more complicated the indicators are, the less accessible and comparable they become. A simple method is defining with one single indicator, disposable income per capita, which will largely facilitate the study because we can compare the data of different historical periods. This paper adopts this defining method. The second question is whether to define the middle-income group with the absolute or relative amount of income per capita. There are great differences between the two methods of definition. Both in themselves and in implications. Both of them are adopted in this paper.

If the absolute amount is used, we can set a standard. For instance, based on the price of 2015, the annual disposable income per capita of RMB 20,000–200,000 is set as the middle income range to review the historical changes of this group. Since this is a rather wide range, it can be narrowed down to RMB 50,000-200,000, but as income per capita has changed dramatically in the past few decades, we may not see a middle-income group if this method is applied to the early period.

If the relative amount is used, there are some internationally recognized methods. For example, the US-based Pew Research Center set 67–200% of median income as the middle income range. In reference to this, this paper sets 70% of median income as the lower limit of middle income and 200% the upper limit. The middle-income group defined in this way has seen considerable income change in history. But at every point it reflects the change in the number of relative middle-income residents and their percentage in total population.

6.2.2 Data

Only the National Bureau of Statistics (NBS) has complete annual surveys and data that show the long-term change of the middle-income group in China, but in most years, its resident income survey was conducted in two sets, one targeting urban residents and the other rural ones. The original data of both sets of samples are never made public, only the average income and expenditure in each set. There are seven groups of urban samples, of which the high-income group, sub-high-income group, minimal-income group and low-income group each accounts for 10% of the households, while the upper-middle-income group, middle-income group and lower-middle-income group 20% each. There are five groups of rural samples, each accounting for 20% of the households. National resident income/expenditure survey encompassing both urban and rural residents started in 2013 and data of 3 years have been made public so far, but they are very roughly divided into only five groups.

The difficulty lies in how to use the two sets of grouped data about urban and rural residents to approximately calculate the size of a national middle-income group. The percentage of urban and rural residents in total population, the average income and average number of family members in each group of the two sets of samples, and other parameters are changing every year, so we cannot just simply add up the two sets of data but have to perform a series of calculations.

Another difficulty is that in the aforementioned data, as proven by some studies, the income of high-income residents is too low, which challenges the accuracy of the calculation.

The grouped data still can be used in spite of these difficulties. First of all, the income gap between urban and rural residents is very wide and the average income of the former is far more than that of the latter, so their income hardly falls in the same range except a small number of people. This makes the calculation easy. We can mix different groups of urban and rural samples and make approximate calculations without major errors. Second, the excessively low income of high-income residents, as shown in the original data, may lead to over-estimation of the number of middle-income residents, but since this happens every year, the calculations still can be used to roughly reflect the historical trend of the percentage of this group.

6.2.3 *Data Calculation and Preliminary Results*

6.2.3.1 Data Calculation

We calculated the size and distribution of the national middle-income group based on the grouped data of urban and rural households (seven urban groups, five rural groups). According to a series of indicators, including household disposable income per capita (net income for rural residents, but close to disposable income), the number of households per group, the number of family members per group, and the percentage of urban and rural population nationwide, we calculated the percentage of every group in total population every year. Table 6.1 shows the calculated percentage in some years. With that and the average income of every group of urban and rural residents published by NBS, we roughly calculated the upper and lower limits of income in each group, and combined and re-grouped the two sets of data, before we proceeded to calculate the national median income and the percentage and distribution of the middle-income group.

Table 6.1 Population Breakdown (%)

	1980	1985	1990	1995	2000	2005	2010	2015
Low-income rural households	18.0	16.8	16.4	15.8	14.2	12.8	11.4	10.0
Lower-middle-income rural households	16.9	15.8	15.4	14.9	13.4	12.1	10.8	9.5
Middle-income rural households	16.0	15.0	14.6	14.1	12.7	11.4	10.2	8.9
Upper-middle-income rural households	15.4	14.3	14.0	13.4	12.0	10.8	9.4	8.2
High-income rural households	14.0	13.0	12.7	12.2	10.9	9.7	8.4	7.2
Minimal-income urban households	2.2	2.8	3.0	3.3	4.2	4.9	5.7	6.5
Low-income urban households	2.1	2.7	2.9	3.2	4.0	4.7	5.6	6.3
Lower-middle-income urban households	4.0	5.1	5.5	6.1	7.7	9.0	10.5	11.7
Middle-income urban households	3.9	4.9	5.3	5.8	7.4	8.5	9.8	11.0
Upper-middle-income urban households	3.8	4.8	5.1	5.6	7.0	8.1	9.3	10.5
High-income urban households	1.8	2.3	2.4	2.7	3.4	3.9	4.5	5.1
Maximal-income urban households	1.7	2.1	2.3	2.5	3.1	3.8	4.4	4.9

6.2.3.2 Percentage of the Middle-Income Group Calculated in Absolute Terms

The results are shown in Fig. 6.4, in which the blue curve means the percentage of middle-income group calculated with the annual income per capita of RMB 20,000–200,000 as the income range, constant price of 2015. As shown, the middle-income group only accounted for 2% of population in 2000, but the percentage shot up rapidly to 47% in 2015. According to this standard and data from NBS, there is no high-income group in China. The red curve means the percentage of middle-income group with the annual income per capita of RMB 50,000-200,000, which was next to zero in 2004 and climbed up to 9% in 2015. The two curves tell us that when we define the middle-income group in absolute terms, the size and percentage of China's middle-income group has quickly increased with economic development. But the trend in Fig. 6.4 does not reflect the change in relative income distribution, and therefore does not reflect the situation of the relative middle-income group at each point.

6.2.3.3 Percentage of the Middle-Income Group in Relative Terms

This paper also defines the middle-income group in the relative range of 70–200% of the national median income. As shown in Fig. 6.5, the percentage of middle-income group in total population increased from 59.1% in 1980 to 62.3% in 1990, but quickly dropped after that and hit the lowest point of around 40% in 2005–2010. In other words, the percentage fell by more than 20 percentage points in 20 years. It began to rebound after 2010 and reached 46.4% in 2015.

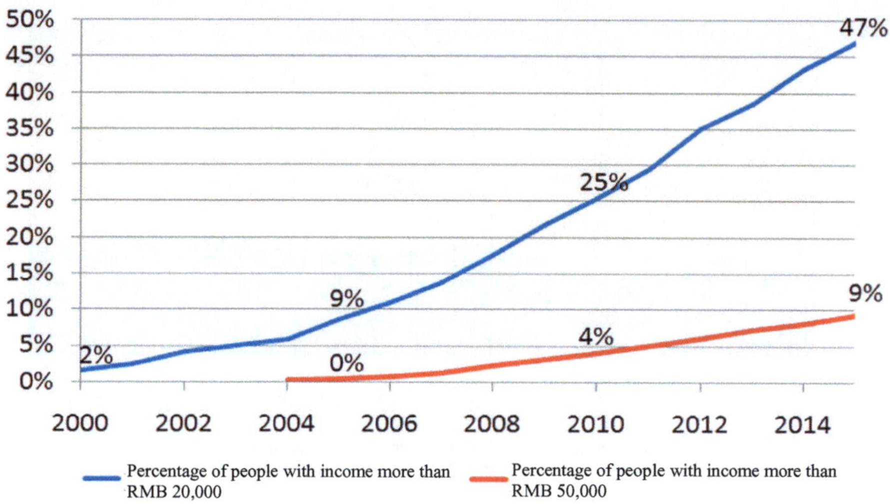

Fig. 6.4 Percentage of the middle-income group in absolute terms

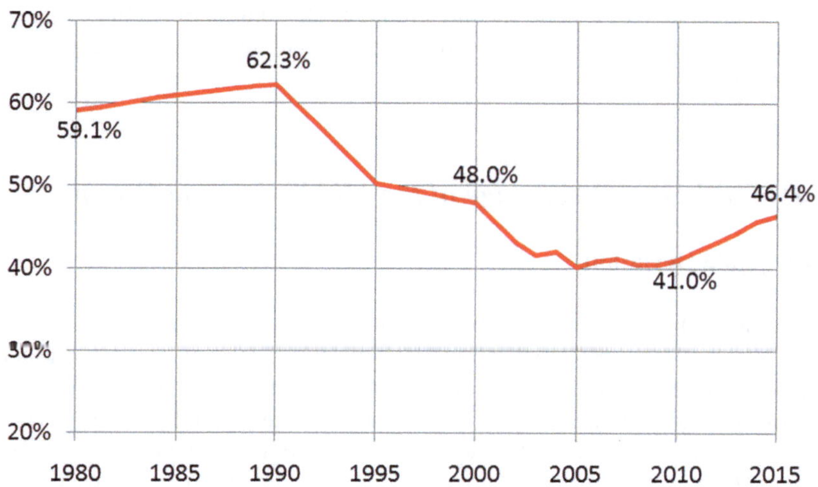

Fig. 6.5 Percentage of the Middle-Income Group in Relative Terms

6.2.3.4 Percentages of Relative High-, Middle- and Low-Income Groups

The percentage of relative high-, middle- and low-income groups is calculated separately, as shown in Fig. 6.6. In 2015, low-income group accounted for about 35% of total population, middle-income group 46% and high-income group less than 19%. In the early period of reform (1980–1990), the percentage of middle-income group increased but that of low- and high-income groups decreased. After 1990, however, the percentage of the latter two groups increased while that of the former decreased

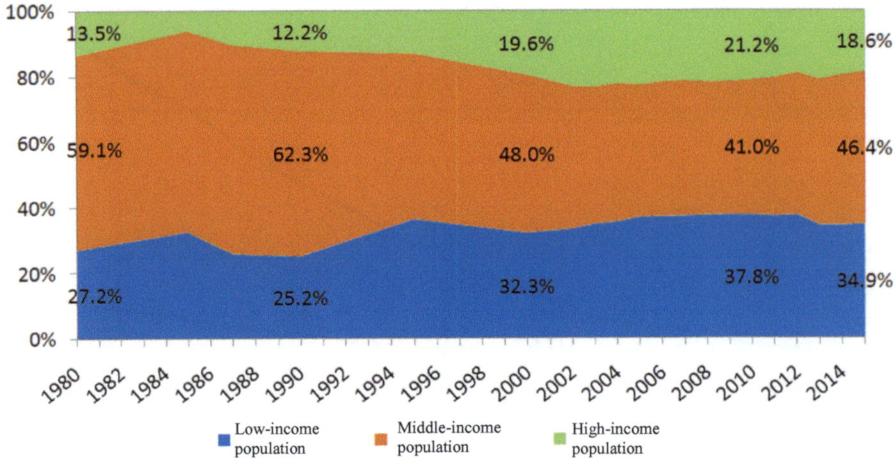

Fig. 6.6 Percentages of high-, middle- and low-income groups

significantly, indicating a widening income gap, a trend that lasted till around 2010, when the percentage of middle-income group hit the bottom. Since then, this group began to expand again whereas the percentage of high- and low-income groups was again on the decline.

6.2.4 *Calibrated Percentage of the Middle-Income Group*

6.2.4.1 Data Deviation

As mentioned above, due to the deviations in original data from NBS, the calculations above will, to some extent, underestimate the percentage of high-income group and over-estimate that of middle-income group. This is because there were omissions of high-income samples in the statistical survey and many high-income residents provide untrue, usually lower-than-actual, figures. Therefore, the real percentage of high-income group is larger and that of the middle-income group smaller. The aforementioned data have to be calibrated to get more truthful and credible results.

We organized three surveys of urban residents' actual income in 2005, 2008 and 2011 respectively, covering tens of cities and towns across the country, and conducted studies of them. The results show that for the top 10% urban households with the highest income, their real income per capita is more than three times as much as the figure in the statistical survey (statistical income), that of middle-income households is slightly more than statistical income, and that of low-income households is basically the same as the statistical income. The three surveys and data analyses come to very close results (Figs. 6.7, 6.8, & 6.9).

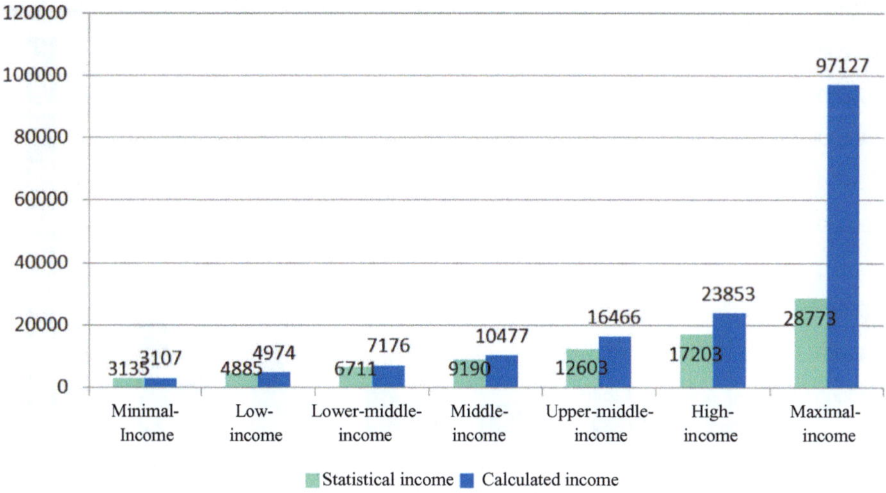

Fig. 6.7 Calculated real income of urban residents, 2005

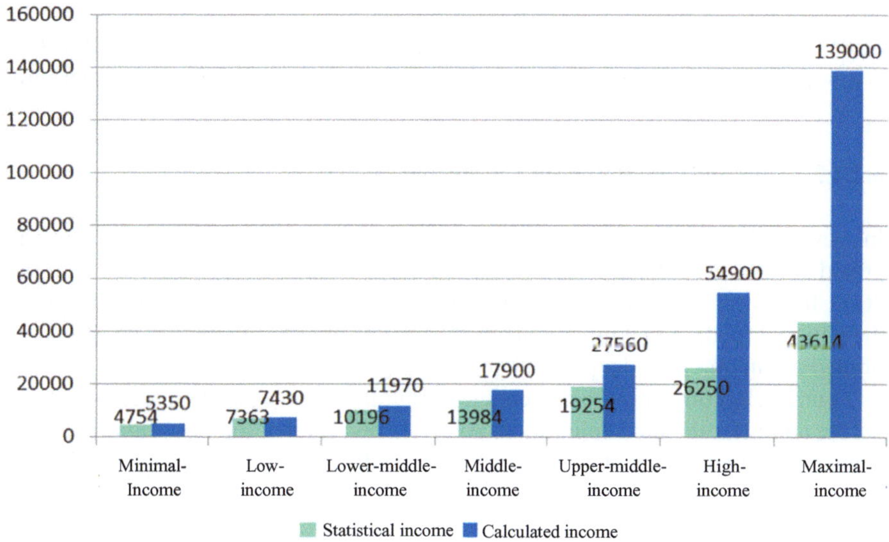

Fig. 6.8 Calculated real income of urban residents, 2008

These studies show that the grouped resident income released by NBS has two omissions: statistical omission in the general sense and gray income. Gray income is from unknown sources, its legitimacy is questioned and it's highly secretive, so it's not included in statistics. It may be illegal, or stands in a gray zone due to loopholes in the legal system. Gray income continuously increased for some time in the past and amounted to an immense number estimated to account for about 12% of

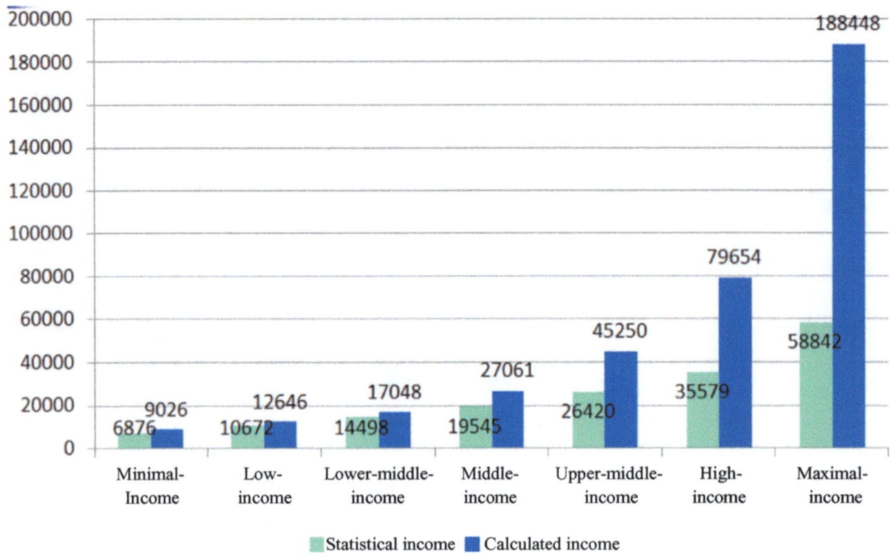

Fig. 6.9 Calculated real income of urban residents, 2011

GDP (Table 6.2), but it has shrunk according to calculations after the 18th CPC National Congress (especially after 2013) thanks to strong anti-corruption measures.

6.2.4.2 Calculations Based on Calibrated Data

In view of the results above and other calculations, this paper estimated and calibrated the income per capita in urban households of middle and higher income since 2000. It also calibrated the income of rural high-income residents and re-calculated the national median income, the income range of middle-income group (70–200% of median income) and its percentage in total population.

Figure 6.10 compares the percentage of middle-income group in total population before and after the data calibration. Analysis reveals that the post-calibration percentage dropped even faster after 1990, especially after 2000, hitting 32% in 2010

Table 6.2 Estimated statistical omission and gray income (RMB 1 trillion)

	2005	2008	2011
Resident income (household survey)	8.3	13.2	19.6
Resident income (capital flow statement)	11.3	18.6	28.5
Statistical omission	3.0	5.4	8.9
Gray income	2.4	4.6	6.2
Gray income/GDP	12.2%	13.6%	12.2%

and then bouncing back to 34.7% in 2015, 12 percentage points lower than the pre-calibration result.

Figure 6.11 shows the distribution of high-, middle- and low-income groups in total population after calibration. A comparison of Figs. 6.11 and 6.6 shows a shrinking middle-income group and growing high-income group.

6.3 Causes of the Changes in the Percentage of the Middle-Income Group

By analyzing the macro-economic data and structural changes in history, institutions and policies, we have found the following causes of the changing percentage of middle-income group.

In the 1980s, reform was implemented in the rural areas and rural residents' income increased rapidly. Later the market was opened up, private economy thrived, urbanization picked up speed, and large amounts of rural residents went to work in cities. As a result, the general income for all residents quickly increased and the middle-income group expanded.

In the 1990s, the income gap continuously widened amid fast economic growth. The high-income group expanded at a faster pace whereas income increase slowed down for farmers and blue-collar workers. Meanwhile, the absence of social security and deficiency of public services also contributed to the rising percentage of low-income group and the falling percentage of middle-income group.

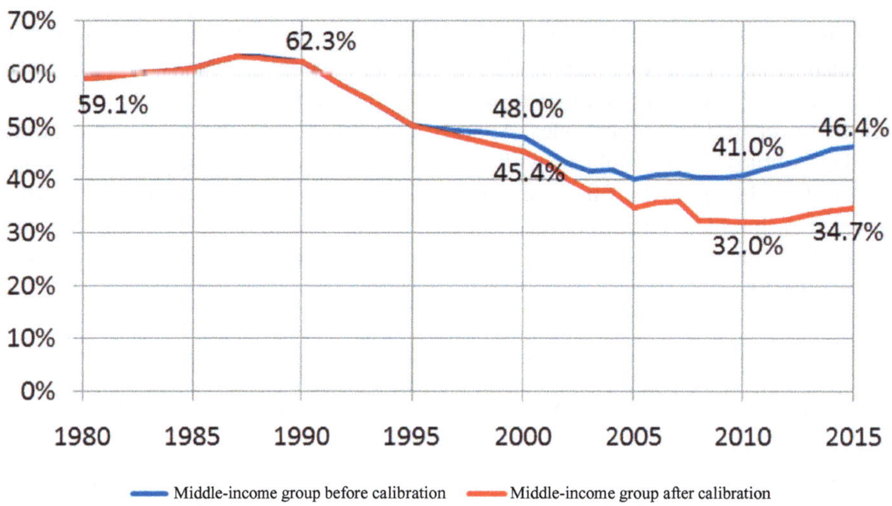

Fig. 6.10 Percentage of the middle-income group in total population before and after calibration

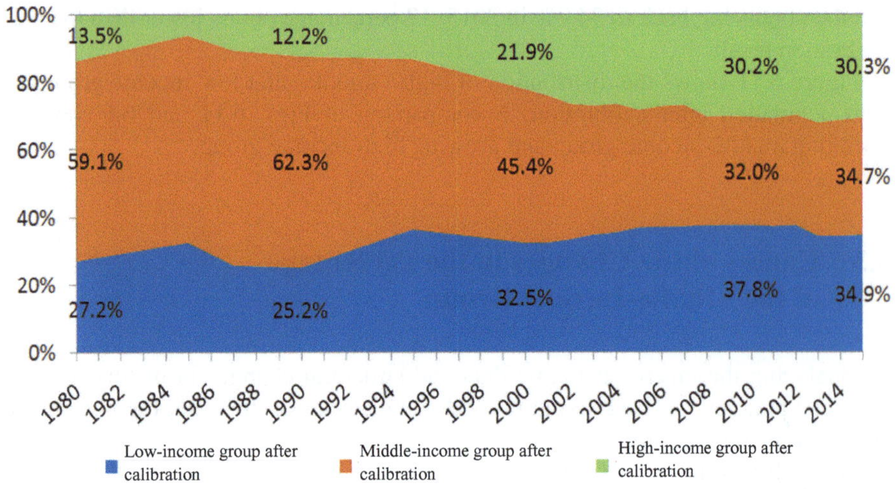

Fig. 6.11 Percentages of high-, middle- and low-income groups after calibration

After 2000, corruption became more serious and income gap continued to widen quickly, leading to the accelerated expansion of high-income group, continuous growth of low-income group, and further shrinkage of middle-income group.

Favorable policies aimed to improve people's livelihood were rolled out after 2010, which, combined with the changed supply and demand of labor force, gave a strong boost to the income of farmers and blue-collar workers. The strong crackdown on corruption in recent years restrained the increase of illegal and gray income and made income distribution fairer, and public services and social security have also been gradually improved. All these have resulted in a larger middle-income group.

Other factors also play a part in the expansion. For instance, the continuous rise of housing and land price has put a heavy economic burden on middle-income residents, and the drastic fluctuations of the problem-ridden capital market have ripped off the lower-middle-income ones. Apart from institutional factors, land and capital market bubbles are also related with the sustained monetary easing, which pumps excess liquidity into the financial and real estate markets constantly and further bloats their bubbles. The effects of these factors may not be reflected in the statistics of resident income, but they do seriously impede the health growth of the middle-income group.

6.4 Suggestions on Expanding the Middle-Income Group

1. The healthy development of the middle-income group should be underpinned by a fair income distribution system and harmonious and stable social relations. Therefore, continued improvement of income distribution is vital and good for long-term economic development.

2. More efforts should be made to improve public service and social security systems, such as medical service, education and housing security.
3. The first priority is to help rural-to-urban residents settle down in cities, cover them in social security programs, and ensure to provide them with equal access to all benefits and facilities enjoyed by urban residents.
4. The land system reform must be accelerated to bring down the excessively high housing price.
5. A standard, transparent and fair capital market should be established.
6. Fair play in the market should be protected to prevent monopoly.
7. A better government-market relation should be forged to keep the former from excessive interference and let the latter play a decisive role in resource allocation.
8. Monetary policies should be neutralized to keep the leverage ratio from rising further and the housing and capital bubbles from further inflation.

Xiaolu Wang, research fellow at China Reform Foundation.

Chapter 7
Study on the Determining Factors in Family Wealth in Urban China

Yongai Jin and Yu Xie

Abstract Using data from the 2010 China Family Panel Studies (CFPS), this paper analyzes the effects of political and market factors on the wealth accumulation of urban families in China. The results indicate that both political and market factors contribute significantly to wealth accumulation, with the former having larger effects on the accumulation of housing assets, while the latter being more influential on the accumulation of non-housing assets (including financial assets, durable consumer goods and productive fixed assets). Furthermore, political capital has greater effects on wealth than on income. Three explanations are proposed. First, families with political capital have benefited greatly from the privatization of public welfare housing. Second, families with political capital have lower household expenses and therefore accumulate more wealth thanks to benefits inside the system. Third, families with political capital may gain higher investment returns, thus converting their savings into wealth more effectively.

Keywords Family wealth · Political capital · Market factors · Family income

7.1 Introduction

There are some studies of the level and distribution of wealth in recent years (e.g. Li et al., 2000; Liang et al., 2010; Li et al., 2005; Yuan & Wang, 2013; Xie & Jin, 2015), all of which come to the conclusion that wealth inequality is quickly worsening in China. But hardly any study has delved into the factors that cause this phenomenon.

Y. Jin
Population Development Studies Center, Renmin University of China, Beijing, China

Y. Xie (✉)
Center for Social Research, Peking University and Center on Contemporary China, Beijing, China
e-mail: lvqs@ssap.cn

F. Cai (ed.), *Income Inequality and Poverty Governance in China*, International Research on Poverty Reduction, https://doi.org/10.1007/978-981-95-5063-0_7

There are many in-depth foreign studies on wealth determining factors, but China has a completely different history and national condition from developed countries when it comes to wealth accumulation. Families in developed countries had accumulated wealth very early in their market economy, but China has experienced different economic development stages in the short span of decades after the People's Republic China was founded in 1949. Before the reform and opening-up was launched, private wealth was strictly restricted in the planned economy system and egalitarianism was implemented across the society. But after the reform and opening-up commenced, market economy began to thrive, efficiency was emphasized, and both private and foreign enterprises emerged across the country. In this process, some people quickly became rich by doing business (Wu, 2002), and some became upstarts with massive amounts of wealth. However, political power's effect on economic status was not weakened. Rather, the market economic reform consolidated the vested interests in that fast-changing period. At the end of the 1980s, China began the housing distribution reform, and those entitled to public welfare housing bought it from the government or their employers at an extremely low price and turned it into their private property (Xi & Xie, 2014; Walder & He, 2014). As the real estate market has been booming since 2000 with housing price soaring sharply, those housing possessors have all made a fortune (Chen & Qiu, 2011).

Although political and market factors are rarely discussed in existing wealth studies, they are under the spotlight in the sociological study of income in China. The 1980s and 1990s witnessed the inception and development of the market economic system in China. Nee (1989, 1991 and 1996) proposed the market transformation theory that as economic reform went deeper, the main factors that decide individual's social and economic status should be those standing for market efficiency, such as human capital, rather than political capital. Studies of factors determining income usually take the CPC membership or cadre status as a political capital or the symbol of re-distribution power, and take the level of education as a market factor (Xie & Hannum, 1996; Hauser & Xie, 2005). Some studies indicate that political capital has declining effects on income (Lin & Wu, 2010; Liu & Wang, 2010) in the course of market transformation but education has a rising return rate (Hauser & Xie, 2005; Jansen & Wu, 2012).

Is it possible to apply the conclusions of income studies to wealth directly? As another kind of economic outcome, wealth looks like a gauge of a family's economic status that can be interchanged with income, but they are actually very different in nature. Wealth is a stock that can result from the accumulation of income and can be inherited and transferred (Gale & Scholz, 1994). In China, there is a special way to obtain wealth: obtaining housing property from the employer. In comparison, income is liquid, which partly comes from wealth, called property income, but mainly from work-based wage. Besides, income can be calculated for each individual but wealth is usually family-based and cannot be split up for each family member. There are studies indicating that the correlation between wealth and income is quite weak, the coefficient being only 0.37 in 2012 (Xie & Jin, 2014). There are even families in urban China that own housing properties worth millions but still live on government minimum living allowance because they have no income. The difference between income and wealth in the way of acquisition and form of existence results in their different determining factors, so conclusions of income studies cannot be directly applied to wealth. As wealth has become an important indicator of a household's economic status, it is necessary to delve into the mechanism behind it.

To make an in-depth analysis of the unique mechanism of family wealth in China and highlight its difference from that of income, this paper analyzes family wealth and income in parallel, and explores how market and political factors act on the former.

7.2 Data and Methodology

7.2.1 Data

This paper uses the data of 2010 CFPS. CFPS is a national, long-term tracking survey, and the one in 2010 was a baseline survey that conducted multi-phased probability sampling on 14,798 households across 25 provincial administrative regions (excluding Xinjiang, Xizang, Inner Mongolia, Ningxia, Hainan, Hong Kong, Macao and Taiwan), which cover 94.5% of the total population in China (Xie et al., 2012; Xie & Lu, 2015). The respondents included all members of the households and the information collected included education, employment, marriage, siblings, children, and details about family wealth. CFPS also collected information about people who did not live in the household at the time of the survey but had economic connections with it and immediate family members. The survey collected as much and detailed information about the family members as possible, laying a sound empirical foundation for studying the mechanism behind the economics of a family.

Starting with the baseline survey in 2010, CFPS has collected detailed information on family properties. Since such data are difficult to obtain, CFPS has adopted remedial measures to avoid missing values as much as possible. It adopts the aggregation method, which means sub-items are listed under each major item, so that the respondents can recall and estimate (Hu et al., 2014). It also adopts the interval method. For example, if the respondents, when asked about their savings, said "I don't know" or refused to answer, the surveyor would continue to ask if the savings were more than RMB 50,000. If they said "yes", they would be asked if the savings were more than RMB 100,000, 250,000 or 500,000. If they said "no", the figure would be lowered to RMB 25,000 or 10,000. This method corrected more than 50% of the missing values (Hu et al., 2014). Although sample surveys cannot capture the information about the extremely rich group, they are meaningful for studying the wealth characteristics of the general public and summarizing the general pattern of wealth distribution.

Missing values are inevitable in social surveys, wealth survey being no exception. This paper makes full use of other information to make up for them. If housing property value is missing, the paper estimates it according to the average price per square meter of the same type of housing in the same community and the housing size collected; if values of other wealth items are missing, such as financial assets and durable consumer goods, the paper substitutes them with the values provided by the household with the closest income in the same community. For details on the handling of missing values, please refer to the paper by Jin and Xie (2014).

7.2.2 *Methodology*

7.2.2.1 Modeling

Traditional income researches usually conduct logarithmic transformation of income and build a simple linear regression model, as shown in Eq. (7.1). Unlike income, net wealth may be negative because of the existence of debts. Existing studies have dealt with wealth as a dependent variable in different ways, either taking net wealth as a dependable variable (Barsky et al., 2002; Smith, 1995; Yamokoski & Keister, 2006), or conducting the inverse hyperbolic sine (IHS) transformation (Meng, 2007), or making a two-step estimation of wealth after dividing it into the positive and negative part (Killewald, 2013). Another method commonly used is conducting logarithmic transformation of wealth (Killewald, 2013), like with income, thus correcting its skewed distribution to meet the hypothesis of normal distribution. The problem with this method is that logarithmic transformation is not applicable for indebted families, so a fixed constant is often added to the wealth of all families to make it positive for indebted families, or their negative wealth is replaced by a very small positive number (Conley & Glauber, 2008; Hall & Crowder, 2011; Keister, 2003). But this leads to another problem that the positive number that replaces the negative wealth value is a subjective choice, which will affect the distribution of wealth and consequently the analytical results (Killewald, 2013). In this paper, indebted families only account for 2.2%,[1] so the most common method of logarithmic transformation has little effect on the result. Therefore, we first set the assets of all indebted families at 0, then add 1 to the wealth of all families before conducting logarithmic transformation, thus building the multiple linear model as follows.

$$\log Y = ?_0 + ?_1 X_1 + ?_2 X_2 + ?_3 X_3 + ?_4 X_4 + ? \tag{7.1}$$

Y stands for income or wealth, X_* stands for explanatory variable, β_* is the coefficient of each variable, and ε is an error term.

There are two methods to estimate Eq. (7.1). The first is Tobit regression. When we analyze different types of family assets, a considerable proportion of the families have no housing or non-housing assets, so their wealth cannot be taken as dependent

[1] The average debts of the indebted families are RMB 41,854, and standard deviation is RMB 88,611.

variable in linear regression, so Tobit regression is used. Tobit regression can analyze the dependent variable of left truncation as it posits a linear relation between a potential variable *y* and the independent variable *x* (Wooldridge, 2010).

The second method is seemingly unrelated regression (SUR), which posits the error term to be related (Zellner, 1962) in order to estimate the model more effectively. The model based on such combined estimation can test whether the variables have the same effects in different models. This paper uses the SUR to compare the different coefficients of independent variables in the wealth model and income model, and the different effects of independent variables in the housing property model and non-housing property model.

7.2.2.2 Sampling

Wealth belongs to the family, but the different family-based independent variables have to be obtained through the information provided about family members. The usual practice is representing the family features with those of the household head (Wu, 2011; Li et al., 2000). This method is commonly used by foreign studies as well, which sometimes take males as default household heads or females in families of single mom or only female members (Schmidt & Sevak, 2006). However, important information may be missed with this method because since wealth is accumulated on the family basis and every family member who is capable of work or participates in economic activities can contribute, the use of household head's information alone may make us neglect the contributions made by other members. Moreover, since they may vary greatly in educational level and profession, there may be deviations if only one person's information is used.

To solve this problem, this paper fully utilizes the comprehensive information collected by CFPS and uses the information on every family member to build the family variables, including average age, average years of education, whether there are children aged 15 or below, whether there are retired elders, family size, whether it is a migrant family,[2] whether anyone holds administrative or managerial positions, whether anyone works in government organs or public institutions, and whether there are CPC members. Only two variables use information about children, which are whether there are children aged 15 or below and the family size, while all other variables use information on adults. Adults are defined as people aged 16 and above and not in school, or in school but married.

To build family variables with personal information, we need to know the details on every adult member, but the CFPS only contains basic information that covers all

[2] A family is considered a migrant one if the *hukou* of those filling the questionnaire for adult members is registered elsewhere. A family is not a migrant one as long as there is one member with a local *hukou*. This approach is in consideration of marriages between locals and non-locals. It must be noted that migrant population is a cross-county or cross-district concept in CFPS. Migrant population within the same district or county and urban residents whose *hukou* is separated from the residence cannot be identified.

members, such as age, educational level and whether they live together. Therefore, more details collected via questionnaires for adult family members[3] are needed in order to deeply analyze the effects of political capital and other factors. However, not every adult member has filled the questionnaire; only those that were home or could be contacted at the time of the survey have, so family variables built in this way may have deviations. In view of this, this paper conducts a sensitivity analysis to make the conclusions more reliable, meaning it analyzes those families in which all eligible members have filled the questionnaire, thus avoiding the deviations caused by the omission of information on one or several adult members.[4]

7.2.2.3 Dependent and Independent Variables

Family wealth consists of the current housing property and other housing properties, financial assets (e.g. savings, stocks, funds and bonds), productive fixed assets (e.g. agricultural machinery, company assets), durable consumer goods and land. Debts are deducted from family wealth. The method proposed by McKinley and Griffin (1993) is used to estimate land assets, namely we assume that 25% of the family's total agricultural income comes from land and the land yield rate is 8%. We can estimate the land value based on that.

The main dependent variable is wealth, or, to be more specific, the logarithm of the average wealth owned by adult family members aged 16 and above. First the net family wealth is divided by the number of adult family members, and the wealth of indebted families is set at 0. Then we add 1 to all wealth values, and conduct logarithmic transformation at last.

As mentioned earlier, this paper analyzes wealth and income in parallel to get to the bottom of the mechanism behind family wealth, so income is another dependent variable. It is the logarithm of the average income of adult family members aged 16 and above. First the net total family income is divided by the number of adult family members, and then logarithmic transformation is conducted.

Categorized family wealth is analyzed in the same way as total wealth. In other words, the value of each type of wealth is divided by the number of adult family members aged 16 and above, negative value is set at 0, and 1 is added to the wealth value of every family before logarithmic transformation is conducted in the end.

The independent variables that represent political and market factors are critical in the model. As the traditional approach goes, family member's CPC membership and the type of their employers are taken to represent the family's political capital. The type of employer means whether any family member works in the CPC or government organs, people's societies, the military, state-owned or collective enterprises or public institutions, or scientific research institutes, which will be generalized

[3] Questionnaire filled separately by adults aged 16 and above who are at home at the time of the survey.

[4] The results are not listed here due to limited length of the paper. Readers can contact the authors for details if they are interested.

as government organs/public institutions hereinafter. In previous studies, working inside the system is a common variable that represents political capital, but it includes work at state-owned or state-controlled enterprises. To remove the effect of market factors as much as possible and highlight that of political capital, and to set off the advantage of working in government organs and public institutions, this paper puts working at CPC and government organs and public institutions under the same category, excluding state-owned enterprises (SOEs).

Market factors are denoted with whether family members engage in self-employment/private business. Education, as an indicator of market efficiency, is represented with the average years of education of all adult family members in the regression model, and educational level should be transformed into years. To be specific, illiteracy is equal to zero year of education, primary school 6 years, middle school 9 years, high school or secondary technical school 12 years, junior college 14 years, college 16 years, and graduate school or higher education 19 years. Existing studies show that the use of different educational levels or years of education does not make a difference on the regression results (Xie & Hannum, 1996).

There is no occupational variable in the model for two reasons. First, occupation has a high correlation to employer; second, there are studies indicating that the decisive factor for social stratification in China is different types of employers (Xie & Wu, 2008), while those of the same type have little occupational difference (Walder & He, 2014).

Age and family structure are demographic factors that affect wealth accumulation, so age, square age, family structure, whether there are children aged 15 and below, family size, square family size and whether there are retired elders are also variables. There are four types of family structure: families where adults of at least three generations live together (grandparents, parents and grandchildren, the last group should also be adults aged 16 and above and not in school, or in school but married); families where adults of two generations live together; those made up of adults of only one generation; and those where grandparents and grandchildren, or adult siblings live together

Besides, the indicator "whether the family is a migrant family" is controlled in the model, and the logarithm of county-level GDP per capita is used to control the difference in regional development.

Table 7.1 is the descriptive statistics of independent and dependent variables.

7.3 Descriptive Statistical Results

The income-wealth relation is an important subject in many wealth researches. Income affects wealth accumulation and, in turn, property income increases family income. Although no agreement has been reached on the complicated relation between income and wealth (Xie & Jin, 2014), the phenomenon that wealth inequality is more serious than income inequality has been widely proven (Keister, 2014; Morgan & Scott, 2007; Keister, 2000). In the United States, wealth also reflects a

Table 7.1 Descriptive statistics of independent and dependent variables

Variable	Average value (%)	Standard deviation
Wealth (RMB 10,000)	10.70	2.62
Income (RMB 10,000)	9.33	1.02
Age (years old)	46.57	12.23
Whether there are children aged 15 and below		
Yes	42.63	–
Family structure		
Adults of three generations live together	5.57	–
Adults of two generations live together	69.19	–
Adults of one generation	24.38	–
Others	0.85	–
Family size (number of people)	3.43	1.51
Whether there are retired elders		
Yes	23.99	–
Years of education (years)	8.64	3.94
Whether any family member holds administrative/ managerial positions		
Yes	12.85	–
Whether any family member works at government organs/ public institutions		
Yes	11.96	–
Whether there are CPC members		
Yes	20.52	–
Whether any family member engages in self-employment/ private business		
Yes	16.76	–
Logarithm of county-level GDP per capita	10.59	1.01
Number of samples	6320	–

Source: Calculated based on 2010 CFPS

much larger racial gap than income (Oliver & Shapiro, 1997; Menchik & Jianakoplos, 1997).

According to data of 2012 CFPS, the Gini coefficient in terms of net family wealth in China was 0.73 (Xie & Jin, 2015), but that in terms of family income was 0.53 (Xie & Zhou, 2014). Moreover, the 90/10 income inequality ratio in terms of net family wealth reached 36.79 in 2012, but that in terms of income was only 13.1 in the same period (Xie et al., 2013). Using the same CFPS data, we display the wealth and income distribution on the Lorentzian curve (Fig. 7.1), on which the wealth curve is obviously right-inclined, meaning a more serious inequality than income distribution.

Another consensus on the wealth-income relation is their low correlation (Keister & Moller, 2000). Data of the United States in the 1980s show a correlation coefficient as low as 0.5, which falls to 0.26 if property income is removed (Lerman &

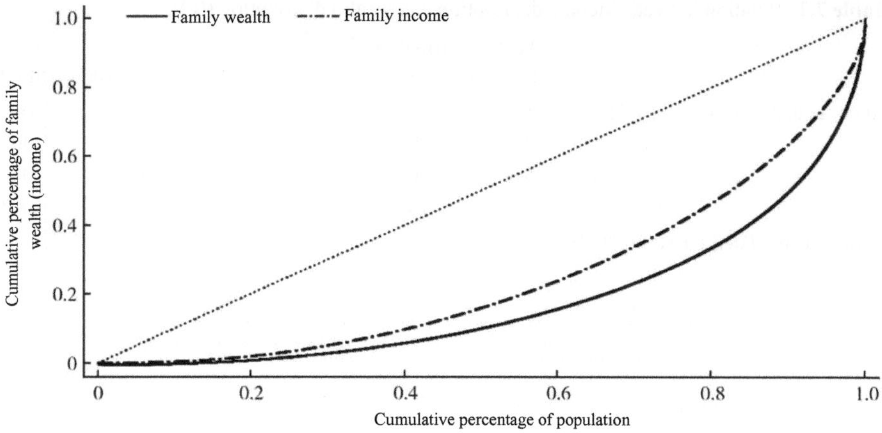

Fig. 7.1 Lorentzian curve of wealth and income. Source: Drawn based on 2010 CFPS

Mikesell, 1988), and this is corroborated by data used in this paper. According to data of 2012 CFPS, the income-wealth correlation coefficient of Chinese families is 0.37, and income is rather loosely distributed on various wealth levels (Table 7.2), except on the bottom and top levels, which correspond to a mildly high percentage of low-income and high-income families respectively. This means the income-wealth correlation is high in families of extremely low or high income, but it is low in the middle class.

Although income and wealth are both indicators of a family's economic status, their relation is more complicated than one may think in the unique social environment of China, and their mechanisms may be different. On the one hand, in the course of market transformation, market factors such as education and market operations affect both income and wealth. On the other hand, the effects on Chinese families' wealth are different from those on their income in that wealth is subject to policy changes, so government workers have easier access to wealth. This can be explained with a controversial phenomenon. Civil servants have a low wage in general, and there have been ever louder calls to raise their wage in recent years, yet the number of people applying to become civil servants has never decreased. The advantage of working in the system cannot be measured with income alone, which is why this paper analyzes the determining factors of wealth and income in parallel.

To display more clearly the disparity between urban families with or without members working in government organs/public institutions and the difference between wealth and income, Fig. 7.2 shows the kernel density curve of wealth and income, which reveals the following points. First, families with members working in government organs/public institutions have a markedly higher average wealth than other families. This goes for their income, too. Second, the first type of families has a more concentrated wealth distribution, which means a less sharp inequality than that among other families. It is the same with their income. Third, wealth distribution differs largely from income distribution, with the latter more concentrated

Table 7.2 Relation between income distribution and wealth distribution (%)

		Wealth distribution				
		0% – 25%	25% – 50%	50% – 75%	75% – 100%	Total
Income distribution	0% – 25%	46.5	29.2	15.7	8.6	100.0
	25% – 50%	25.7	29.3	27.6	17.5	100.0
	50% – 75%	17.6	26.2	30.7	25.5	100.0
	75% – 100%	10.2	15.3	26.0	48.5	100.0

Source: Calculated based on 2010 CFPS

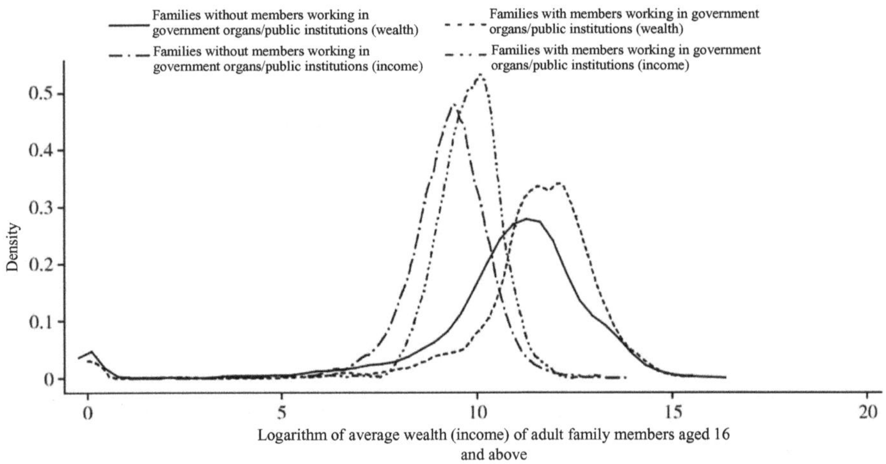

Fig. 7.2 Kernel density curve by employer type (Urban). Note: The type of kernel function used is epanechnikov, with the bandwidth of 0.2333. Source: Drawn based on 2010 CFPS

and the former more scattered, indicating a more serious inequality in wealth than in income.

Table 7.3 preliminarily explores the difference in the distribution pattern of wealth and income. It is clear that compared with income disparity, the disparity in wealth is even more drastic. Families with members working in government organs/public institutions have 106.8% more wealth than other families, but only 83.7% more income. Families with CPC members also have a bigger edge over those without in wealth (112.7% more) than in income (69.7% more). This means families with political capital have greater advantages in wealth than in income, which indicates different mechanisms behind wealth and income. This is another reason why this paper analyzes wealth and income in parallel.

Table 7.3 also shows how the engagement in market economy and educational level affects family wealth and income. As mentioned earlier, wealth varies more greatly than income regarding the type of employers and CPC membership. In other words, families that have members working in government organs/public institutions or being CPC members have more wealth advantages than income advantages, but this is not true with the engagement in market activities. On the contrary,

Table 7.3 Relation between political/market factors and family wealth/income

	Wealth			Income		
	No (RMB)	Yes (RMB)	Higher (%)	No (RMB)	Yes (RMB)	Higher (%)
Whether any family member works in government organs/public institutions	33,285	68,829	106.8	9806	18,015	83.7
Whether any family member is CPC member	31,187	66,350	112.7	9482	16,096	69.7
Whether any family member engages in self-employment/ private business	36,018	37,979	5.4	10,238	12,177	18.9
Whether any family member completes high school or higher education	26,184	48,773	86.3	8015	13,513	68.6

Note: Wealth and income refers to the average wealth (income) of adult family members aged 16 and above. Sampling weight is used in the calculations
Source: Calculated based on 2010 CFPS

families that have members engaged in self-employment/private business have fewer wealth advantages than income advantages as their family wealth is only 5.4% more than that of other families as opposed to 18.9% more income. The educational variable is the highest educational level in the family and is divided into two groups: high school and above, and middle school and below. Results show that educational level has the same effect pattern as political capital, namely has larger wealth advantages than income advantages. Though educational level represents market efficiency factors, it is highly related with whether a family has political capital, and the result is reasonable as the effect of political capital is not controlled. Further analysis will be made later with other variables being controlled.

It is shown that political capital factors and market efficiency factors display different effects on wealth and income, for the former with much more advantages in wealth than in income, while the engagement in market activities displays larger income advantages. The underlying causes and mechanisms are worth further discussion.

7.4 Regression Results

Part III preliminarily describes the possible effects imposed by political and market factors on family wealth, and reveals the different mechanisms of wealth and income. This paper will also explore the effects of these two types of factors while other variables are controlled. This part will use the traditional approach of conditional mean estimation and analyze wealth and income separately with multiple linear regression models.

7.4.1 *Different Effects of Political Factors on Wealth and Income*

Table 7.4 shows the results of the regression analysis of wealth and income. This paper uses several key variables to measure political factors' effects on wealth and income, and the results show that being a CPC member and holding administrative/managerial positions has notably greater effects on wealth than on income, but the years of education, self-employment and working in CPC or government organs/public institutions have almost the same effects on wealth and income ("coefficient difference significance test" in Table 7.4).

While other variables are controlled, having CPC members increases 30% family wealth and 12% income. Although CPC membership is not a direct indicator of political status, it has a bearing on promotion and establishment of social relations (Bian & Logan, 1996; Xie & Hannum, 1996; Zhou, 2000; Hauser & Xie, 2005). As CPC membership can help individuals obtain more opportunities of promotion and other material resources in the system (Ma, 2012), researchers usually take it as a measurement of political capital or redistribution power. The regression coefficient shows that working in government organs/public institutions increases 36% family wealth and 27% income, but the two coefficients are not significantly different in a statistical sense.

All in all, political capital has more advantages in wealth than in income, which may be attributed to three factors. First, after the housing reform commenced in the late 1980s, families with political capital, such as with CPC membership, obtained large and good-quality apartments (Walder & He, 2014), and their wealth advantages have been fortified by the soaring housing price since 2000. Second, the income-expense gap varies. Even when families have similar income, those with political capital spend much less because they enjoy various benefits from the employer (such as reimbursement and allowances). The widening income-expense gap leads to the accumulation of wealth. Third, families with political capital have more chances of making higher investment returns and turning them into savings or wealth. For instance, housing property can be converted into investment property or, if sold, into bank savings or financial assets.

It must be explained that according to some empirical studies, CPC membership no longer affects family income when the type of employer in the system and cadre status are controlled (Davis et al., 2005; Liu, 2005; Wu & Wu, 2009), but it does according to this paper. This paper adopts the total family income, which includes wage income, income from nonfarm operation, transfer income, property income and all other forms of income. While CPC membership has little effect on the forms of income that is more seriously affected by market factors (e.g. wage income), it still has significant effects on total family income according to our results.

Table 7.4 Comparison of multiple linear regression results on wealth and income

	Property		Income		Coefficient difference significance test
	Coefficient	Standard deviation	Coefficient	Standard deviation	Chi-square value & significance
Age	0.034	0.021	−0.010	0.008	–
Square age	−0.000	0.000	0.000	0.000	–
Whether there are children aged 15 or below					
Yes	0.205*	0.082	0.202***	0.033	–
Family structure (reference: Adults of three generations live together)					
Adults of two generations live together	−0.018	0.121	0.126**	0.044	–
Adults of one generation	0.287	0.188	0.176*	0.070	–
Others	−0.022	0.330	0.223*	0.105	–
Family size	0.110	0.094	−0.083*	0.035	–
Square family size	−0.012	0.008	−0.000	0.003	–
Whether there are retired elders					
Yes	0.047	0.103	0.456***	0.050	–
Whether it is a migrant family					
Yes	−0.731***	0.191	0.159**	0.050	–
Years of education	0.090***	0.015	0.071***	0.005	2.11
Whether any family member works at government organs/public institutions					
Yes	0.309**	0.114	0.238***	0.029	0.42
Whether any family member holds administrative/managerial positions					
Yes	0.665***	0.107	0.376***	0.032	8.64**
Whether there are CPC members					
Yes	0.264**	0.082	0.115***	0.031	3.60 +
Whether any family member engages in self-employment or private business					
Yes	0.309**	0.094	0.245***	0.033	0.51
Logarithm of county-level GDP per capita	0.462***	0.105	0.203***	0.027	8.12**

(continued)

Table 7.4 (continued)

	Property		Income		Coefficient difference significance test
	Coefficient	Standard deviation	Coefficient	Standard deviation	Chi-square value & significance
Constant	3.287**	1.173	6.679***	0.361	
Number of samples	6320		6320		
R^2	0.092		0.303		

Note: (1) ***p < 0.001, **p < 0.01, *p < 0.05 and +p < 0.1; (2) "Others" under family structure refer to scenarios where adult siblings live together, adult grandchildren live with grandparents, among others; (3) Standard deviations cluster at county level; (4) Seemingly Unrelated Regression (SUR) is used to test the significance of difference in independent variable coefficients between the two models

Source: Calculated based on 2010 CFPS

7.4.2 *Different Effects Imposed by Political Capital and Market Factors*[5] *on Family Wealth*

The regression model helps us quantify the different effects imposed by political capital and market factors on family wealth. Educational level has significant positive effect on family wealth. One more year of education increases family wealth by 9%. While other conditions are the same, families without CPC members need 2.9 more years of education, basically the jump from primary school to middle school or from middle school to high school, to catch up with those with membership in terms of wealth. The difference is more obvious in terms of employer. Families with members working in government organs or public institutions have 36.2% more wealth than other families, which is equivalent to 3.4 more years of education. The

[5] Putting political factors and market factors (e.g. employer and self-employment/private business) in the same regression model may lead to overlapping. For instance, a person may work in a government organ/public institution but also engages in self-employment/private business. But in fact, this kind of families takes up a very small proportion, only 0.9 percent, in urban China, thus with basically zero effect on the conclusion. By putting employer and self-employment/private business in the same model, we divide the families into four groups: those with no member working in government organs/public institutions or engaged in market activities (reference group), those with members working in government organs/public institutions but not engaged in self-employment/private business (the second group), those with members engaged in self-employment/private business but not working in government organs/public institutions (the third group), and those with members both working in government organs/public institutions and engaged in market activities (the fourth group). The comparison between the second group and the reference group shows the effects of pure political factors, and that between the third group and the reference group shows the effects of pure market factors, but the results are no different than when the two variables are in separate models. It is the same with the CPC membership variable. Since there are two variables of political factors and two of market factors, the variables are put in the model separately for simplification.

CPC membership and employer fully showcase the advantages brought by political capital in obtaining economic resources (Table 7.4).

To better explain the different effects imposed by political capital and market factors on family wealth, this paper further divides wealth into housing property (the residence the family lives in and others) and other properties (financial assets, productive fixed assets and durable consumer goods). Table 7.5 shows the Tobit regression results on the two kinds of properties. Political factors (employer and CPC membership) have significant effects on both housing and non-housing properties with similar intensity ("coefficient difference significance test" in Table 7.5). Market factors (educational level and self-employment/private business) also have significant effects on both kinds of properties, but more intensely on non-housing properties than on housing properties. As shown in Table 7.5, the influence coefficient of the years of education on housing properties is 0.11, but that on non-housing properties is 0.18, while the influence coefficient of self-employment/private business on the two kinds of properties is 0.33 and 0.84 respectively, indicating a significant disparity. This means that with the rapid development of market economy in China today, market factors are critical for the accumulation of non-housing properties.

In the meantime, a close look at the housing property model reveals greater effects from political factors (the regression coefficient of CPC membership and working in government organs/public institutions is 0.66 and 0.40) and smaller effects from market factors (the regression coefficient of self-employment/private business is 0.33). The results of non-housing property model are just the opposite, in which the influence coefficient of self-employment/private business reaches 0.84, while that of CPC membership and working in government organs/public institutions is 0.41 and 0.37. This fully demonstrates the important role played by political factors in the accumulation of housing properties and that by market factors in the accumulation of non-housing properties.

7.4.3 *Effects of Other Structural Factors on Family Wealth*

This part discusses the effects imposed by several important structural factors on housing property. The first factor is regional difference. Not only income, but also wealth displays huge regional differences in China. According to Xie and Jin (2015), the volume of wealth and degree of wealth inequality varies greatly from province to province, which accounts for over 20% of the general wealth disparity. The regression results in Table 7.4 show that county-level economic development significantly affects family wealth, and regional factors have more significant effects on wealth than on income. Therefore, regional difference is significant on the wealth inequality in China.

The second structural factor is the migrant population resulting from the *hukou*-based urban-rural dichotomy, a special phenomenon given China's special social system. The results of this paper as well as other studies indicate that the income of

Table 7.5 Tobit regression results by type of property

	Housing property		Non-housing property		Coefficient difference significance test
	Coefficient	Standard deviation	Coefficient	Standard deviation	Chi-square value & significance
Age	0.181***	0.051	−0.035	0.030	–
Square age	−0.001**	0.001	0.001 +	0.000	–
Whether there are children aged 15 or below					
Yes	−0.065	0.159	0.622***	0.139	–
Family structure (reference: Adults of three generations live together)					
Adults of two generations live together	0.091	0.212	0.095	0.244	–
Adults of one generation	0.550	0.350	0.452	0.315	–
Others	−1.507 +	0.814	0.601	0.618	–
Family size	0.747***	0.222	−0.167	0.161	–
Square family size	−0.056**	0.020	−0.019	0.015	–
Whether there are retired elders					
Yes	−0.387	0.236	0.579***	0.172	–
Whether it is a migrant family					
Yes	−2.685***	0.419	0.292	0.232	–
Years of education	0.108***	0.028	0.183***	0.022	5.05*
Whether any family member works at government organs/public institutions					
Yes	0.402 +	0.228	0.373*	0.184	0.01
Whether any family member holds administrative/managerial positions					
Yes	0.836***	0.171	0.919***	0.155	0.12
Whether there are CPC members					
Yes	0.658**	0.206	0.407**	0.156	0.87
Whether any family member engages in self-employment or private business					
Yes	0.332 +	0.177	0.842***	0.161	4.47*
Logarithm of family income	0.060 +	0.032	0.100***	0.021	1.19

(continued)

Table 7.5 (continued)

	Housing property		Non-housing property		Coefficient difference significance test
	Coefficient	Standard deviation	Coefficient	Standard deviation	Chi-square value & significance
Logarithm of county-level GDP per capita	0.321 +	0.177	0.434***	0.11	0.55
Constant	−2.871	2.040	0.195	1.421	–
Number of samples	6320		6320		

Note: Points (1) to (4) are the same as in Table 4; effect on family income is controlled in these two models
Source: Calculated based on 2010 CFPS

migrant population is not much different from (Zhou, 2014), or even higher than (Zhou et al., 2013), that of local population. But migrant families in cities stand at an obvious disadvantage when it comes to wealth accumulation, with only 48% of the wealth owned by urban families when other variables are controlled. Most migrants cannot afford to buy an apartment in the city, so they have much fewer housing assets than the locals. Meanwhile, they have to spend part of their income on rent, which reduces their savings and makes it harder for them to invest in the financial market. Therefore, migrant population is in serious disadvantage from the wealth perspective. This provides a new angle for future studies on the economic integration of migrant population: to pay more attention to their family wealth, not just income.

At last, a brief analysis will be made on the effects of other control variables on wealth (Table 7.4). The age has an inverse U-shaped effect on wealth, but not significant, nor is the effect of square age. We need to be very careful when explaining this phenomenon in China. Some studies explain this inverse U-shaped effect with the life cycle theory, but we need to keep in mind that the private wealth accumulation only started after the reform and opening-up was launched in 1978, and the housing privatization reform was carried out in the 1990s. If we divide the Chinese population into three age groups, including the elderly, middle-aged and young, the younger elders in the first group may have accumulated a certain amount of assets through housing privatization and the allocation of welfare housing, but the older they get, the less likely wealth accumulation becomes. The middle-aged group, in comparison, has accumulated huge amounts of wealth thanks to the market economic reform and housing reform, whereas the young group, which has just begun to work, has not had enough time to accumulate wealth and has not experienced the period for welfare housing either. Therefore, the inverse U-shaped pattern only reflects the difference in age but is not enough to prove the life cycle theory on wealth accumulation, which requires data over a long period of time. If we use cross-sectional data, the wealth accumulation experienced by the three age groups must be similar in order to simulate the accumulation process over a lifetime.

The type of family structure and family size don't have independent, significant effects on family wealth, but families with children aged 15 and below have obviously more wealth than other families. This may be because (1) they have higher income than others and (2) they have spent less and saved more for the children's future education.

7.5 Further Discussion of Regression Results

In China, private wealth is quickly accumulated after the reform and opening-up. Wealth accumulation and level is affected by many factors. In China's development history, factors that affect income also affect wealth accumulation since income minus expenditure is savings. People with higher education have more chances of making higher income, so educational level represents the potential of wealth acquisition while also directly affecting the acquisition through investment. On the other hand, wealth accumulation of Chinese families is also deeply susceptible to the policy and social environment. After the housing reform was implemented, urban families with members working in the system bought welfare housing from their employers at extremely low prices. The housing unit became their private property and the largest component of family wealth, and the system separation became an important factor in family wealth. Another contributing factor that is discussed most overseas is inheritance (Gale & Scholz, 1994), but it has little effect in China because private wealth is a fairly recent phenomenon in the country, and very most people who have obtained huge amounts of wealth since the 1980s are still alive.

In present-day urban China, political factor plays an important role in the accumulation of family wealth. Data show that political factor has more advantages in wealth than in income, which means the wage gap cannot explain the wealth gap which is more driven by political identity. Besides, as far as wealth is concerned, one family member being a CPC member or working in government organs/public institutions is equivalent to having three more years of education. Why is that? This paper explains from three perspectives.

First, from the housing perspective, the housing reform that began in the late 1980s turned the apartments most urban families were living in into their private property. This unexpected, external factor, which was somewhat like a legacy, gave those families a sudden property within a short time without them having to accumulate their income. While being a kind of asset itself, housing also saves rent for those who own it, who then can either put the money in banks or invest it, thus forming another kind of assets.

Second, from the consumption perspective, income minus consumption is savings that may become wealth. The group with political capital, such as those working in the system, has great income advantages, but even greater wealth advantages. When income is controlled, this group still has more wealth, probably because they are entitled to plenty of benefits or allowances from the employer and consequently spend less. Although this factor is not as directly influential as housing, it amounts to a fortune over time.

Third, families with political capital are able to make better investments in, for instance, the real estate market or the emerging financial market. Housing affects wealth accumulation (Killewald & Zhu, 2015). With the housing price hike in Chinese cities, families with housing invest in real estate, accumulate more wealth, and further push up the price, which makes it harder for unhoused families to buy it and worsens housing inequality (Chen & Qiu, 2011). Families with political capital have more money to make financial investment and increase the value of their current assets.

The 2010 CFPS collects detailed data on housing, income and expenditure, which preliminarily provide the empirical verification for the explanations above. Let us first take a look at housing property right. 88.7% of the families with CPC members own an apartment as opposed to 79.2% of those without; 21.8% of the families with CPC members have other housing properties except the one currently inhabited as opposed to 16.9% of those without. As to the effect of employer (Fig. 7.3), families with members working in government organs/public institutions have the highest housing ownership (88%) after those with members engaged in agriculture, followed by those with members working in state-owned enterprises (SOEs, 82.8%) and those with retirees (81.9%). Families with members engaged in self-employment/private business have the highest ownership of other housing properties, but the lowest ownership of inhabited housing (76.2%). This is probably because they are migrants and have housing properties in the rural hometown. Families with members working in government organs/public institutions rank next in the ownership of other housing properties (23.5%).

The second explanation is the income-expense gap. The numbers above show that families with political capital have major income advantages, which become wealth advantages when income is converted into savings or investment. This paper tries further to analyze how consumption affects family wealth accumulation while income is the same. If family members work in government organs/public institutions, the benefits such as various reimbursements and allowances from the employer largely reduce the family expenditure and increase savings. If income minus expenditure leaves family wealth (savings = income–expenditure), the lower expenditure, the higher savings given the same income. Of course there may be two reasons for the high savings when income is controlled—(1) low expenditure and high surplus, and (2) other investments, such as stock value increase or real estate investment. Since data about these two factors cannot be fully separated, we decide to combine the second explanation (expenditure) and the third one (investment).

Following this thought, we use the family's financial assets to represent its savings, conduct Tobit regression[6] with the logarithm of savings as a dependent variable, and get the regression forecast. The horizontal axis stands for the logarithm of

[6]The independent variables are the same as in previous models. Control variables also include employer, CPC membership, years of education, self-employment/private business and wage income.

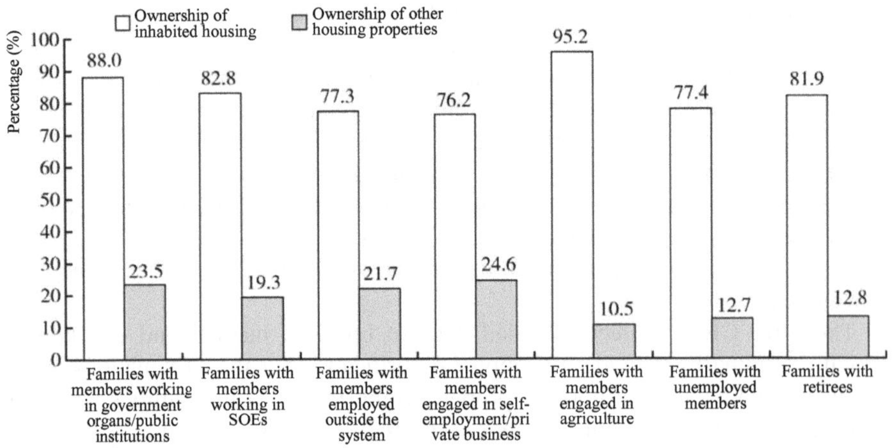

Fig. 7.3 Difference in ownership of inhabited housing and other housing properties by type of employer. Source: Calculated based on 2010 CFPS

the average income of family members aged 16 and above and the vertical axis the regression forecast. Figs. 7.4 and 7.5 are fitting charts based on the type of employer and CPC membership, which show that with their income being the same, families with members working in government organs/public institutions have much more financial assets than those without. Likewise, families with CPC members also have much more financial assets than those without. This means that while other factors are controlled, families with political capital have more savings than other families even with the same income, and possible explanations, as said before, are low expenditure and better investment.

As to expenditure, families with political capital spend quite a large amount of money actually. Consumption data in CFPS show that these families spend a lot on education and entertainment, so their high savings must be attributed to the allowances, reimbursements and other benefits from their employers. We will discuss expenditure and investment separately in the future if relevant data are available.

7.6 Conclusions

Using the CFPS data, this paper analyzes family wealth and family income in parallel, discusses the effects imposed by political factors and market factors on family wealth in urban China, and comes to the following conclusions.

1. In urban China, political capital has far more advantages in wealth than in income, and income difference cannot fully explain the wealth disparity resulting from political capital.

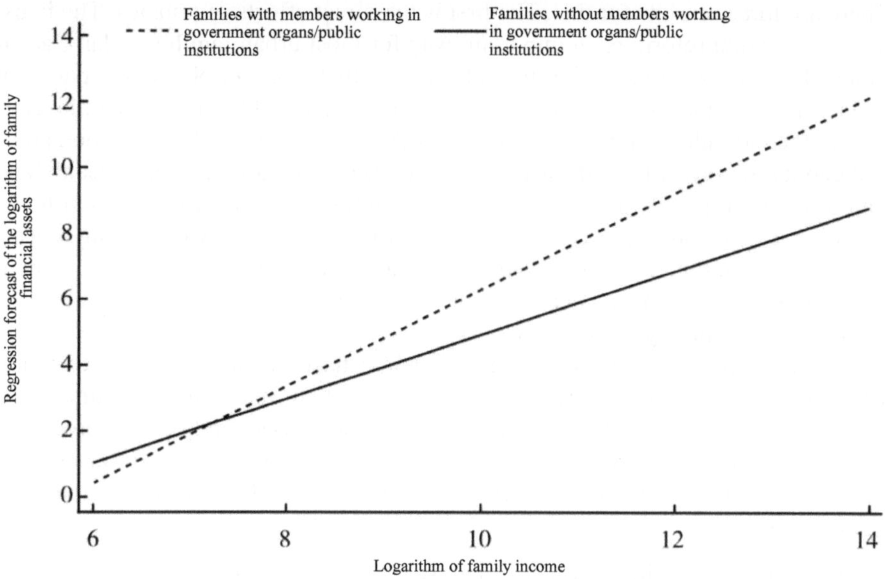

Fig. 7.4 Difference in financial assets for families with the same income but different types of employers. Note: Family income represents the logarithm of the average income of adult family members aged 16 and above; family financial assets represent the logarithm of their average financial assets. Source: Calculated based on 2010 CFPS

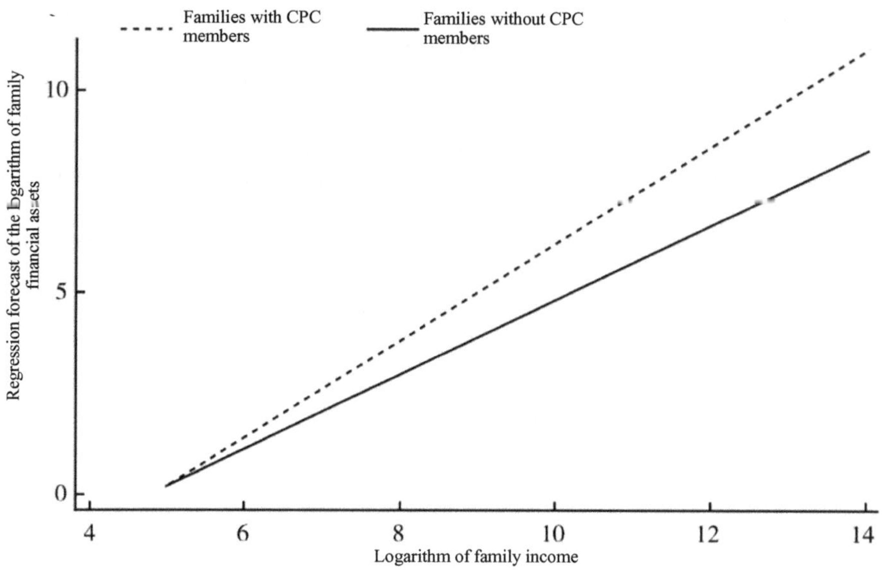

Fig. 7.5 Difference in financial assets for families with the same income but different CPC membership. Note: Family income represents the logarithm of the average income of adult family members aged 16 and above; family financial assets represent the logarithm of their average financial assets. Source: Calculated based on 2010 CFPS

There are three reasons for this. The first is the direct effects of policies. The housing privatization reform is an important way for most urban families to have accumulated private wealth. During the reform, whether one can obtain an apartment and its size and quality are directly related to the nature and level of the employer as well as the individual's rank in the employer (Walder & He, 2014). Therefore, political capital directly affects the acquisition and accumulation of family wealth, and families with it quickly accumulate private wealth through the acquisition of housing. Later as the housing price in cities begins to soar, families with housing properties further accumulate wealth through real estate investment, whereas those without find it more difficult to buy an apartment. The widening gap in housing assets leads to the rising inequality in family wealth.

Second, urban families with political capital have advantages in expenditure, which refer to the benefits provided inside the system, including reimbursements and allowances. As a result, they can spend less and consequently save more.

Third, families with political capital are more likely to make good investment decisions in the real estate market or financial market, thus accumulating more wealth.

2. In urban China, where market economy is developing rapidly while traditional political power has not been weakened yet, political capital and market factors jointly affect the accumulation of family wealth. Families with members working in government organs/public institutions, with CPC members, with better education and engaged in market activities have notable advantages in wealth accumulation.
3. However, political factors and market factors have different effects on different kinds of property, the former with more effects on housing assets while the latter on non-housing assets. This, on the one hand, reflects the role of policies and systems in Chinese urban families' accumulation of private wealth, since those with political capital have acquired a large amount of wealth through the privatization of public housing. On the other hand, it also reflects the important role played by market factors in the accumulation of market-related wealth, including financial assets and productive fixed assets, in the course of market economy reform.
4. Structural factors, which consist of differences in geography and *hukou*, are important factors that affect the wealth accumulation of Chinese urban families.

Of course family wealth accumulation is a very complicated process, which seems more elusive against the special social background in China. More empirical studies are needed to fill the huge blank in this field.

References

Barsky, R., Bound, J., Charles, K. K., & Lupton, J. (2002). Accounting for the black-white wealth gap: A nonparametric approach. *Journal of the American Statistical Association, 97*(459), 663–673.

Bian, Y/ & Logan, J. (1996). "Market transition and the persistence of power: The changing stratification system in urban China". *American Sociological Review*, 61 (5), 739–758.

Chen, Y., & Qiu, Z. (2011). How high housing price affects household saving rate and wealth inequality. *Economic Research Journal, 10*, 25–38.

Conley, D. & Glauber, R. (2008). *Wealth mobility and volatility in black and white*. Center for American Progress. Accessed on Nov. 15, 2014, https://cdn.americanprogress.org/wp-content/up1oads/issues/2008/07/pdf/wealth_mobility.pdf

Davis, D., Bian, Y., & Wang, S. (2005). Material rewards to multiple capitals under market-socialism in China. *Social Transformations in Chinese Societies, 1*, 31–58.

Gale, W., & Scholz, J. K. (1994). Intergenerational transfers and the accumulation of wealth. *Journal of Economic Perspectives, 8*(4), 145–160.

Hall, M., & Crowder, K. (2011). Extended-family resources and racial inequality in the transition to homeownership. *Social Science Research, 40*(6), 1534–1546.

Hauser, S., & Xie, Y. (2005). Temporal and regional variation in earnings inequality: Urban China in transition between 1988 and 1995. *Social Science Research, 34*(1), 44–79.

Hu, J., Xie, Y., & Sun, Y. (2014). Design of China family panel studies questionnaire. In Y. Xie, X. Zhang, J. Li, X. Yu, & Q. Ren (Eds.), *China family panel studies 2014* (pp. 166–208). Peking University Press.

Jansen, W., & Wu, X. (2012). Income inequality in Urban China, 1978-2005. *Chinese Sociological Review, 45*(1), 3–27.

Jin, Y. & Xie, Y. (2014). *CFPS 2012 and technical report on wealth data 2010*. In the series of CFPS technical report, No. CFPS-29, Accessed Mar 1, 2015, from http://www.isss.edu.cn/cfps/d/file/wd/jsbg/TR2012/2014-12-22/303ebb3bd405f33c3d1bd2741ba2d045.pdf

Keister, L. (2000). *Wealth in America: Trends in wealth inequality*. Cambridge University Press.

Keister, L. (2003). Religion and wealth: The role of religious affiliation and participation in early adult asset accumulation. *Social Forces, 82*(1), 173–205.

Keister, L. (2014). The one percent. *Annual Review of Sociology, 40*(1), 347–367.

Keister, L., & Moller, S. (2000). Wealth inequality in the United States. *Annual Review of Sociology, 26*, 63–81.

Killewald, A. (2013). Return to being black, living in the red: A race gap in wealth that goes beyond social origins. *Demography, 50*(4), 1177–1195.

Killewald, A. & Zhu, F. (2015). *Does your home make you wealthy?* Paper Presented at 2015 Annual Meeting of Population Association of America.

Lerman, D., & Mikesell, J. (1988). Rural and urban poverty: An income/net worth approach. *Review of Policy Research, 7*(4), 765–781.

Li, S., Wei, Z., & Ding, S. (2005). Empirical analysis of unequal wealth distribution of Chinese residents and its reasons. *Economic Research Journal, 6*, 4–15.

Li, S., Wei, Z., & Gustafsson, B. (2000). Wealth distribution of urban residents in China. *Economic Research Journal, 3*, 16–23.

Liang, Y., Huo, Z., & Liu, K. (2010). Empirical study of wealth distribution among urban and rural residents in China. *Economic Research Journal, 10*, 33–47.

Lin, Z., & Wu, X. (2010). Institutional evolution, change of class structure and income inequality in China: 1978-2005. *Chinese Journal of Sociology, 6*, 1–40.

Liu, X. (2005). Multiple drivers of social stratification in current China: An explanation from the perspective of power derivative theory. *Social Sciences in China, 4*, 101–114.

Liu, H., & Wang, Y. (2010). Does political capital increase or decrease benefits as market economy develops? *China Economic Quarterly, 3*, 891–908.

Ma, D. (2012). A relational view of organizational restructuring: The case of transitional China. *Management and Organization Review, 8*(1), 51–75.
McKinley, T., & Griffin, K. (1993). The distribution of land in rural China. *The Journal of Peasant Studies, 21*(1), 71–84.
Menchik, P., & Jianakoplos, N. A. (1997). Black-white wealth inequality: Is inheritance the reason? *Economic Inquiry, 35*(2), 428–442.
Meng, X. (2007). Wealth accumulation and distribution in urban China. *Economic Development and Cultural Change, 55*(4), 761–791.
Morgan, S., & Scott, J. (2007). Wealth inequality and the prospects for increasing intergenerational transfers. *Social Science Research, 36*(3), 1105–1134.
Nee, V. (1989). A theory of market transition: From redistribution to markets in state socialism. *American Sociological Review, 54*(5), 663–681.
Nee, V. (1991). Social inequalities in reforming state socialism: Between redistribution and markets in China. *American Sociological Review, 56*(3), 267–282.
Nee, V. (1996). The emergence of a market society: Changing mechanisms of stratification in China. *American Journal of Sociology, 101*(4), 908–949.
Oliver, M., & Shapiro, T. (1997). *Black wealth, white wealth: A new perspective on racial inequality*. Routledge.
Schmidt, L., & Sevak, P. (2006). Gender, marriage, and asset accumulation in the United States. *Feminist Economics, 12*(1–2), 139–166.
Smith, J. (1995). Racial and ethnic differences in wealth in the health and retirement study. *Journal of Human Resources, 30*, S158–S183.
Walder, A., & He, X. (2014). Public housing into private assets: Wealth creation in Urban China. *Social Science Research, 46*, 85–99.
Wooldridge, J. (2010). *Econometric Analysis of Cross Section and Panel Data* (2nd ed.). MIT Press.
Wu, X. (2002). *Embracing the market: Entry into self-employment in transitional China, 1978-1996*. Population Studies Center, University of Michigan. Accessed on Dec.1, 2014, http://deepblue.lib.umich.edu/bitstream/handle/2027.42/39897/wp512.pdf
Wu, X. (2011). Income and wealth inequality of Chinese urban households: 1995-2002. *Population Research, 6*, 13–26.
Wu, Y., & Wu, X. (2009). Occupational, gender segregation and income stratification in cities. *Sociological Studies, 4*, 88–111.
Xi, S., & Xie, Y. (2014). Market transition theory revisited: Changing regimes of housing inequality in China, 1988-2002. *Sociological Science, 1*, 277–291.
Xie, Y., & Hannum, E. (1996). Regional variation in earnings inequality in reform-era Urban China. *American Journal of Sociology, 101*(4), 950–992.
Xie, Y., & Jin, Y. (2014). Family Wealth. In Y. Xie, X. Zhang, J. Li, X. Yu, & Q. Ren (Eds.), *China family panel studies 2014* (pp. 25–46). Peking University Press.
Xie, Y., & Jin, Y. (2015). Household wealth in China. *Chinese Sociological Review, 47*(3), 203–229.
Xie, Y., & Lu, P. (2015). The sampling design of the China family panel studies (CFPS). *Chinese Journal of Sociology, 1*(4), 471–484.
Xie, Y., Qiu, Z. & Lv, P. (2012). *Sampling design for dynamic CFPS*. In the series of CFPS technical report, No. CFPS-1, Accessed Mar 1, 2015, from http://www.isss.edu.cn/cfps/d/file/wd/jsbg/2010jsbg/c70c703752f7f6f24e27b5a8a85c1cba.pdf
Xie, Y., & Wu, X. (2008). Danwei profitability and earnings inequality in Urban China. *The China Quarterly, 195*, 558–581.
Xie, Y., Zhang, X., Xu, Q., & Zhang, C. (2013). Income Distribution. In Y. Xie, X. Zhang, J. Li, X. Yu, & Q. Ren (Eds.), *China family panel studies 2013* (pp. 27–53). Peking University Press.
Xie, Y., & Zhou, X. (2014). Income inequality in Today's China. *Proceedings of the National Academy of Sciences, 111*(19), 6928–6933.
Yamokoski, A., & Keister, L. (2006). The wealth of single women: Marital status and parenthood in the asset accumulation of young baby boomers in the United States. *Feminist Economics, 12*(1–2), 167–194.

Yuan, P., & Wang, L. (2013). Unequal housing distribution among Chinese urban residents and study of contributors and contribution rate. *Statistical Research, 12*, 69–76.
Zellner, A. (1962). An efficient method of estimating seemingly unrelated regressions and tests for aggregation bias. *Journal of the American Statistical Association, 57*(298), 348–368.
Zhou, X. (2000). Economic transformation and income inequality in urban China: evidence from panel data. *American Journal of Sociology, 105*(4), 1135–1174.
Zhou, X. (2014). Increasing returns to education, changing labor force structure, and the rise of earnings inequality in urban China, 1996-2010. *Social Forces, 93*(2), 429–455.
Zhou, H., Duan, B., & Hu, Y. (2013). Population flow. In Y. Xie, X. Zhang, J. Li, X. Yu, & Q. Ren (Eds.), *China family panel studies 2013* (pp. 250–280). Peking University Press.

Yongai Jin, associate professor at Population Development Studies Center, Renmin University of China.

Yu Xie, professor at Center for Social Research, Peking University and Center on Contemporary China, Princeton University.

Chapter 8
Income Polarization between Urban and Rural Residents in China and its Decomposition: 1988–2007

Chen Wang, Guanghua Wan, and Hui Cao

Abstract China's rapid economic development has come with serious problems in income distribution. The rising income inequality has attracted a lot of attention, but few studies focus on income polarization. Serious income polarization not only solidifies income classes, but also brings adverse effects on social stability. This paper estimates the trends of income bi-polarization and multi-polarization using the data from China Household Income Project (CHIP), and decomposes them by income source with the Shapley method. The paper makes the following findings. First, income polarization declined from 1988 onwards, but increased again from 1995 to 2007, staying on a high level even though slightly lower than that of 1988. Second, the largest contributor to aggravating income bi-polarization and multi-polarization is wage while transfer income from collectively and state-owned enterprises mitigates income bi-polarization in rural areas, and property income mitigates both income bi-polarization and multi-polarization in urban area. Third, in rural areas, wage aggravates income bi-polarization and multi-polarization in 1988–2002; in urban areas, wage and operational income aggravate bi-polarization while operational income and government subsidy mitigate income multi-polarization in 1995–2007.

Keywords Bi-polarization · Multi-polarization · Decomposition of polarization

---

C. Wang
School of Urban and Regional Science, Shanghai University of Finance and Economics, Shanghai, China

G. Wan
Research Institute for Indian Ocean Economies, Yunnan University of Finance and Economics, Kunming, China

H. Cao (✉)
School of Economics, Shanghai University, Shanghai, China
e-mail: lvqs@ssap.cn

F. Cai (ed.), *Income Inequality and Poverty Governance in China*, International Research on Poverty Reduction, https://doi.org/10.1007/978-981-95-5063-0_8

8.1 Introduction

Income distribution in China has received a lot of attention and given birth to many relevant studies (Wang et al., 2014). The researchers, using data from different sources and various gauges of income inequality, have analyzed in great depth China's income distribution issue in every aspect. Some studies use the CHIP data (Li et al., 2011; Sicular et al., 2007; Zhao, 2001) and some the data from the National Bureau of Statistics (NBS) of China (Ravallion & Chen, 2007), some examine the Gini coefficient (Li et al., 2011) and some the Theil index (Kanbur & Zhang, 2005; Wan, 2013), and some make spatial adjustment of price during calculations but some do not. Yet their results have something in common. First, income inequality is quite serious in China, where the official Gini coefficient was 0.491 in 2008 and 0.473 in 2013 (Li et al., 2011). Second, income inequality temporarily shrank in the early years of reform and opening-up, but has been on the rise ever since the mid-1980s until 2008, when it dropped slightly. Third, there are many factors that cause the unequal income distribution in China, but the biggest contributor is the urban-rural inequality. According to the study by Wan (2007), the urban-rural inequality in income distribution can explain 70–80% of regional inequality. Lin et al. (2010) drew a similar conclusion with the percentage of 79.46%, while Sicular et al. (2007) and Gustafsson and Li (1998) found that urban-rural inequality in income distribution can explain about one third of the unequal income distribution among Chinese households. But these studies have two shortcomings. On the one hand, they are focused on, or limited to, measuring the inequality or income gap, but very few analyze the causes (Liu, 2010; Wan, 2004; Wan, 2007; Wan et al., 2005) and consequences (Wan, 2013). Studying the causes for inequality or decomposing it is of great importance in that the results can be helpful for formulating targeted policies to make income distribution more equal in China.

But income distribution encompasses more aspects than just inequality, such as income mobility, measuring the size of the middle class, and so on, of which income bi-polarization, a familiar subject among the public, is of special importance. Generally speaking, bi-polarization means the poor get poorer and the rich richer, which implies a shrinking middle class and an unstable social structure. But in fact, income polarization can mean two poles (the rich and the poor) as well as multiple poles. In present-day China, for example, farmers are at the bottom of the income ladder, people with urban *hukou* on top of the ladder, and a large number of migrant workers in the lower-middle section.

To be more precise, income polarization refers to the process in which income is concentrated in the hands of a small number of people (Foster & Wolfson, 2010). It results in the solidification of income classes and, worsening of poor income mobility, and contradicts with a major feature of a stable society, namely an olive-shaped income distribution structure. Foreign studies show that income polarization undermines economic growth (Ezcurra, 2009), people's health (Blanco & Xavier, 2010) and social stability, and even causes social unrest (Duclos et al., 2004; Esteban & Ray, 1994). According to this logic, China's income polarization, either with two or multiple poles, may be more harmful than income inequality. Therefore, analyzing this phenomenon and its determining factors is of great importance for maintaining social stability and harmony and promoting economic development.

This paper studies the income bi- and multi-polarization in rural and urban China and answers a series of questions: What is the trend of income polarization in rural and urban areas, up, down or not much change? How does income from different sources affect the degree and change of income polarization in urban and rural areas? Based on CHIP data of 1988, 1995, 2002 and 2007 and using the method of bi-polarization measurement proposed by Foster and Wolfson (2010) and that of multi-polarization measurement proposed by Duclos et al. (2004), this paper estimates the degree of income polarization in China and conducts Shapley decomposition of the estimated results.

The next part will review existing literature on income polarization. Part III will give an elaborate introduction to the data, measurement method and decomposition method used. Part IV estimates the degree of income bi–/multi-polarization in rural and urban China in 1988–2007, decomposes it by source of income, and analyzes its change and determining factors. Part V presents our conclusions.

8.2 Literature Review on Income Polarization

Polarization means the income is concentrated in the hands of a few groups, which leads to the social stratification (Gradín, 2000) and the "hollowing out of the middle class" regarding income distribution (Zhang & Kanbur, 2001). Polarization also means the difference in income class affects people-to-people relation. In other words, people in different classes are emotionally distant from each other because they have little in common, whereas those in the same income class have more in common or a higher degree of recognition. Esteban and Ray (1994) described this phenomenon in the "alienation–recognition" framework, the former referring to the alienating features and the latter recognizing features of polarization. When social polarization reaches a high level, class solidification will be serious and inter-class frictions are highly probable, which undermines social stability and causes turmoil (Duclos et al., 2004; Esteban & Ray, 1994). There is limited literature on the measurement and decomposition of income polarization. The measurement method in the real sense originated in the 1990s (Esteban & Ray, 1994; Wolfson, 1994) and became mature in 2004 (Duclos et al., 2004). The measurement of income polarization will be expounded in the next part.

Studies of income polarization have increased in recent years with the development of measurement methods. Gasparini et al. (2008) analyzed the income polarization in Latin American and Caribbean countries in 1989–2004. Ezcurra (2009) studied the situation in 61 regions of eight European countries in 1993–2003. Wang et al. (2015) estimated the income polarization trend in 31 European countries in 2004–2012 and the effects on it imposed by tax, transfer payment and other income sources. Gochoco-Bautista et al. (2013) analyzed the income polarization trends in eight Asian countries. Some scholars studied the income polarization in a specific country, such as Gradín (2002) and Kwack and Lee (2007). As to income polarization in China, Hong (2010) calculated the polarization index of eight regions according to each province's population and GDP in 1978–2008, and found it to be on the rise ever since the reform and opening-up. Hong decomposed the polarization changes into the results of effects from GDP per capita, ranking and percentage of population. Wang and Wan (2015) found from the grouped income data in statistical yearbooks and CHIP data that income polarization has become more serious in the last few decades, with that in the western region being more serious than in the coastal region and that among rural residents more serious than among urban residents. The aggravated polarization in 2002–2007 was mainly caused by the changing distribution of property income and transfer payment. Luo (2010) echoed that Chinese people's income distribution has been polarized at a fast pace. While income polarization of urban residents is of a high speed, that of rural residents is of greater severity. Luo also found that going out as migrant workers has great effects on rural polarization while employment and economic transformation on urban polarization. Yao and Ye (2012) analyzed rural residents' income in different provinces in 1997–2009, and found that regional polarization in rural China strengthened with volatility before 2006 and weakened after that, with wage being the principal factor. Guo (2004), Xu and Wang (2008), Araar (2008) and Bonnefond and Clément (2012) have conducted research on China's income polarization in recent years.

Very little literature has offered explanations for polarization. Existing literature either analyze the determining factors of polarization based on macro data, or cover a limited period, or focus only on the rural population. This paper, using CHIP data, estimates the national, urban and rural income inequality and polarization in 1988–2007, and decomposes its changes by sources of income.

8.3 Data and Research Methods

8.3.1 Data

Data used in this paper come from the CHIP of 1988, 1995, 2002 and 2007. They are collected through the income distribution survey of Chinese urban and rural households conducted by the income distribution team at the China Institute for Income Distribution, using the multi-phased stratified probability sampling method (Gao, 2008). The income concept here is defined in the same way as that used by the National Bureau of Statistics (NBS): net income per capita for rural residents and disposable income for urban ones.

Based on CHIP data, this paper studies the rural and urban groups separately. The rural net income in 1988, 1995 and 2002 can be divided into the following items: wage income and pension ($RY1$), income from work at township enterprises

(*RY*2), operational income (*RY*3), converted income from the production and sale of agricultural products (*RY*4), property income (*RY*5), rent from privately owned housing (*RY*6), transfer income from collectively or state-owned enterprises (*RY*7) and other income including private transfer payment (*RY*8). They add up to form the net income of rural residents (*RY*). Due to the adjustment of statistical specifications, the rural net income of 2007 is divided into the following items: wage income (*NRY*1), income from primary industry (*NRY*2), income from secondary industry (*NRY*3), income from tertiary industry (*NRY*4), property income (*NRY*5), and after-tax transfer income (*NRY*6). The sum from *NRY*1 to *NRY*6 is the net income of rural residents.

According to the work by Griffin and Zhao (1991), the urban disposable income in 1988 is divided into the following items: wage income (*UY*1), pension income (*UY*2), income of the unemployed (*UY*3), operational income (*UY*4), property income (*UY*5), other income including private transfer payment (*UY*6), aftertax subsidy other than housing subsidy and voucher (*UY*7), voucher subsidy (*UY*8), housing subsidy (*UY*9), and rent from privately owned housing (*UY*10). They add up to form the disposable income of urban residents (*UY*). As statistics of income of the unemployed (*UY*3) was changed and the voucher subsidy (*UY*8) is canceled after 1988, the income in 1995, 2002 and 2007 is categorized differently, and urban disposable income is divided into the following items: wage income (*UY*1), pension income (*UY*2), operational income (*UY*4), property income (*UY*5), other income including private transfer payment (*UY*6), subsidy other than housing subsidy and voucher (*UY*7), housing subsidy (*UY*9), and rent from privately owned housing (*UY*10). They add up to form the disposable income of urban residents (*UY*).

8.3.2 Measurement and Decomposition of Income Polarization

8.3.2.1 Measurement of Bi-Polarization

Income polarization consists of bi-polarization and multi-polarization, the former closely related with the hollowing-out of the middle class (Wolfson, 1994). Many studies have tried to evaluate the importance of the middle class, but they have not reached an agreement on the measuring method. Thurow (1984) defined the middle class as the group whose income is 75–125% of the median income, but Blackburn and Bloom (1985) expanded the scope to 60–225%. Davis and Huston (1992), Lawrence (1984) and Birdsall (2007) also discussed the scope of the middle class.

This paper uses the bi-polarization measurement proposed by Foster and Wolfson (2010), which is the most extensively used and recognized indicator so far:

$$P_G = \left(I_G^B - I_G^W\right)\left(\overline{x} / m\right) \tag{8.1}$$

In this equation, $\overline{x}$, m, I_G^B and I_G^W respectively stand for the average value, median, inter-class Gini coefficient and intra-class Gini coefficient of income x. The group whose income is lower than the median is designated as the low-income group and that whose income is higher than the median the high-income group. P_G is a relative bi-polarization indicator. Some scholars proposed absolute bi-polarization indicator (Chakravarty et al., 2007) and other types of bi-polarization indicators (Chakravarty & D'Ambrosio, 2010; Lasso de la Vega et al., 2010; Rodriguez & Salas, 2003; Wang & Tsui, 2000). Another bi-polarization indicator commonly-used was put forward by Silber et al. (2007):

$$P_A = \left(I_G^B - I_G^W\right) / I_G^{TOT} \tag{8.2}$$

I_G^{TOT} stands for the overall Gini coefficient.

8.3.2.2 Measurement of Multi-Polarization

Multi-polarization is a more extensive concept than bi-polarization. It measures to what extent the income distribution converges into a few groups rather than two like in bi-polarization. Multi-polarization encompasses bi-polarization and allows two or more income groups in the spectrum. Many scholars proposed measuring methods for multi-polarization, such as Esteban and Ray (1994), Zhang and Kanbur (2001), Reynal-Querol (2002), Duclos et al. (2004), Lasso de la Vega and Urrutia (2006), Esteban et al. (2007), Gigliarano and Mosler (2009), and Poggi and Silber (2010).

The measurement of income multi-polarization started with Esteban and Ray (1994), who believed political or social frictions and struggles are closely related with polarization, a process in which individuals are divided into different groups. Individuals in the same group have similar traits while different groups differ from each other. The higher inter-group heterogeneity and intra-group homogeneity are, the more likely it is to cause social unrest. Therefore, they put forth the "recognition—alienation" analytical framework, and held that income groups in the polarizing process have a high level of intra-group recognition and inter-group alienation. On that basis, they concluded that multi-polarization instead of income inequality is the cause for social struggles.

Another problem with multi-polarization measurement is how to divide the income groups. Many methods actually rely on the researchers to draw a line, such as Esteban and Ray (1994), Zhang and Kanbur (2001) and Poggi and Silber (2010), but this approach has its shortcomings. For instance, dividing income groups based on the median may lead to high-income individuals being put in the low-income group, and vice versa. To address this, Duclos et al. (2004) divided the groups based on an income density function, whereby the number of groups is determined by data. This paper uses the method of Duclos et al. (2004) to gauge multi-polarization:

$$DER = P_\alpha(f) = \iint f(x)^{1+\alpha} f(y)\left|x-y\right| dxdy \tag{8.3}$$

In this equation, α is a parameter that reflects the sensitivity of the multi-polarization indicator (*DER*), $0.25 \le \alpha \le 1$.

To use the *DER* index to measure the polarization of actual income distribution, Duclos et al. (2004) presented Eq. (8.3) as follows:

$$DER = P_\alpha(F) = \int_y f(y)^\alpha a(y) dF(y) \tag{8.4}$$

In which

$$a(y) = \mu + y(2F(y) - 1) - 2\int_{-\infty}^{y} x dF(x) \tag{8.5}$$

Suppose there is a random sample of independent and identically distributed income y_i (i = 1, ..., n), the samples are sequenced upward according to the income ($y_1 \le \cdots \le y_i \le \cdots \le y_n$), the income distribution function is $F(y)$, and the discrete version of *DER* is:

$$P_\alpha(\hat{F}) = \left(\frac{1}{n}\right) \sum_{i=1}^{n} \hat{f}(y_i)^\alpha \hat{a}(y_i) \tag{8.6}$$

In which

$$\hat{a}(y_i) = \hat{\mu} + y_i\left[\left(\frac{1}{n}\right)(2i-1) - 1\right] - \left(\frac{1}{n}\right)\left[2\sum_{j=1}^{i-1} y_j + y_i\right] \tag{8.7}$$

Here $\hat{\mu}$ means the average value of samples and $\hat{f}(y_i)^\alpha$ in Eq. (8.6) is non-parametric kernel density estimation.

8.3.2.3 Decomposition of Polarization

This paper decomposes income bi-polarization and multi-polarization by income source with the Shapley decomposition method, which is often used in the decomposition of Gini coefficient (Chantreuil & Trannoy, 2013; Sastre & Trannoy, 2002). Shorrocks (2013) pointed out that the Shapley method can be used to decompose any equation, not just the Gini coefficient, including poverty rate (Kolenikov & Shorrocks, 2005), R^2 of regression equation (Israeli, 2007), and maximum likelihood ratio (D'Ambrosio et al., 2011). The Shapley method takes into account all possible paths in the decomposition process, and the result is the average of all the results of those paths, so its result is not affected by the path.

We use a simple example to explain the principle of Shapley decomposition. We posit two income sources x and y, whose average value is $\overline{x}$ and $\overline{y}$. The bi-polarization indicator P_G is denoted as $P_G(x, y)$. We change the income sources in two ways. In one way we change x first and then y; in the other way we change y first and then x, and the average of their sum is the contribution of source x.

$$C(x)=\frac{1}{2}\{P_G(x;y)-P_G(x=\overline{x};y)\}+\frac{1}{2}\{P_G(x;y=\overline{y})-P_G(x=\overline{x};y=\overline{y})\} \quad (8.8)$$

In which, the value of $P_G(x=\overline{x};y=\overline{y})$ is 0. When income source x is changed, its value is set at $\overline{x}$ for all individuals. Likewise, the contribution of income source y to polarization for P_G is as follows:

$$C(y)=\frac{1}{2}\{P_G(x;y)-P_G(x;y=\overline{y})\}+\frac{1}{2}\{P_G(x=\overline{x};y)-P_G(x=\overline{x};y=\overline{y})\} \quad (8.9)$$

Adding Eq. (8.8) and (8.9), we get

$$P_G(x,y)=C(x)+C(y) \quad (8.10)$$

When there are more than two income sources, we can calculate the marginal contribution of each source in the same way. This decomposition method also applies to multi-polarization.

8.4 Income Polarization and Inequality of Urban and Rural Residents

Table 8.1 estimates the income bi-polarization, multi-polarization and inequality of urban and rural residents. In rural areas, the trend of bi-polarization and income inequality is rather consistent in 1988–2007, mitigating in 1988–1995 and aggravating in 1995–2007. Bonnefond and Clément (2012) came to a similar conclusion. Therefore, we infer that the aggravated income bi-polarization and inequality may be caused by the widening gap between the high-income and low-income rural groups. Moreover, bi-polarization and multi-polarization display the same trend most of the time since 1988 except in 2002–2007, when bi-polarization strengthens a little but multi-polarization basically remains the same. In general, rural multi-polarization has improved since 1988.

The situation in urban areas is different. From 1988 to 1995, bi-polarization falls but income inequality increases; the situation in 1995–2002 is just the opposite, with Gini coefficient down and bi-polarization up. The two indicators still display opposite trends in 2002–2007, with aggravated income inequality and mitigated bi-polarization. In general, urban income inequality increases (from 0.237 to 0.383) in 1988–2007, but bi-polarization improves a little (from 0.344 to 0.320). According to the equation that measures bi-polarization, bi-polarization is increasing function of inter-group inequality and decreasing function of intra-group inequality. So we

Table 8.1 Income bi-polarization, multi-polarization and inequality between urban and rural residents, 1988–2007

Year	Bi-polarization indicator P_G	Multi-polarization indicator $DER(\alpha = 1)$	Gini coefficient
Rural areas			
1988	0.348	0.100	0.370
1995	0.307	0.069	0.356
2002	0.330	0.083	0.364
2007	0.345	0.082	0.384
Urban areas			
1988	0.344	0.079	0.237
1995	0.271	0.073	0.343
2002	0.365	0.104	0.301
2007	0.320	0.043	0.383

Source: Calculated based on CHIP data of 1988, 1995, 2002 and 2007

infer that the aggravated urban income inequality is caused by the widening gap between high-income and low-income groups. A comparison between bi-polarization and multi-polarization shows a similar trend. The latter decreases in 2002–2007 much more drastically than the former, meaning income concentration in a few groups is mitigated in 2007.

To further explain the changes in bi-polarization and multi-polarization, we will decompose them by source of income. As there are plenty of explanations for the change of Gini coefficient, this paper will focus on that of bi-polarization and multi-polarization.

8.4.1 Decomposition of Bi-Polarization by Source of Income

Very little literature has discussed how each source of income affects bi-polarization and multi-polarization. We first decompose bi-polarization by source of income. Negative value means the source will mitigate bi-polarization while positive value means it will strengthen it. Table 8.2 shows that the biggest contributor to rural bi-polarization in 1988 is rent from privately owned housing (*RY*6), accounting for 83.1%, followed by converted income from the production and sale of agricultural products (*RY*4, accounting for 22.8%) and operational income (*RY*3, accounting for 20.1%). The income source that mitigates bi-polarization is transfer income from collectively or state-owned enterprises (*RY*7, accounting for −16.3%). This is consistent with existing literature, which generally holds that nonfarm income aggravates inequality and contributes more to bi-polarization than agricultural income (Bonnefond & Clément, 2012).

In urban areas, wage income (*UY*1) contributes most to bi-polarization, accounting for 85.3%. The aggravating effect of wage on income inequality is discussed in

Table 8.2 Decomposition of bi-polarization indicator P_G by source of income in urban and rural areas, 1988

Rural income sources	Contribution of each source	Urban income sources	Contribution of each source
*RY*1	0.028 (8.0%)	*UY*1	0.293 (85.3%)
*RY*2	−0.018 (−5.0%)	*UY*2	−0.018 (−5.2%)
*RY*3	0.070 (20.1%)	*UY*3	−0.030 (−8.8%)
*RY*4	0.080 (22.8%)	*UY*4	−0.013 (−3.9%)
*RY*5	−0.030 (−8.6%)	*UY*5	−0.013 (−3.9%)
*RY*6	0.289 (83.1%)	*UY*6	0.0003 (0.1%)
*RY*7	−0.057 (−16.3%)	*UY*7	0.110 (32.0%)
*RY*8	−0.014 (−4.1%)	*UY*8	0.015 (4.3%)
Bi-polarization indicator P_G	0.348 (100%)	Bi-polarization indicator P_G	0.344 (100)

Note: Contribution (percentage) of each income source is in the parentheses
Source: Calculated based on CHIP data of 1988

plenty of literature, such as Bonnefond and Clément (2012). This is because wage is the principal source of income for urban residents and it varies greatly from industry to industry. High-income industries usually have a high threshold. Unlike in rural areas, transfer subsidy (*UY*6, *UY*7, *UY*8) aggravates bi-polarization of the year, probably because transfer subsidy is so inefficient and has so many operational flaws that it is allocated to groups that should not be subsidized and leads to cumulative refunding. Income sources that mitigate bi-polarization that year include pension (*UY*2), income of the unemployed (*UY*3), operational income (*UY*4) and property income (*UY*5). At that time, the Chinese pension system was underdeveloped, so its effect was negligible.

Table 8.3 shows the decomposition of bi-polarization in 1995, when bi-polarization in rural areas is more serious than in urban areas. In rural areas, four income sources mitigate bi-polarization, namely property income (*RY*5), rent from privately owned housing (*RY*6), transfer income from collectively and state-owned enterprises (*RY*7) and other income including private transfer payment (*RY*8), of which transfer income from collectively and state-owned enterprises (*RY*7) has the largest mitigating effect. On the other hand, income sources that aggravate bi-polarization include operational income (*RY*3, accounting for 67.8%) and wage income and pension (*RY*1, accounting for 43.6%), the latter making a much bigger contribution, which is worth noting. The contribution made by income from work at township enterprises (*RY*2) goes from negative to positive, which is probably due to

Table 8.3 Decomposition of bi-polarization indicator P_G by source of income in urban and rural areas, 1995

Rural income sources	Contribution of each source	Urban income sources	Contribution of each source
*RY*1	0.134 (43.6%)	*UY*1	0.201 (74.2%)
*RY*2	0.026 (8.3%)	*UY*2	−0.015 (−5.4%)
*RY*3	0.208 (67.8%)	*UY*4	−0.062 (−22.9%)
*RY*4	0.072 (23.4%)	*UY*5	−0.003 (−0.9%)
*RY*5	−0.018 (−5.8%)	*UY*6	−0.028 (−10.3%)
*RY*6	−0.042 (−13.8%)	*UY*7	−0.028 (−10.4%)
*RY*7	−0.070 (−22.9%)	*UY*9	0.101 (37.3%)
*RY*8	−0.002 (−0.6%)	*UY*10	0.104 (38.4%)
Bi-polarization indicator P_G	0.307 (100%)	Bi-polarization indicator P_G	0.271 (100%)

Note: Contribution (percentage) of each income source is in the parentheses
Source: Calculated based on CHIP data of 1995

the thriving of those enterprises. Since only a few rural residents work in township enterprises, income from it aggravates bi-polarization.

In urban areas, three income sources aggravate bi-polarization, namely wage income (*UY*1), housing subsidy (*UY*9) and rent from privately owned housing (*UY*10), of which wage income (*UY*1) is the largest contributor, accounting for 74.2%. The rest five income sources all mitigate bi-polarization. The top three contributors, operational income (*UY*4), other income including private transfer payment (*UY*6), and aftertax subsidy other than housing subsidy and voucher (*UY*7), account for −22.9%, −10.3% and − 10.4% respectively.

Table 8.4 shows rural and urban bi-polarization in 2002. Compared with 1995, urban areas see more serious bi-polarization (0.365) than rural areas (0.330) in 2002, which consists with current literature (Bonnefond & Clément, 2012). This is because the market-oriented reform in China was first implemented in rural areas and then spread to cities. The main contributors to aggravated rural bi-polarization include wage income (*RY*1), which accounts for 49.5%, representing a slight increase from 1995, followed by operational income (*RY*3), rent from privately owned housing (*RY*6) and converted income from the production and sale of agricultural products (*RY*4), accounting for 28.5%, 20.3% and 18.2% respectively. The main contributors to aggravated bi-polarization in urban areas in 2002 are wage income (*UY*1) and pension income (*UY*2), while the effect of housing subsidy (*UY*9) is negligible. All other income sources have mitigating effects, especially

Table 8.4 Decomposition of bi-polarization indicator P_G by source of income in urban and rural areas, 2002

Rural income sources	Contribution of each source	Urban income sources	Contribution of each source
*RY*1	0.163 (49.5%)	*UY*1	0.466 (127.6%)
*RY*2	−0.007 (−2.1%)	*UY*2	0.061 (16.7%)
*RY*3	0.094 (28.5%)	*UY*4	−0.049 (−13.5%)
*RY*4	0.060 (18.2%)	*UY*5	−0.015 (−4.2%)
*RY*5	−0.001 (−0.2%)	*UY*6	−0.003 (−0.7%)
*RY*6	0.067 (20.3%)	*UY*7	−0.066 (−18.2%)
*RY*7	−0.074 (−22.3%)	*UY*9	0.001 (0.2%)
*RY*8	0.027 (8.1%)	*UY*10	−0.029 (−7.9%)
Bi-polarization indicator P_G	0.330 (100%)	Bi-polarization indicator P_G	0.365 (100%)

Note: Contribution (percentage) of each income source is in the parentheses
Source: Calculated based on CHIP data of 2002

government subsidy (*UY*7). Pension income (*UY*2) makes negative contribution to bi-polarization in 1995 but turns positive in 2002, because China did not have a real urban pension system until 1997. Even then the system had a very limited coverage and pension for civil servants and endowment insurance for urban employees were vastly different, which aggravated bi-polarization.

Compared with 2002, the year 2007 saw more serious bi-polarization in rural areas than in urban areas (Table 8.5). This is partly because the rural middle-income group is shrinking as a large number of rural residents move to the cities, and partly because the urban poor population is much smaller whereas a lot of rural residents still live under the poverty line. In rural areas, total wage income (*NRY*1 + *NRY*2 + *NRY*3 + *NRY*4) aggravates bi-polarization, but income from the secondary industry (*NRY*3) offsets the aggravation to some extent (−5.1%). Except income from secondary industry (*NRY*3) and transfer income (NRY6), the other income sources do not mitigate bi-polarization. Similarly, wage income (*UY*1) is the main income source that aggravates urban bi-polarization, while other income including private transfer payment (*UY*6) and government subsidy (*UY*7) play a major role in mitigation.

Table 8.5 Decomposition of bi-polarization indicator P_G by source of income in urban and rural areas, 2007

Rural income sources	Contribution of each source	Urban income sources	Contribution of each source
*NRY*1	0.232 (67.0%)	*UY*1	0.279 (87.2%)
*NRY*2	0.107 (31.0%)	*UY*2	−0.018 (−5.7%)
*NRY*3	−0.018 (−5.1%)	*UY*4	0.009 (2.9%)
*NRY*4	0.037 (10.8%)	*UY*5	−0.002 (−0.5%)
*NRY*5	0.003 (0.9%)	*UY*6	−0.027 (−8.4%)
*NRY*6	−0.016 (−4.6%)	*UY*7	−0.034 (−10.5%)
Bi-polarization indicator P_G	0.345 (100%)	*UY*9	0.042 (13.2%)
		*UY*10	0.070 (21.8%)
		Bi-polarization indicator P_G	0.320 (100%)

Note: Contribution (percentage) of each income source is in the parentheses
Source: Calculated based on CHIP data of 2007

8.4.2 Decomposition of Multi-Polarization by Source of Income

How do the various income sources affect multi-polarization? Multi-polarization and bi-polarization are measured in different ways. Multi-polarization involves more than two income concentration points, and the division of income groups is based on the data features instead of human decision. Therefore, the income sources that aggravate or mitigate bi-polarization do not necessarily have the same effect on multi-polarization. Table 8.6 shows that all income sources aggravate rural multi-polarization in 1988, with rent from privately owned housing (*RY*6) and converted income from the production and sale of agricultural products (*RY*4) being the largest and second largest contributor, accounting for 31.6% and 31.5% respectively. In urban areas, operational income (*UY*4) mitigates multi-polarization (−12.6%), while the three main aggravators are wage income (*UY*1), pension income (*UY*2) and aftertax subsidy other than housing subsidy and voucher (*UY*7).

Table 8.7 shows that the situation in rural areas in 1995 is similar to that in 1988, with all income sources aggravating multi-polarization. Operational income (*RY*3) makes the largest contribution of 29.5%, followed by 24.9% of converted income from the production and sale of agricultural products (*RY*4). In urban areas, all income sources aggravate multi-polarization of the year, particularly wage income (*UY*1), except housing subsidy (*UY*9) and rent from privately owned housing

Table 8.6 Decomposition of multi-polarization indicator *GER*(α = 1) by source of income in urban and rural areas, 1988

Rural income sources	Contribution of each source	Urban income sources	Contribution of each source
*RY*1	0.011 (10.6%)	*UY*1	0.040 (50.7%)
*RY*2	0.004 (4.0%)	*UY*2	0.016 (19.9%)
*RY*3	0.012 (11.6%)	*UY*3	0.001 (0.6%)
*RY*4	0.032 (31.5%)	*UY*4	−0.010 (−12.6%)
*RY*5	0.001 (1.0%)	*UY*5	0.004 (5.0%)
*RY*6	0.032 (31.6%)	*UY*6	0.011 (14.5%)
*RY*7	0.0004 (0.4%)	*UY*7	0.013 (16.2%)
*RY*8	0.009 (9.3%)	*UY*8	0.005 (5.7%)
Multi-polarization indicators *DER*	0.100 (100%)	Multi-polarization indicators *DER*	0.074 (100%)

Note: Contribution (percentage) of each income source is in the parentheses
Source: Calculated based on CHIP data of 1988

Table 8.7 Decomposition of multi-polarization indicator *GER*(α = 1) by source of income in urban and rural areas, 1995

Rural income sources	Contribution of each source	Urban income sources	Contribution of each source
*RY*1	0.006 (9.0%)	*UY*1	0.039 (53.8%)
*RY*2	0.007 (10.4%)	*UY*2	0.024 (33.6%)
*RY*3	0.020 (29.5%)	*UY*4	0.001 (1.8%)
*RY*4	0.017 (24.9%)	*UY*5	0.005 (6.4%)
*RY*5	0.002 (3.1%)	*UY*6	0.006 (8%)
*RY*6	0.0001 (0.2%)	*UY*7	0.007 (9.1%)
*RY*7	0.005 (7.1%)	*UY*9	−0.005 (−6.7%)
*RY*8	0.011 (15.7%)	*UY*10	−0.004 (−6.1%)
Multi-polarization indicators *DER*	0.069 (100%)	Multi-polarization indicators *DER*	0.073 (100%)

Note: Contribution (percentage) of each income source is in the parentheses
Source: Calculated based on CHIP data of 1995

(*UY*10), whose mitigating effect is −6.7% and − 6.1% respectively. The mitigating effect of housing subsidy validates the government benefit policy.

Table 8.8 shows that in 2002, only property income (*RY*5) and transfer income from collectively or state-owned enterprises (*RY*7) mitigate rural multi-polarization, while operational income (*RY*3), rent from privately owned housing (*RY*6) and wage income and pension (*RY*1) aggravate it most, accounting for 31.5%, 27.5% and 21.6% respectively. In contrast, property income (*UY*5) aggravates multi-polarization in urban areas while aftertax subsidy other than housing subsidy and voucher (*UY*7) mitigates it. Like in 1988 and 1995, wage income (*UY*1) and pension (*UY*2) remain the top two contributors to urban multi-polarization in 2002.

Table 8.9 shows that the rural situation in 2007 is similar to that in 1988 and 1995. Total wage income (*NRY*1 + *NRY*2 + *NRY*3 + *NRY*4), property income (*NRY*5) and aftertax transfer income (*NRY*6) all aggravate multi-polarization. In urban areas, housing subsidy (*UY*9) and operational income (*UY*4) mitigate multi-polarization while the rest income sources aggravate it, with wage income (*UY*1) and pension (*UY*2) being the largest and second largest contributor by contributing 91.5% and 56.2% respectively. The results are not much different from those about bi-polarization.

Generally speaking, wage income is the primary source that aggravates bi-polarization in both rural and urban areas in all years. Except in 2007, operational income always aggravates bi-polarization in rural areas and mitigates that in urban areas. Government subsidy mitigates bi-polarization in 1995, 2002 and 2007. It must be particularly pointed out that property income does not aggravate bi-polarization. It only does so in rural areas in 2007. In contrast, most income sources aggravate rural multi-polarization. Moreover, wage income is the main aggravator of bi-polarization and multi-polarization in both urban and rural areas. This is probably owing to the huge wage difference among different industries, and whether an individual can engage in a high-income industry has much to do with his/her family background, meaning those who do enter high-income industries are usually from wealthy families (Chen et al., 2009).

8.4.3 Decomposition of Changes in Bi-Polarization and Multi-Polarization

As time goes by, which factors are decisive on bi-polarization and multi-polarization? Which factors aggravate or mitigate them? In fact, the income source that is decisive on polarization in a certain year does not necessarily have important effects on the change of polarization. For example, in a certain year, wage income has major effects on bi-polarization and also aggravates multi-polarization, but it does not necessarily aggravate multi-polarization in a period of time. In view of this, next we will discuss the factors that affect the change of bi-polarization and multi-polarization.

Table 8.8 Decomposition of multi-polarization indicator *GER*($\alpha = 1$) by source of income in urban and rural areas, 2002

Rural income sources	Contribution of each source	Urban income sources	Contribution of each source
*RY*1	0.018 (21.6%)	*UY*1	0.043 (41.1%)
*RY*2	0.0002 (0.3%)	*UY*2	0.034 (32.9%)
*RY*3	0.026 (31.5%)	*UY*4	0.006 (5.9%)
*RY*4	0.012 (14.6%)	*UY*5	0.001 (0.6%)
*RY*5	−0.004 (−5.3%)	*UY*6	0.008 (7.4%)
*RY*6	0.023 (27.5%)	*UY*7	−0.008 (−7.2%)
*RY*7	−0.002 (−2.2%)	*UY*9	0.010 (9.5%)
*RY*8	0.010 (12.0%)	*UY*10	0.010 (9.7%)
Multi-polarization indicators *DER*	0.083 (100%)	Multi-polarization indicators *DER*	0.082 (100%)

Note: Contribution (percentage) of each income source is in the parentheses
Source: Calculated based on CHIP data of 2002

Table 8.9 Decomposition of multi-polarization indicator *GER*($\alpha = 1$) by source of income in urban and rural areas, 2007

Rural income sources	Contribution of each source	Urban income sources	Contribution of each source
*NRY*1	0.047 (56.8%)	*UY*1	0.039 (91.5%)
*NRY*2	0.011 (13.0%)	*UY*2	0.024 (56.2%)
*NRY*3	−0.002 (−2.9%)	*UY*4	−0.007 (−15.7%)
*NRY*4	0.011 (12.8%)	*UY*5	0.003 (6.9%)
*NRY*5	0.006 (7.0%)	*UY*6	0.006 (14.9%)
*NRY*6	0.011 (13.3%)	*UY*7	0.004 (9.4%)
Multi-polarization indicators *DER*	0.082 (100%)	*UY*9	−0.041 (−96.2%)
		*UY*10	0.014 (33.0%)
		Multi-polarization indicators *DER*	0.043 (100%)

Note: Contribution (percentage) of each income source is in the parentheses
Source: Calculated based on CHIP data of 2007

Tables 8.10 and 8.11 show the contribution made by each income source to the change of bi-polarization and multi-polarization in urban and rural areas. Since the rural income information in 2007 is different from that in 1988, 1995 and 2002, the analysis of rural polarization change does not include 2007. For urban areas, the income information in 1988 is different from that in 1995, 2002 and 2007, so analysis of urban polarization change starts from 1995.

Bi-polarization in rural areas slightly declines in 1988–2002, during which wage income and pension (*RY*1) plays the main aggravating role while rent from privately owned housing (*RY*6) plays the main mitigating role (Table 8–10). Bi-polarization decreases from 1988 to 1995 mainly because of changes in rent from privately owned housing (*RY*6). In that period, wage income and pension (*RY*1), income from work at township enterprises (*RY*2), operational income (*RY*3) and property income (*RY*5) are the main factors that aggravate bi-polarization. However, the increase in 1995–2002 somewhat offsets the decline in the previous period, and rent from privately owned housing (*RY*6) is the main aggravator of bi-polarization in this period.

Bi-polarization in urban areas strengthens in 1995–2007 (Table 8.10) primarily due to wage income (*UY*1) and operational income (*UY*4), although housing subsidy (*UY*9) and rent from privately owned housing (*UY*10) offset part of the uptrend. The overall aggravation stems from that in 1995–2002, mainly driven by wage income (*UY*1). Operational income (*UY*4) is the only factor that aggravates bi-polarization in both periods.

Rural multi-polarization declines to a very small extent in 1988–2002 (Table 8.11) under the combined mitigating effects of income from work at township enterprises (*RY*2), converted income from the production and sale of agricultural products (*RY*4), property income (*RY*5), rent from privately owned housing (*RY*6), and transfer income from collectively or state-owned enterprises (*RY*7). The multi-polarization indicator falls by 0.031 in 1988–1995 due to the decrease in converted income from the production and sale of agricultural products (*RY*4) and rent from privately owned housing (*RY*6). But it rises by 0.014 in 1995–2002, which partly offsets the decline in the previous period, and the rise is primarily caused by the increase in wage income and pension (*RY*1) and rent from privately owned housing (*RY*6).

Multi-polarization declines in urban areas from 1995 to 2007, which is caused by operational income (*UY*4), property income (*UY*5), aftertax subsidy other than housing subsidy and voucher (*UY*7), and housing subsidy (*UY*9). In the first period (1995–2002), all income sources contribute to the aggravation except property income (*UY*5) and aftertax subsidy other than housing subsidy and voucher (*UY*7). In the second period (2002–2007), however, multi-polarization mitigates due to wage income (*UY*1), pension income (*UY*2), operational income (*UY*4), other income including private transfer payment (*UY*6), and housing subsidy (*UY*9), despite the aggravating effect from property income (*UY*5). This is consistent with the conclusion drawn by Wang and Wan (2015).

Table 8.10 Change of bi-polarization indicator P_G in rural and urban areas (by income source)

Rural areas	1988–1995	1995–2002	1988–2002	Urban areas	1995–2002	2002–2007	1995–2007
P_G beginning of period	0.348	0.307	0.348	P_G beginning of period	0.271	0.365	0.271
P_G end of period	0.307	0.330	0.330	P_G end of period	0.365	0.320	0.320
P_G change	−0.041	0.024	−0.018	P_G change	0.094	−0.045	0.049
*RY*1's contribution	0.106	0.030	0.136	*UY*1's contribution	0.264	−0.187	0.078
*RY*2's contribution	0.043	−0.033	0.010	*UY*2's contribution	0.076	−0.079	−0.004
*RY*3's contribution	0.138	−0.114	0.024	*UY*4's contribution	0.013	0.058	0.071
*RY*4's contribution	−0.008	−0.011	−0.019	*UY*5's contribution	−0.013	0.014	0.001
*RY*5's contribution	0.012	0.017	0.029	*UY*6's contribution	0.025	−0.024	0.001
*RY*6's contribution	−0.332	0.109	−0.222	*UY*7's contribution	−0.038	0.033	−0.005
*RY*7's contribution	−0.013	−0.003	−0.017	*UY*9's contribution	−0.101	0.042	−0.059
*RY*8's contribution	0.013	0.028	0.041	*UY*10's contribution	−0.133	0.099	−0.034

Source: Calculated based on CHIP data of 1988, 1995, 2002 and 2007

Table 8.11 Changes in multi-polarization indicator *DER* in rural and urban areas (by income source)

Rural areas	1988–1995	1995–2002	1988–2002	Urban areas	1995–2002	2002–2007	1995–2007
DER beginning of period	0.100	0.069	0.100	*DER* beginning of period	0.073	0.104	0.073
DER end of period	0.069	0.083	0.083	*DER* end of period	0.104	0.043	0.043
DER change	−0.031	0.014	−0.017	*DER* change	0.031	−0.061	−0.030
*RY*1's contribution	−0.004	0.012	0.007	*UY*1's contribution	0.004	−0.003	0.000
*RY*2's contribution	0.003	−0.007	−0.004	*UY*2's contribution	0.010	−0.010	0.000
*RY*3's contribution	0.009	0.006	0.014	*UY*4's contribution	0.005	−0.013	−0.008
*RY*4's contribution	−0.014	−0.005	−0.020	*UY*5's contribution	−0.004	0.002	−0.002
*RY*5's contribution	0.001	−0.007	−0.005	*UY*6's contribution	0.002	−0.001	0.001
*RY*6's contribution	−0.032	0.023	−0.009	*UY*7's contribution	−0.014	0.012	−0.003
*RY*7's contribution	0.005	−0.007	−0.002	*UY*9's contribution	0.015	−0.051	−0.037
*RY*8's contribution	0.002	−0.001	0.001	*UY*10's contribution	0.014	0.004	0.019

Source: Calculated based on CHIP data of 1988, 1995, 2002 and 2007

8.5 Conclusions

As the Chinese economy thrives, the country has seen problems in its income distribution, among which income polarization is worthy of close attention. This paper, using the CHIP data of 1988–2007, studies the trend of income bi-polarization and multi-polarization in rural and urban areas, and analyzes how much each income source affects bi-polarization and multi-polarization and their changes with the Shapley decomposition method.

The results of this paper show that in 2007, rural bi-polarization and multi-polarization is less serious than in 1988 but more serious than in 1995. In both periods, wage income is the biggest contributor to aggravated bi-polarization and multi-polarization, followed by operational income and converted income from the production and sale of agricultural products, while transfer income from collectively and state-owned enterprises mitigates bi-polarization. From 1988 to 2002, the two major factors that affect the change of bi-polarization are the aggravating effect of wage income and pension and the mitigating effect of rent from privately owned housing. Except wage income, property income and other income including private transfer payment, all other income sources mitigate multi-polarization in that period.

In urban areas, bi-polarization in 2007 is less serious than in 1988, but far more serious than in 1995, while multi-polarization has mitigated with fluctuations since 1988. Like in rural areas, wage income is the principal contributor to aggravated bi-polarization and multi-polarization, while property income plays a role in mitigation all the time.

Urban bi-polarization aggravates in 1995–2007, mainly caused by wage income and operational income, but multi-polarization mitigates in that period, driven by operational income, aftertax subsidy other than housing subsidy and voucher and housing subsidy.

This paper shows that the deterioration of income distribution may originate in intra-group or inter-group difference. As income polarization and income inequality may go in opposite directions, not differentiating the two may mislead the policy makers. The Chinese economy has developed at a fast rate for 30 years, but has also seen many problems. International experience tells us that sustained development is impossible in any country if there is serious inequality in income distribution, and ineffective distribution policies may very well be counterproductive. Therefore, researchers should conduct meticulous and accurate analysis of income distribution to help the government make effective and targeted policies.

References

Araar, A. (2008). On the decomposition of polarization indices: Illustrations with Chinese and Nigerian household surveys. *Cahier de Recherche Working Paper*.

Birdsall, N. (2007). Do no harm: Aid, weak institutions and the missing middle in Africa. *Development Policy Review, 25*(5), 575–598.

Blackburn, M., & Bloom, D. (1985). What is happening to the middle class? *American Demographics, 7*(1), 18–25.
Blanco, C., & Xavier, R. (2010). Polarization and health. *Review of Income and Wealth, 56*(1), 171–185.
Bonnefond, C., & Clément, M. (2012). An analysis of income polarization in rural and urban China. *Post-Communist Economies, 24*(1), 15–37.
Chakravarty, S., & D'Ambrosio, C. (2010). Polarization orderings of income distributions. *Review of Income and Wealth, 56*(1), 47–64.
Chakravarty, S., Majumder, A., & Roy, S. (2007). A treatment of absolute indices of polarization. *The Japanese Economic Review, 58*(2), 273–293.
Chantreuil, F., & Trannoy, A. (2013). Inequality decomposition values: The trade-off between marginality and consistency. *The Journal of Economic Inequality, 11*(1), 83–98.
Chen, Z., Lu, M., & Sato, H. (2009). Who enter high-income industries? Effect of connections, household registration and productivity. *Economic Research Journal, 10*, 121–132.
D'Ambrosio, C., Deutsch, J., & Silber, J. (2011). Multidimensional approaches to poverty measurement: An empirical analysis of poverty in Belgium, France, Germany, Italy and Spain, based on the European panel. *Applied Economics, 43*(8), 951–962.
Davis, J., & Huston, J. (1992). The shrinking middle-income class: A multivariate analysis. *Eastern Economic Journal, 18*(3), 277–285.
Duclos, J. Y., Esteban, J., & Ray, D. (2004). Polarization: Concepts, measurement, estimation. *Econometrica, 72*(6), 1737–1772.
Esteban, J. M., Gradín, C., & Ray, D. (2007). An extension of a measure of polarization, with an application to the income distribution of five OECD countries. *Journal of Economic Inequality, 5*(1), 1–19.
Esteban, J. M., & Ray, D. (1994). On the measurement of polarization. *Econometrica, 62*(4), 819–851.
Ezcurra, R. (2009). Does income polarization affect economic growth? The case of the European regions. *Regional Studies, 43*(2), 267–285.
Foster, J., & Wolfson, M. (2010). Polarization and the decline of the middle class: Canada and the U.S. *The Journal of Economic Inequality, 8*(2), 247–273.
Gao, Q. (2008). Social benefits in Urban China: Determinants and impact on income inequality in 1988 and 2002. *Research Paper*, No. 2006/117, United Nations University.
Gasparini, L., Horenstein, M., Molina, E., & Olivieri, S. (2008). Income polarization in Latin America: Patterns and links with institutions and conflict. *Oxford Development Studies, 36*(4), 461–484.
Gigliarano, C., & Mosler, K. (2009). Constructing indices of multivariate polarization. *Journal of Economic Inequality, 7*(4), 435–460.
Gochoco-Bautista, M., Bautista, C., Maligalig, D., & Sotocinal, N. (2013). Income polarization in Asia. *Asian Economic Papers, 12*(2), 101–136.
Gradín, C. (2000). Polarization by sub-populations in Spain, 1973–91. *Review of Income and Wealth, 46*(4), 457–474.
Gradín, C. (2002). Polarization and inequality in Spain: 1973–1991. *Journal of Income Distribution, 11*(1–2), 34–52.
Griffin, K. & Zhao, R. (1991). *Chinese household income project 1988: Original sampling description*. In DSDR (Data Sharing for Demographic Research), Inter-university Consortium for Political and Social Research, Ann Arbor, Michigan.
Guo, T. (2004). Study of changing trend of spatial polarization of regional economy in China in the last 50 years. *Economic Geography, 6*, 743–747.
Gustafsson, B., & Li, S. (1998). Inequality in China at the end of the 1980s: Locational aspects and household characteristics. *Asian Economic Journal, 12*(1), 35–63.
Hong, X. (2010). Regional difference, polarization and mobility in China. *Economic Research Journal, 12*, 82–96.

Israeli, O. (2007). A Shapley-based decomposition of the R-square of a linear regression. *Journal of Economic Inequality, 5*(2), 199–212.

Kanbur, R., & Zhang, X. (2005). Fifty years of regional inequality in China: A journey through central planning, reform, and openness. *Review of Development Economics, 9*(1), 87–106.

Kolenikov, S., & Shorrocks, A. (2005). A decomposition analysis of regional poverty in Russia. *Review of Development Economics, 9*(1), 25–46.

Kwack, S. Y., & Lee, Y. S. (2007). The distribution and polarization of income in Korea, 1965–2005: Historical analysis. *Journal of Economic Development, 32*(2), 1–39.

Lasso de la Vega, C., & Urrutia, A. (2006). An alternative formulation of the Esteban-Gradín-Ray extended measure of polarization. *Journal of Income Distribution, 15*, 42–54.

Lasso de la Vega, C., Urrutia, A., & Díez, H. (2010). Unit consistency and bipolarization of income distributions. *Review of Income and Wealth, 56*(1), 65–83.

Lawrence, R. (1984). Sectoral shifts and the size of the middle class. *The Brookings Review, 3*(1), 3–11.

Li, S., Luo, C. & Sicular, T. (2011). Overview: Income inequality and poverty in China, 2002–2007. *CIBC Working Paper Series*. No. 2011–10, Department of Economics, The University of Western Ontario.

Lin, T., Zhuang, J., Yarcia, D., & Lin, F. (2010). Decomposing income inequality: People's Republic of China, 1990–2005. In Z. Juzhong (Ed.), *Poverty, inequality, and inclusive growth in Asia: Measurement, policy issues, and country studies* (pp. 367–386). Anthem Press.

Liu, X. (2010). Decomposition of China's income inequality, 1995–2006. *The Chinese Economy, 43*(4), 49–72.

Luo, C. (2010). Polarization of resident income distribution. *Chinese Journal of Population Science, 6*, 49–60.

Poggi, A., & Silber, J. (2010). On polarization and mobility: A look at polarization in the wage-career profile in Italy. *Review of Income and Wealth, 56*(1), 123–140.

Ravallion, M., & Chen, S. (2007). China's (uneven) Progress against poverty. *Journal of Development Economics, 82*(1), 1–42.

Reynal-Querol, M. (2002). Ethnicity, Political systems and civil war. *Journal of Conflict Resolution, 46*(1), 29–54.

Rodriguez, J., & Salas, R. (2003). Extended bi-polarization and inequality measures. *Research on Economic Inequality, 9*, 69–83.

Sastre, M., & Trannoy, A. (2002). Shapley inequality decomposition by factor components: Some methodological issues. *Journal of Economics, 77*(1), 51–89.

Shorrocks, A. (2013). Decomposition procedures for distributional analysis: A unified framework based on the Shapley value. *Journal of Economic Inequality, 11*(1), 99–126.

Sicular, T., Yue, X., Gustafsson, B., & Li, S. (2007). The urban-rural income gap and inequality in China. *Review of Income and Wealth, 53*(1), 93–126.

Silber, J., Hanoka, M., & Deutsch, J. (2007). On the link between the concepts of kurtosis and bipolarization. *Economics Bulletin, 4*(36), 1–6.

Thurow, L. (1984). The disappearance of the middle class. *The New-York Times, Feb., 5*, F3.

Wan, G. (2004). Explaining regional income inequality in rural China: A decomposition method based on regression equation. *Economic Research Journal, 8*, 117–127.

Wan, G. (2007). Understanding regional poverty and inequality trends in China: Methodological issues and empirical findings. *Review of Income and Wealth, 53*(1), 25–34.

Wan, G. (2013). Urbanization and inequality: Analytical method and case study of China. *Economic Research Journal, 5*, 73–86.

Wan, G., Lu, M., & Chen, Z. (2005). Globalization and regional income gap: Evidences from China. *Social Sciences in China, 3*, 17–26.

Wang, J., Koen, C., Kees, G. & Wang, Chen. (2015). *Decomposing income polarization and tax-benefit changes across 31 European countries and Europe wide, 2004–2012*. Department of Economics Research Memorandum, Leiden University.

Wang, Y. Q., & Tsui, K. Y. (2000). Polarization orderings and new classes of polarization indices. *Journal of Public Economic Theory, 2*(3), 349–363.
Wang, C., & Wan, G. (2015). Income polarization in China: Trends and changes. *China Economic Review, 36*, 58–72.
Wang, C., Wan, G., & Yang, D. (2014). Income inequality in the People's Republic of China: Trends, determinants, and proposed remedies. *Journal of Economic Surveys, 28*(4), 686–708.
Wolfson, M. (1994). When inequalities diverge. *American Economic Review, 84*(2), 353–358.
Xu, X., & Wang, H. (2008). Bi-polarization in primary income distribution in China and its causes. *Economic Research Journal, 2*, 106–118.
Yao, X., & Ye, R. (2012). Regional income polarization and changing constituents in rural China: A new dynamic decomposition formula and its application. *Statistics & Information Forum, 3*, 56–60.
Zhang, S. B., & Kanbur, R. (2001). What difference do polarization measures make? An application to China. *Journal of Development Studies, 37*(3), 85–98.
Zhao, R. (2001). Increasing income inequality and its causes in China. In C. Riskin, R. Zhao, & S. Li (Eds.), *China's retreat from equality: Income distribution and economic transition* (pp. 25–43). M. E. Sharpe.

Chen Wang, research fellow at School of Urban and Regional Science, Shanghai University of Finance and Economics.

Guanghua Wan, professor at Research Institute for Indian Ocean Economies, Yunnan University of Finance and Economics.

Hui Cao, associate professor at School of Economics, Shanghai University.

Chapter 9
Research on Household Wealth Inequality in China: Retrospect and Prospect

Shi Li and Haiyuan Wan

Abstract Household wealth is a key measure of a country's economic competitiveness and individual income level. The distribution of wealth is key to the evaluation of social equity in a country. On the basis of literature review, this paper examines the definition of wealth, data sources, and methodology in previous studies on wealth distribution in China and responds to the estimation results and some arguments on wealth inequality in China. Furthermore, it summarizes the key issues and challenges that exist in the estimation of wealth inequality in previous studies and puts forward suggestions for future research.

Keywords Wealth level · High-income groups · Sample omission · Wealth inequality

In the era of the planned economy, China implemented a package of systems aimed at eliminating the propertied class. In the 1950s, it launched land reform to establish collective land ownership, deprived the propertied class of their private property, and eliminated private ownership of the means of production to build a proletarian society. In order to accumulate capital for industrialization, a series of systems and policies that stripped farmers of land were put into effect, leaving a vast majority of farmers in poverty without any property. In the meantime, low-wage policies were adopted in cities and towns, keeping the wages of workers at low levels for a long time. Only a few urban households had savings, but the amount was paltry.[1]

[1] Even in the early days of reform and opening up, the main form of assets was still savings, the amount of which was quite insignificant. For example, total household savings in China were RMB40.6 billion in 1979, including RMB20.26 billion for urban residents and RMB20.36 billion for rural residents, or RMB117.5 and RMB25.8 per person, respectively. This is estimated based

S. Li · H. Wan (✉)
China Institute for Income Distribution, Beijing Normal University, Beijing, China
e-mail: lvqs@ssap.cn

F. Cai (ed.), *Income Inequality and Poverty Governance in China*, International Research on Poverty Reduction, https://doi.org/10.1007/978-981-95-5063-0_9

After the reform and opening-up policy was introduced in 1978, private property rights were restored and effectively protected. The new systems and policies give legitimacy to the ownership of private property, paving the way for household wealth accumulation. These systems and policies include allowing for and encouraging the development of private businesses, protecting the legitimacy of private property rights, privatizing public housing, and promoting the development of the stock market and real estate market. With the rapid growth of China's economy and the hikes in people's income in the past 30-plus years, the wealth of Chinese households has also seen a dramatic increase.

However, the wealth gap between households has widened quickly in this process.[2] China has transformed from a proletarian society to a society that has seen explosive growth in private property and more importantly, from an egalitarian society to a society with huge wealth gaps. In the 1980s and 1990s, wealth disparities were not obvious. For example, in 1995, the Gini coefficient based on wealth distribution was 0.40, which was even lower than that based on income distribution (Li et al., 2005; Li & Zhao, 2008). Even at the beginning of the twenty-first century, China's wealth gap was still less striking than that of many other countries.[3] However, according to relevant research (Li & Wan, 2015; Xie & Jin, 2014; Xie & Xiang, 2014), by 2010, China's Gini coefficient based on wealth distribution had exceeded 0.73, much higher than that based on income distribution.[4] Suffice it to say that the changes in the landscape of household wealth accumulation and distribution have given impetus to China's economic development, but very wide gaps, especially illegitimate sources of wealth, have posed a great threat to economic development and social stability and given rise to social contradictions. Against the backdrop of slowing economic growth, uneven distribution of wealth may be a breakpoint for social contradictions, resulting in a higher risk of social instability (Li et al., 2000; Li et al., 2008).

Currently, there are still many issues to be addressed in wealth distribution research in China. For example, what is the general landscape of wealth distribution in China? How big is the wealth gap? What are the causes of the widely acknowledged

---

on data in *China Finance Statistics 1950–1985* (Overall Planning Department of Ministry of Finance of China, China Financial & Economic Publishing House, 1987) and *China Statistical Abstract 1987*.

[2] This paper does not make distinctions between assets, property, and wealth.

[3] According to relevant estimation results, China's Gini coefficient based on wealth distribution was 0.55 in 2002 (Li et al., 2005; Li & Zhao, 2008). However, Davies et al. (2008) calculate the wealth gaps in 26 countries in 2000 and finds that only the Gini coefficient of Japan (0.547) was slightly lower than that of China (0.550), while the coefficients of other countries were much higher. Switzerland topped the list with 0.803, followed by the U.S. with 0.801.

[4] According to income inequality estimates, China's Gini coefficient based on income distribution was around 0.5. For example, it was 0.481 in 2010 (National Bureau of Statistics, 2013). Based on the 2010 data from China Family Panel Studies (CFPS) conducted by Institute of Social Science Survey, Peking University, Li and Wan (2015) estimate the coefficient at 0.74. Using the family panel data in 2012, Xie and Xiang (2014) conclude that the Gini coefficient based on income distribution was 0.49 and that based on wealth distribution 0.73 (Xie & Jin, 2014). Apparently, the latter was much higher than the former.

widening of the wealth gap? How do income gap and wealth gap affect each other as the two are interconnected? While the income gap has been preliminarily contained, what will happen to the wealth gap in the future? How will the public respond to the widening of wealth gap? Will they pay more attention to the income gap or wealth gap? How much impact does the wealth gap have on economic development and social stability? Due to the limitations of data, existing studies fail to provide solid answers to these questions. Even though a few studies try to answer some of these questions, because of the different data sources, definitions of wealth, and wealth inequality measurement methods, their research results are still debatable. In this context, it is necessary to sort out and analyze the issues in household wealth research, especially research on the dynamic changes in household wealth growth and gaps. On the basis of literature review, this paper comprehensively sorts out the important issues in wealth inequality research, examines the rationality of different research results, draws some conclusions on household wealth levels and inequality in China, and offers some suggestions for future research.

9.1 Definition of Household Wealth

9.1.1 Composition of Household Wealth

Existing studies are divided over how to define and measure household wealth (Table 9.1). It is commonly acknowledged in the world that household wealth involves two types: total wealth and net wealth. The former includes financial assets, real estate, productive fixed assets, consumer durables, land, and other assets, while the latter is total wealth minus liabilities. When measuring the stock of household wealth, most studies choose net wealth over total wealth, such as Li and Wan (2015) and Xie and Jin (2014), while some opt for total wealth, such as Gan et al. (2012). From the perspective of the basic economic theory, using net wealth is more reasonable in order to better measure the effect of household consumption on wealth; in contrast, using total wealth cannot truly reflect people's actual wealth status and runs against international practices in income distribution and wealth distribution research.

There are also differing opinions about wealth composition. First, different studies have different choices about what kind of assets should be included. For example, according to the National Bureau of Statistics (2013), household wealth is composed of financial assets, real estate, operating assets, and worth of consumer durables, while Li and Wan (2015) hold that household wealth includes not only the above four types but also land, liabilities, and other assets. Second, there are varying definitions of the components of wealth. The National Bureau of Statistics (2013) defines operating liquid assets as productive assets, while Li and Wan (2015) define them as financial assets. However, they both agree that gold (excluding gold jewelry), other artifacts, and collectibles are financial assets. In addition, vehicles used

Table 9.1 Empirical studies on household wealth inequality in China

Author	Subject matter	Data	Sampling period	Definition of wealth	Data processing method	Gini coefficient based on wealth distribution	Main conclusions
Mckinley (1993)	Characteristics of rural wealth distribution	CHIP rural data only	1988	Net household wealth	Cross-sectional data, without inter-regional PPP adjustment	0.34 nationwide and 0.31 in rural areas in 1988	Wealth gap was smaller than income gap; the wealth level of rural households was much lower than that of their urban counterparts.
Li et al. (2000)	Distribution of urban household wealth	CHIP urban data only	1995	Net household wealth per capita; housing worth is based on the privatization of all public housing	Cross-sectional data, without inter-regional PPP adjustment	0.40 nationwide in 1995 and 0.52 in urban areas	Wealth gap began to reverse and exceed income gap; urban wealth growth was significantly faster than that of rural areas, and rural wealth inequality was higher.
Brenner (2001)	Distribution of rural household wealth	CHIP rural data only	1995	Net household wealth per capita, excluding samples with zero or negative values and public housing	Cross-sectional data, without inter-regional PPP adjustment	0.33 in rural areas in 1995	Rural wealth gap was higher than urban gap, and rural household wealth was far lower.
Urban survey team of the National Bureau of Statistics (2003)	Urban household wealth holdings	Urban survey data only	2002	Net household wealth per capita, but only including financial assets, real estate, present worth of consumer durables, and operating assets; samples with zero or negative values were retained	Cross-sectional data, without inter-regional PPP adjustment	In 2002, 48.5% of households had wealth between RMB150,000 and RMB300,000, 34.8% below RMB150,000, and 16.7% above RMB300,000	The average urban household wealth totaled RMB228,300, including RMB79,800 of financial assets; housing accounted for 47.9% of total household wealth, the highest among all components.

Meng (2007)	Distribution of urban household wealth	Urban survey data only	1995, 1999, 2002	Net household wealth per capita, excluding samples with zero or negative values	Cross-sectional data, without inter-regional PPP adjustment	The Gini coefficient for per capita net wealth in 1995, 1999, and 2002 was 0.50, 0.52, and 0.56, respectively	There was little change in the distribution of wealth from 1995 to 2002. The increase in wealth mainly came from accumulation of non-savings wealth.
Li et al. (2005)	Wealth distribution and its causes	CHIP nationwide data	1995, 2002	Net household wealth per capita, excluding samples with zero or negative values	CPI adjustment, without inter-regional PPP adjustment	0.40 in 1995; 0.55 in 2002	The Gini coefficient for wealth expanded by 38%; urban-rural gap accounted for 37% of total wealth gap.
Li and Zhao (2008)	Changes in wealth inequality	CHIP nationwide data	1995, 2002	Net household wealth per capita, excluding samples with zero or negative values	CPI adjustment, without inter-regional PPP adjustment	0.40 in 1995; 0.55 in 2002	The widening of national wealth gap was mainly driven by the widening of urban-rural gap.
Luo et al. (2009)	International comparison on wealth distribution	From previous studies	1995, 2002	Net household wealth per capita, excluding samples with zero or negative values	Annual CPI adjustment, without inter-regional PPP adjustment	0.40 in 1995 and 0.55 in 2002, higher than similar countries	Wealth distribution was not highly uneven, which was expanding fast; wealth inequality was higher than most countries in the world.
Li et al. (2008)	Wealth changes	National aggregate data	2006	Net household wealth, excluding samples with zero or negative values	Cross-sectional data, without interregional PPP Adjustment	0.686 nationwide and 0.45 in urban areas in 2006	Wealth gap continued widening, but at a slower pace.

(continued)

Table 9.1 (continued)

Author	Subject matter	Data	Sampling period	Definition of wealth	Data processing method	Gini coefficient based on wealth distribution	Main conclusions
Chen et al. (2009)	Housing prices, household savings rate, and wealth inequality	Aronad data, urban households only	2005, 2007	Household rather than individual total worth; samples with negative values were retained; analysis was focused on real estate	Two rounds of cross-section data, without annual or interregional adjustment	0.56 in urban areas in 2005 and 0.58 in urban areas in 2007	Wealth gap edged up; improvements in data processing and measurement methods.
Gan et al. (2012)	Urban household wealth holdings only	CHFS urban data only	2010	Net household wealth, excluding samples with zero or negative values	Cross-sectional data, without inter-regional PPP adjustment	In 2011, urban household worth was RMB2.476 million, and per capita wealth was six times that in the U.S.	In urban household wealth, housing accounted for the highest proportion, followed by non-financial assets and financial assets.
Xie and Jin (2014)	Wealth structure, distribution, and changes	CFPS nationwide data for 2010 and 2012	2010, 2012	Net household wealth, interpolating abnormal wealth values and using Pareto functions for processing	Panel data, CPI adjustment, without inter-regional PPP adjustment	In 2012, national average net household wealth was RMB439,000, and the Gini coefficient was 0.73.	Wealth inequality in China was rising rapidly, with urban housing accounting for 80% of total wealth; housing inequality was the main factor of wealth inequality in China.
Li and Wan (2015)	National wealth, structure, distribution, and causes for 2-year changes	CHIP nationwide data for 2002 and CFPS nationwide data for 2010	2002, 2010	Net household wealth per capita; samples with zero or negative values were retained; wealth outliers were treated	Annual and interregional CPI and PPP adjustment	In 2010, the Gini coefficient was 0.739 nationwide, 0.706 in rural areas, and 0.632 in urban areas.	The present worth of households per capita was RMB142,000, wealth stock growing rapidly, and wealth became polarized; the proportion of housing surged, resulting in a distorted wealth structure.

Source: Prepared by the authors based on relevant studies

for operation and production are categorized as operating assets and productive fixed assets, respectively, while other precious metals, gold jewelry, antiques and paintings, and jewels as consumer durables and other assets. In general, there is still some disagreement about how different components of wealth should be further divided, such as how to classify productive housing, how to discount long-term bank loans, and which category gold jewelry belongs to. According to the National Bureau of Statistics (2013), gold jewelry is a type of consumer durables, while Xie and Jin (2014) categorizes it as financial asset, and Li and Wan (2015) as other assets.

9.1.2 Definition of Land as Property

Among all the components of wealth, there are different views about whether land should be regarded as a type of property for rural residents. Chen (2000) thinks that it should not be included in farmers' property because farmers contract land that belongs to the government or collectives at village or township levels and is thus not owned by farmers in the legal sense; in reality, farmers cannot buy and sell land at will as they can do with other types of property, so land cannot be counted as part of farmers' property. As to this view, Li (2000) points out that land-based property rights are composed of a couple of rights, of which rights to revenue from land and residual claims are the most important from the standpoint of wealth distribution research. Although farmers in China have no right to dispose of land at random, they enjoy relatively complete rights to revenue and residual claims and therefore at least partially own land-based property rights. Moreover, it is difficult to explain wealth distribution and income distribution in rural China without regarding land as part of farmers' property. Therefore, it is vital and necessary to include land in farmers' property. Li et al. (2005) and Li and Wan (2015) use the gross income from agricultural operations to reckon farmers' income from land and then estimate the worth of households' land as property.

9.1.3 The Relationship Between Wealth and Income

It is generally believed that income is a flow, and wealth is a stock, i.e., income minus necessary spending. Thus, income and wealth are significantly positively correlated. In reality, however, income and wealth are not monotonically increasing. The combination of high income levels yet low wealth levels peaks at one's midlife, that is, workers may earn a high salary but not hold much wealth because of high spending. Likewise, as the stock of wealth is not directly taxed in China, it is often passed on to the next generation through inheritance, who therefore possesses considerable wealth easily. This results in deviation between wealth and income. In addition, while stemming from the flow of income, the stock of wealth can also generate new income, so the relationship between wealth and income is further reinforced through such income. China's statistical system for property-related income is still flawed. For example, if interest from a bank deposit is not taken out when it is mature, interest accrued in the first period and the recurring interest will not be counted as property-related income in the current period. As a result, property-related income is underestimated, and the relationship between wealth and income is further distorted. On the whole, there is virtually no systematic research on their relationship.

9.2 The Problem of Sample Omission for High-Income Groups

Among all the issues in wealth distribution research, data quality is the biggest concern and the most controversial for researchers. Since different studies use different data sources and data collection methods, it is unlikely to draw conclusions that everyone agrees with. In general, as high-income groups make up a fraction of the entire population, it is difficult to get an effective sample through simple random sampling. Moreover, as people in the high income bracket are generally reluctant to take part in surveys and some may conceal their true wealth from others, it is difficult to obtain a sufficient sample through random sampling, leading to bias in wealth distribution research. Therefore, scholars in the field of wealth distribution research give much attention to how to improve and supplement the data for high-income groups based on household surveys.

9.2.1 Supplementation Through the Pareto Distribution Function

Due to the lack of high-quality wealth data, household survey data thus becomes the first choice for researchers and was most widely used in previous studies (Davies et al., 2008). However, studying wealth distribution by simply using household survey data may lead to arguments. With the growing concentration of wealth accumulation, underrepresentation of the richest group has become a prominent issue. The conclusions drawn based on household survey data can be seriously biased. In response, many researchers have adopted a variety of techniques to correct deviations in traditional household surveys, one of which is to supplement the data through the Pareto distribution function. At the end of the nineteenth century, Italian economist Vilfredo Pareto observed from a large number of real-world phenomena that the distribution of wealth obeys a power law, that is, in a free market, 80% of a country's wealth would be concentrated in the hands of only 20% of the population (the 80–20 rule). Wang and Zhou (2006) and Xie and Jin (2014) estimate the wealth of the richest people (such as those on the billionaires lists of Forbes and Hurun) by means of the Pareto distribution function and reckon the wealth of those at the top through the Pareto parameter estimation. Based on the estimates, together with weighted household survey data, they get a full picture of wealth distribution and thus estimate the level of wealth inequality.

9.2.2 Extrapolation from Inheritance Tax Data

Due to the sample omission for the richest group and the concealment of true wealth, it is very difficult to estimate the distribution of wealth. In recent years, experts around the world have started doing so using inheritance tax data and have achieved great success. For example, Atkinson (2013) and Saez and Gabriel (2014) creatively collect the marginal tax rates and actual tax records of various countries and use the actual tax data, especially real estate tax and inheritance tax, to get relatively accurate and complete data on the wealth of rich people. Adopting this method, Piketty (2014) estimates the wealth inequalities of over 20 countries with well-established inheritance tax systems, including the United States, Britain, and Japan. It is found that the richest 10% held over 60% of wealth in the eighteenth century and their share of wealth, after a downward trend for more than a century, has seen a sharp rise in recent years and is possible to return to the level of social stratification in the Middle Ages. Although this method of estimation is relatively accurate and reasonable, it will not work in China since an inheritance tax system has not been put in place in the country.

9.2.3 Revision to Household Survey Data

It is generally believed that although high income groups are underrepresented in household survey data, it can accurately reflect the wealth of low- and middle-income groups. Therefore, some studies propose to revise household survey data by indirectly adjusting high-income group samples. On the one hand, the size of high-income group samples may be insufficient through random sampling; on the other hand, there are random errors in the survey process, resulting in a portion of abnormal samples. Since these two problems exist randomly, if a reasonable number of abnormal samples are retained, then the co-existence of underestimation and overestimation may offset part of the original error of estimate. In the studies on the distribution of household wealth in 2010 using China Family Panel Studies (CFPS) data, it is found that the wealth values of 0.3% of the samples are abnormally high, and there was an obvious mutation in the distribution curve. For these abnormal observed values, Li and Wan (2015) choose to retain those questionable abnormal samples while eliminating the outliers. For the same data, Xie and Jin (2014) adopt another method, i.e., simply removing all wealth outliers and supplementing the extreme values by using the Pareto distribution function. However, Chen et al.

(2009) point out that the method of excluding such samples to avoid the impact of extreme values on wealth distribution is somewhat subjective and is liable to underestimate wealth inequality. Additionally, no matter which method is adopted, the estimation results of the two are basically the same.

9.2.4 Correction Through Tax Payment Data for High-Income Earners

The lack of high-income group samples in wealth distribution research can lead to the underestimation of wealth inequality. However, such samples are not easily available, so some studies try to use income data instead of wealth data to indirectly supplement the samples. For example, Torche and Seymour (2008) add high-income taxpayer data from tax authorities to regular household income survey samples to get the parameter relationship between the omitted sample and survey sample and extend by analogy such parameter relationship to wealth distribution research. On this basis, the wealth data for rich people can be extrapolated and then added to the wealth distribution curve. It goes without saying that there are some problems with this method. For example, most of previous studies extrapolate income from high-income group samples rather than estimate wealth from income. This is because income flows are implicit and dynamically changing, while wealth is a relatively stable stock that is easier to calculate. In addition, the parameter relationship between high-income and low-income groups in income distribution may not be consistent with that in wealth distribution. Therefore, it may be inappropriate to directly use income in wealth research by analogy. Nonetheless, on the basis of properly addressing these problems, using high-income taxpayer data from tax authorities to estimate the overall wealth distribution is still a research direction worth exploring in the future.

9.2.5 Reckoning Through Data from Government Authorities

In response to the increasingly complex composition of household wealth, many countries have established cross-sectoral, multi-tiered information platforms to facilitate the sharing of personal wealth information among government authorities. Such platforms integrate administrative information and data from various authorities, such as demographics from public security authorities, financial assets information from banking and securities regulators, automobile information from transportation and vehicle authorities, housing information from housing and urban-rural development authorities, information on enterprises and business assets from industry and commerce authorities, and tax information from local tax authorities, thereby incorporating the wealth information of households such as housing, tax, vehicles, and operating assets. Data from government authorities is relatively accurate, objective, authentic, and authoritative, making it possible to estimate the true wealth of households. On the one hand, such data can be directly summed to estimate the distribution of household wealth; on the other hand, it can be compared with the self-reported wealth data in household surveys to deduce the rate of hidden wealth among households at different levels of wealth and thereby estimate true wealth of the richest groups (Yao, 2014). Generally, given the relatively high accuracy and credibility of administrative data, using it to estimate the distribution of wealth is also becoming an effective attempt.

9.2.6 Prediction Through Individual Behavior Data

Some studies extrapolate the stock of household wealth through the close correlation between individual behavior and wealth. For example, the higher the level of wealth, the lower the proportion of consumption in wealth stock. Therefore, on the basis of grouping by wealth level, some studies estimate the consumption propensity of each group, then predict the consumption propensity of the richest groups, and deduce their wealth levels (Wang, 2010). This method still has some deficiencies. For example, there may be no linear relationship between consumption and wealth, so this prediction method is not feasible (Luo et al., 2011). Some behavioral economics studies try to estimate the stock of wealth from donation data. Davies et al. (2006) collect publicly available donation information and donor wealth data to calculate the donation propensity coefficient of each group and then estimate the wealth level of the top group. In addition to behavioral data on consumption and donations, first-hand behavioral data obtained from practitioners in various fields can also be used. For example, we can contact legal consultants to get the number and information of people who consulted with law firms about inheritance over the years, make the wealth distribution curve of the rich population based on the wealth distribution of these samples, and thereby estimate the wealth gap.

9.3 Estimates of Household Wealth Inequality in China

International research on wealth inequality estimates has a long history, and the focus is shifting from country-specific studies to international comparative studies (Davies et al., 2010). Recent international research shows that amid globalization in the past 20 years, wealth inequality in the world and major developed countries has been rising (Piketty, 2014). In contrast, research on the distribution of household wealth in China has a relatively short history. Mostly based on empirical analysis, such research relies more on household wealth information and representative wealth data in household surveys.

9.3.1 Estimates Based on CHIP Data

Since the late 1980s, household wealth information and data has been collected in household surveys, which constitutes the main source of data for household wealth research in China. The income distribution team of the Institute of Economics, Chinese Academy of Social Sciences carried out the first Chinese Household Income Project (CHIP) in 1988 and collected adequate information on the wealth of rural residents. Using the 1988 CHIP data, Mckinley (1993) examines the distribution of wealth among rural residents in 1988, and the paper represents an important result of early research on the distribution of wealth in China. The subsequent household surveys collect information on household wealth more comprehensively. For example, those 1995 and 2002 gathered information not only on financial assets, productive assets, and worth of consumer durables of households but also related to the worth of real estate, providing a basis for systematically estimating the total and net household wealth. Li et al. (2000) use the data to examine the distribution of wealth among urban households in 1995 and through function estimation, calculate the Gini coefficient based on wealth distribution in 1988 and 1995 at 0.34 and 0.40, respectively. The above-mentioned two studies fill the void in China's wealth distribution research. They use microscopic survey data to estimate the country's total wealth and distribution structure and give a more accurate estimate of wealth inequality in China, providing empirical evidence for analyzing the characteristics of wealth distribution in late 1980s and early 1990s. Based on the CHIP data for 1995 and 2002, a series of academic papers have been published, such as Li et al. (2005), Zhao and Ding (2008), Meng (2007), Li and Zhao (2008), and Luo et al. (2009). They find that during the 7 years, household wealth in China increased rapidly, and the average annual growth rate of net wealth reached 11.5%. In addition, wealth disparities widened notably, mainly driven by the rapid widening of the gap between urban and rural areas. For example, from 1995 to 2002, the average annual growth rate of rural household wealth was merely 1.8%, while that of urban household wealth was as high as 18.9% (Brenner, 2001). Some of these studies are listed in Table 9.1.

In general, these studies adopt quite similar definitions and classification criteria of wealth and conduct a valuable analysis of the growth and distribution of household wealth in China from the late 1980s to the beginning of the twenty-first century. However, these studies still have deficiencies. For example, when estimating wealth gaps, they disregard the differences in purchasing power between urban and rural areas and between regions, thus to some extent overestimating the actual wealth inequality between urban and rural areas and even across the country. Using household survey data to estimate wealth inequality has not fundamentally solved the underestimation problem for high-income group samples. Additionally, data collected by surveys in different years is still cross-sectional data, making it impossible to study wealth mobility and intergenerational wealth gaps.

9.3.2 Estimation Results of the National Bureau of Statistics

In addition to non-official wealth surveys, the urban survey team of the National Bureau of Statistics (NBS) selected 3997 households as effective samples in eight provinces (municipalities) including Hebei in 2003 to get an idea of urban household wealth. It was found that in 2002, the average value of household wealth in China totaled RMB228,300, of which financial assets, real estate, present worth of consumer durables, and operating assets reached RMB79,800, RMB109,400, RMB11,500, and RMB27,700, accounting for 34.9%, 47.9%, 5%, and 12.2%, respectively. The Gini coefficient for urban household wealth calculated based on this set of survey data was 0.51 (Urban survey team of the National Bureau of Statistics, 2003).

However, this survey should not suffice to gain a full picture of household wealth in China. First, it only looked at the distribution of wealth in urban areas while excluding that in rural areas, let alone national distribution of wealth. Second, it only collected information on four types of wealth including financial assets, housing, consumer durables, and operating assets while disregarding household liabilities and other assets. Moreover, operating assets as defined in the survey are not equal to productive fixed assets in the traditional sense, making it difficult to compare its definition of wealth with internationally recognized definitions. In addition, this survey did not answer the question regarding the representation of high-income groups or touch on such issues as wealth mobility, urban-rural disparities, and regional disparities. Therefore, in comparison, the CHIP survey data is more suitable for studying the general landscape of household wealth distribution in China.

9.3.3 Research Results of Special Surveys

In response to the absence of studies on the representation of the rich groups, "investor behavior survey data" targeted at higher-income groups was used alternatively. Chen et al. (2009) use the data from the investor behavior survey conducted by Beijing Aordo Investment Consulting Center in 2005 and 2007 to analyze the wealth gap among urban households in the 2 years. Their estimates show that the richest 1% of households held more than 8% of wealth, and the richest 5% and 10% held over 23% and 36%, respectively. In contrast, the poorest 10% of households had negative wealth; in 2005, the proportion of urban households with negative wealth was 2.22% and in 2007, it rose to 5.43%. Moreover, the Gini coefficient based on urban household wealth distribution in China was 0.56 in 2005 and edged up to 0.58 in 2007, reflecting that wealth inequality was widening. However, as the survey aims to study investor behavior rather than wealth distribution, plenty of omissions and missing values existed in wealth questionnaires. Moreover, the study only examines the distribution of wealth among urban households and has a relatively small sample size (e.g., 1123 in 2007), making it impossible to effectively deduce the national wealth distribution. In addition, it disregards the price and consumption levels in different years and regions.

Some studies are specifically designed to collect wealth data of the probably richest people to deduce the distribution of household wealth. For example, the Credit Suisse Research Institute (2010) uses the wealth data in Forbes' list to estimate the wealth of Chinese households and the distribution of wealth and made international comparisons accordingly. In 2010, average wealth per adult in China was USD17,126, and the Gini coefficient based on wealth distribution was 0.69, compared to about 0.61 in the U.S. and Canada and less than 0.495 in African countries over the same period. Moreover, in most parts of the U.S., Canada, and Africa, the proportion of housing in household wealth was on a downward trend, while that in China was increasing rapidly. However, the problem with this study is that the samples collected may not be the wealthiest people in reality and estimating the stock and distribution of wealth in this way has no solid methodological basis. Moreover, the definition of wealth in this study differs greatly from the traditional concept of wealth. As to the treatment of samples, it only takes into account the wealth of adults rather than per capita wealth of all households and individuals.

9.3.4 Analysis Results Based on Data of Other Household Surveys

Although some researchers try to address the representation of high-income group samples through various methods and have made some progress in this regard, the reality is that their attempts still have many problems. For this reason, recent studies are going back to traditional micro survey data. For example, Gan et al. (2012) use micro survey data to estimate some relevant indicators of household wealth in China and conclude that average household wealth in China in 2010 was RMB2,476,000, including RMB112,000 financial assets, RMB1,457,000 other non-financial assets, and RMB930,000 housing assets. However, there are several problems with this study. First, it calculates total household wealth instead of household wealth per capita, which is inconsistent with traditional studies and international practices. Second, it excludes negative and zero wealth samples, implying obvious overestimation of household wealth. Third, although it calculates household wealth and makes a household balance sheet accordingly, it neither analyzes the specific sources and composition of the household wealth gap nor explains why the wealth gap widened. Finally, it concludes that per capita wealth in China was six times that in the U.S., drawing much media attention at home and abroad and raising a lot of doubts.[5]

[5] See: Yao, S.J. Reflection on Malpractices and Flippancy in Academia: Discussions About Net Household Wealth of RMB2.47 Million, September 2012, http://blog.sina.com.cn/s/blog_66ccfca601016ppc.html

Using the CFPS data, Xie and Jin (2014) inquire into the level, distribution, structure, and main social determinants of household wealth in China. According to the study, in 2012, net household wealth in China was RMB439,000; the wealth of the 25th and 75th percentiles of households was RMB63,000 and RMB347,000, respectively; that of the top 10th and 1th percentiles was RMB736,000 and RMB1,176,000, while that of the highest 1th percentile exceeded RMB3,245,000; the Gini coefficient for net household wealth was 0.73.

In addition to cross-sectional studies in certain years, Li and Wan (2015) use CHIP and CFPS data to make comparisons of confidence intervals to estimate the wealth level and distribution of urban and rural households in the 2 years, and analyze the changes in wealth gap and the causes. It is found that in 2002 and 2010, net household wealth per capita in China was RMB32,000 and RMB143,000, respectively; the Gini coefficient based on wealth distribution grew from 0.538 to 0.739, up 37%; in 2002 and 2010, real estate made up the lion's share of household wealth, accounting for 57.1% and 73.5%,[6] respectively. During this period, the proportion of real estate in total wealth increased by over 16%, while the worth of real estate surged by five times. Moreover, after the housing price factor was excluded, wealth inequality dropped significantly, and the Gini coefficient based on net household wealth declined from 0.739 to 0.663, down 10.3%. They conclude that within less than 10 years, Chinese households' wealth level, wealth structure, and wealth distribution underwent significant changes, such as rapid increases in wealth, fast widening of wealth gaps, deformation of wealth structure, and polarized wealth distribution, which would have negative impacts on China's social fabric and economic development.

9.4 Conclusions and Prospects

Due to the underrepresentation of high income groups, how to estimate the wealth level and distribution of the rich people has become a difficult issue in wealth level and inequality research. Moreover, because of the different methods adopted in different studies, the estimation results about even the same subject matter are discrepant. In view of that, this paper sorts out Chinese and foreign literature on the definition, classification, data sources, and estimation methods of household wealth, compares the conclusions drawn using different processing methods, summarizes several common conclusions, and puts forward suggestions for future research.

[6] Such wealth structure is not common in other countries. At the end of 2004, real estate accounted for 41% of net household wealth in Britain, and the ratio was only 39% in the U.S. (Muellbauer, 2007).

9.4.1 Pareto Distribution Function and Inheritance Tax Data Are Effective Tools to Estimate Wealth Inequality

By combing through Chinese and foreign literature and the realities in China, we find that using the Pareto distribution function to estimate the wealth of the rich people has a methodological basis and is widely accepted by scholars around the world. Therefore, it has become a common method to estimate wealth inequality. In addition, some scholars use historical data on inheritance to indirectly estimate the distribution of wealth based on the specific conditions of each country. This approach is relatively simple and reliable. However, it is only applicable to countries where the inheritance tax is in place and historical data on inheritance is available. Hence, it is not quite applicable to China.

9.4.2 Using Household Survey Data Is the Second-Best Choice

Although using household survey data may lead to underestimation of wealth equality in varying degrees, it is still a practical choice given that it is impossible to have completely accurate wealth distribution data. In the actual process of wealth estimation, the deviation caused by underrepresentation of high-income households will be somewhat offset by the abnormal samples of high-income groups. In addition, using the Pareto distribution function method to supplement high-income group samples can also effectively ease this problem. Therefore, using household survey data to estimate wealth inequality is still the second-best choice. Especially when the changes in wealth levels and the dynamic evolution of wealth distribution are drawing more attention, the problem of underestimation of the rich groups in household survey data becomes less important.

9.4.3 Using Data from Government Authorities Is an Effective Attempt

Data from government authorities is relatively accurate, authentic, and authoritative, and the data of different authorities can also be used for mutual verification, making it an effective tool for estimating real wealth levels. Moreover, the data from government authorities can be compared with the self-reported wealth data in household surveys, which can help estimate the rate of hidden wealth among households in the different quantiles and thereby the true wealth of the richest groups. Overall, because of the relatively high accuracy and credibility of data from government authorities, using such data is becoming an effective attempt to estimate the distribution of wealth.

9.4.4 Several Relationships that Need to Be Handled Properly in Household Wealth Inequality Estimations

In wealth inequality research, the following relationships need to be handled properly. First, with regard to the definition and classification of wealth, it is important to distinguish between assets, wealth, and income and align the definition of household wealth with international standards; otherwise, international comparisons would become meaningless. Second, it is necessary to properly deal with the relationships between total amount and components of wealth, wealth and income, wealth and employment, wealth and consumption, and wealth and individual behavior, and to take advantage of the relationships between these variables to indirectly estimate the distribution of wealth among high-income groups. Third, it is necessary to make full use of the relationship between wealth level and demographic characteristics and compare the wealth variables of individuals with relevant information of other family members so as to remove outliers and accurately estimate wealth levels and wealth inequality.

9.4.5 Some Facts About Household Wealth Inequality in China

Although different studies come to different conclusions about household wealth inequality in China, there are still some common findings. First, household wealth in China has seen rapid growth, and the growth rate of wealth per capita exceeded that of national income per capita and disposable income per capita. Second, household wealth inequality has been increasing at an extraordinary pace. Despite the problem of sample omission for high-income groups in wealth inequality estimations, household wealth disparities across the country, within urban areas, within rural areas, and between urban and rural areas, have expanded significantly over the years. The Gini coefficient reached about 0.73 in 2012, a very high level, indicating that China has become one of the countries with the highest level of wealth inequality in the world. Third, the wealth structure of Chinese households has undergone great changes. Household wealth is increasingly concentrated in real estate, while the proportion of financial assets has dropped considerably, and productive fixed assets count for very little. Fourth, housing prices significantly affect wealth growth and wealth inequality. Just as inflation generally goes against low-income groups, rising housing prices tend to be more unfavorable to those at the lower levels of wealth.

In conclusion, the implications of the rapid increase of household wealth inequality are worthy of attention. For other countries, it may take decades or even hundreds of years for the wealth structure to be distorted and the wealth gap to widen to such extent, while in China, it takes less than 10 years. Although the impact on social stability is still hard to estimate, we believe that the psychological impact on the public should not be underestimated. In particular, when the legitimacy of the sources of some groups' wealth is in question, the dramatic wealth gap and rapid increase of wealth inequality will undoubtedly pose a threat to social stability.

References

Atkinson, A. (2013). *Wealth and inheritance in Britain from 1896 to the present.* Working Paper.

Brenner, M. (2001). Re-examining the distribution of wealth in rural China. In C. Riskin, R. W. Zhao, & S. Li (Eds.), *China's retreat from equality: Income distribution and economic transformation* (pp. 245–275). M. E. Sharpe.

Chen, Z. S. (2000). In-depth research on income disparities in China. *Economic Research Journal (Jingji Yanjiu), 7*, 68–72.

Chen, Y. B., Huo, Z., & Chen, J. (2009). Disaster risk and wealth distribution of urban households in China. *Economic Research Journal (Jingji Yanjiu), 11*, 144–158.

Credit Suisse Research Institute. (2010). *Global wealth data book.* www.credit-suisse.com

Davies, J. et al. (2006). *Estimating the world distribution of household wealth.* Paper Presented at the 29th General Conference of The International Association for Research in Income and Wealth, Joensuu, Finland.

Davies, J. et al. (2008). *The world distribution of household wealth.* WIDER Discussion Paper.

Davies, J., et al. (2010). The level and distribution of global household wealth. *The Economic Journal, 121*, 223–254.

Gan, L., et al. (2012). *China household finance survey report.* Southwestern University of Finance and Economics Press.

Li, S. (2000). Further discussion on several issues in income distribution research. *Economic Research Journal (Jingji Yanjiu), 7*, 72–76.

Li, P. L., Chen, G. J., Zhang, Y., & Li, W. (2008). *Social harmony and stability in China today.* Social Sciences Academic Press.

Li, S., & Wan, H. Y. (2015). Evolution of wealth inequality in China. *China Economic Journal, 8*(3), 264–287.

Li, S., Wei, Z., & Ding, S. (2005). Empirical analysis of uneven household wealth distribution in China and its causes. *Economic Research Journal (Jingji Yanjiu), 6*, 4–15.

Li, S., Wei, Z., & Gustafsson, A. B. (2000). Wealth distribution of urban households in China. *Economic Research Journal (Jingji Yanjiu), 3*, 16–23.

Li, S., & Zhao, R.W. (2008). *Changes in the distribution of wealth in China 1995–2002.* World Institute for Development Economic Research Paper.

Luo, C. L., Li, S., & Zhao, R. W. (2009). Wealth distribution in China and international comparison. *Economist (Jingji Xuejia), 9*, 90–99.

Luo, C.L., Yue, X.M., & Li, S. (2011). A question into the estimation of gray income. *Comparative Studies (Bi Jiao)*, 1.

McKinley, T. (1993). The distribution of wealth in rural China. In K. Griffin & R. W. Zhao (Eds.), *The distribution of income in China* (pp. 116–134). Macmillan Press.

Meng, X. (2007). Wealth accumulation and distribution in urban China. *Economic Development and Cultural Change, 55*, 761–791.

Muellbauer, J. (2007). *Housing and personal wealth in a global context.* WIDER Research Paper.

National Bureau of Statistics. (2013). *Gini coefficient of China 2003–2012.* http://politics.People.com.cn/n/2013/0118/c1001-20253603.html

Piketty, T. (2014). *Capital in the twenty-first century*. Harvard University Press.

Saez, E., & Gabriel, Z. (2014). *The distribution of wealth, capital income and rates of returns in the U. S. since 1913.* Working Paper.

Torche, F., & Seymour, S. (2008). Household wealth in Latin America. In J. Davies (Ed.), *Personal wealth from a global perspective*. Oxford University Press.

Urban Survey Team of the National Bureau of Statistics. (2003). *Wealth: Solid foundation for a moderately prosperous society*. Taiyuan: Shanxi Economic Press.

Wang, X. L. (2010). Gray income and national income distribution. *Comparative Studies (Bi Jiao), 48*, 1–29.

Wang, H. G., & Zhou, K. G. (2006). Is the inequity of income distribution of rural and urban households underestimated: A test based on Pareto distribution. *Statistical Research (Tongji Yanjiu), 4*, 8–15.

Xie, Y., & Jin, Y. G. (2014). Household wealth. In Y. In Xie, X. B. Zhang, J. X. Li, X. J. Yu, & Q. Ren (Eds.), *China livelihood development report 2014* (pp. 25–46). Peking University Press.

Xie, Y., & Xiang, Z. (2014). Income inequality in today's China. *Proceedings of the National Academy of Sciences, 19*, 6928–6933.

Yao, K. (2014). Ensuring fairness and justice of livelihood policies with a new type of verification mechanism. *Red Flag Manuscript (Hongqi Wengao), 16*, 30–31.

Zhao, R. W., & Ding, S. (2008). Research on household wealth distribution in China. In S. In Li, T. L. Shi, & A. B. Gustafsson (Eds.), *Research on income distribution in China III* (pp. 255–285). Beijing Normal University Press.

Shi Li, professor at China Institute for Income Distribution, Beijing Normal University.

Haiyuan Wan, research fellow at China Institute for Income Distribution, Beijing Normal University.

Chapter 10
The Income Redistribution Effect of China's Social Security System

Shi Li

10.1 Introduction

As is known to all, China is now at a new stage of development, and its economy has entered a new normal. Social security will play an increasingly important role in stabilizing economic growth, balancing income distribution, alleviating poverty and maintaining social stability. The goal of social security is to achieve the fair distribution of social resources through social solidarity, reduce income fluctuations caused by risky economic activities, and protect some population groups from falling into poverty. The experience of developed countries shows that with economic development, social security is an effective way of income redistribution comparable to government taxation.

However, China's social security system, still at the stage of development and reform, has quite limited impact on income distribution. It needs further improvement to achieve full coverage, narrow the gap among different population groups, and eventually further play its role in income redistribution.

In the past three decades, China's GDP and household income have both been growing rapidly. Between 1978 and 2008, the average growth rate of GDP was close to 10%, and the average growth rate of household income in urban and rural areas reached 8%. In recent years, the economic growth rate has declined, but remained above 6%, which was quite good compared to other countries'. By the end of 2015, with its GDP per capita reaching USD 7500 according to the current exchange rate, China became an upper middle-income country. Despite the remarkable economic growth, the development of China's social development, especially its social security and welfare, has been much less impressive, basically unable to help regulate income distribution. The social security system is currently highly fragmented and

S. Li (✉)
China Institute for Income Distribution, Beijing Normal University, Beijing, China
e-mail: lvqs@ssap.cn

F. Cai (ed.), *Income Inequality and Poverty Governance in China*, International Research on Poverty Reduction, https://doi.org/10.1007/978-981-95-5063-0_10

disparity in the benefits it offers to different groups of people is serious, even contributing to a wider income gap.

Although hugely successful in poverty alleviation, China has not achieved as much in narrowing the income gap. Whether in urban areas, rural areas, or across the country, the income gap is much greater than that in the early stage of the economic reform. The current Gini coefficient of the entire country is estimated to be about 0.47.[1] Although lower than the peak level of 2008, it is still much higher than the 0.30[2] of the early 1980s. At the same time, the Gini coefficient of rural China increased from 0.26 in 1980 to 0.40 in 2013, and the urban Gini coefficient increased from 0.16 in 1978 to 0.39 in 2013 (see Fig. 10.1).

Over the past 40 years, China's poverty rate dropped significantly, but poverty is still a serious social problem. By the end of 2015, China still had more than 50 million poor people in rural areas measured by standard income; and the figure would be even higher if by the multidimensional poverty criteria is used as there are still a

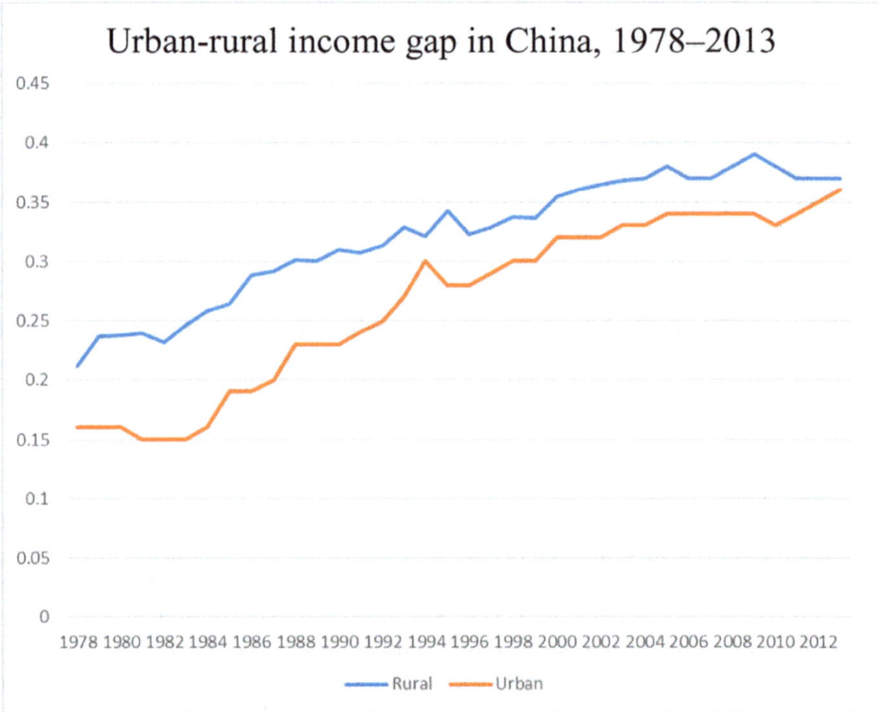

Fig. 10.1 Urban-rural income gap in China, 1978–2013. Source: Annual Report on Income Distribution of Chinese Residents 2015

[1] The Gini coefficient was estimated to be 0.47 by China Institute for Income Distribution based on data collected in 2013; while the Gini coefficient announced by the National Bureau of Statistics in 2015 was 0.464.

[2] See Adelmen & Sunding, 1987.

large number of rural households whose income is higher than the poverty line, but are plunged into poverty due to health problems or natural disasters.

The share of consumption in GDP has been falling since the mid-1990s, partly because of the decrease in the share of labor income, and partly the decline in the average consumption propensity. The decrease in consumption propensity is due to the increased uncertainty concerning the cost of healthcare, education and housing, and this is especially true for those who are not covered by social security. In response to the global financial crisis, the government has strived to stimulate domestic demand since the second half of 2008, but relevant measures adopted stressed increasing investment rather than consumption. Actually a wider coverage of social security, narrower gaps in social security benefits, and increased overall security level will help stimulate the propensity to consume.

China sees an accelerating pace in population aging. According to the data from the National Bureau of Statistics (NBS), in 2014, among the 1.367 billion people, China had 212 million people aged 60 and above and 137 million aged 65 and above, accounting for 15.5% and 10.1% of the total population, respectively. According to international standards, China has undoubtedly become an aging country, and will continue to age in the next few years. The pace of population aging poses a serious challenge to China's old-age care system, requiring a more sustainable and fair system in this regard.

To address the above-mentioned economic and social problems, it is a wise choice for the Chinese government to include a full-coverage and fair social security framework in the 13th Five-Year Plan. This idea has been widely welcomed in the Chinese society. However, how to make the social security system more effective in regulating income distribution and alleviating poverty remains a top priority in the reform of the social security system.

Section 2 is to discuss the major challenges in current China. These challenges are closely related to the huge income gap, uneven income distribution and inadequate social security reform. A sound social security system will help narrow the income gap and meet these challenges. Sect. 3 is to discuss some key functions of social security, with an emphasis on its role in regulating income distribution and alleviating poverty. In Sect. 4, results of empirical analyses will be examined, to show the impacts of various social security policies on income redistribution in China. Due to the limitation of data, focus is placed on the impact of the old-age care system on income redistribution, which is the core of this article. Sect. 5 presents a comparative study of the income redistribution effect of the different social security systems of China and European countries. The last section is the conclusion policy recommendations.

10.2 Social and Economic Challenges Facing China Today

The social and economic challenges that China is facing right now include an excessive income gap, poverty, a sharp decline in consumption propensity, increased social conflicts and instability. Without doubt, these challenges must be fully recognized and effectively addressed.

10.2.1 Large Income Gap

Thirty years ago, China was a country where egalitarianism prevailed, but since the early 1980s, the nation's income gap has expanded dramatically. As a developing country, China has different economic and social policies for urban and rural areas, with favorable policies for cities. This has resulted in huge differences in income levels, social security, access to social services, and living standards between urban and rural households (Gustafsson et al., 2008; Riskin et al., 2001). In terms of income inequality, different estimates all point to an increasing urban-rural income disparity in China. For example, according to the estimates based on comparable sample data, the Gini index of urban China increased from 0.16 in 1978 to 0.37 in 2013, and the Gini coefficient of rural areas during the same period increased from 0.22 to 0.38, as shown in Fig. 10.1. The urban-rural income gap first widened and then narrowed over the past 15 years. As shown in Fig. 10.2, the nominal per capita income of urban households was 2.9 times that of rural households in 2001 and 3.34 times in 2009, a record high. In the years that followed, the urban-rural income gap declined slowly, leaving the per capita income of urban households less than three times that of rural households in the most recent 2 years. The gap is still wider than that in the early days of the reform and opening up, though.

The Gini coefficient, which reflects the income gap, was basically on the rise during the first 30 years of the reform and opening up (1978–2008), going up from 0.30 in the early 1980s to the peak of 0.491 in 2008. Then, the expanding trend of the income gap was curbed, and the Gini coefficient dropped. By 2015, the Gini coefficient had fallen below 0.47 (see Fig. 10.3). However, the income gap is still wide today in China, and the problem of unfair income distribution has not been

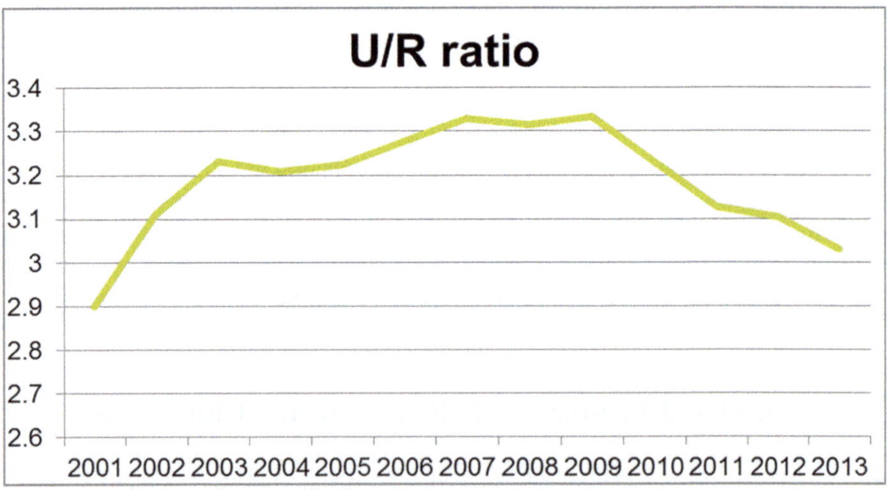

Fig. 10.2 Urban-rural income gap in China, 2001–2013. Source: China Statistical Abstract 2014, p.101

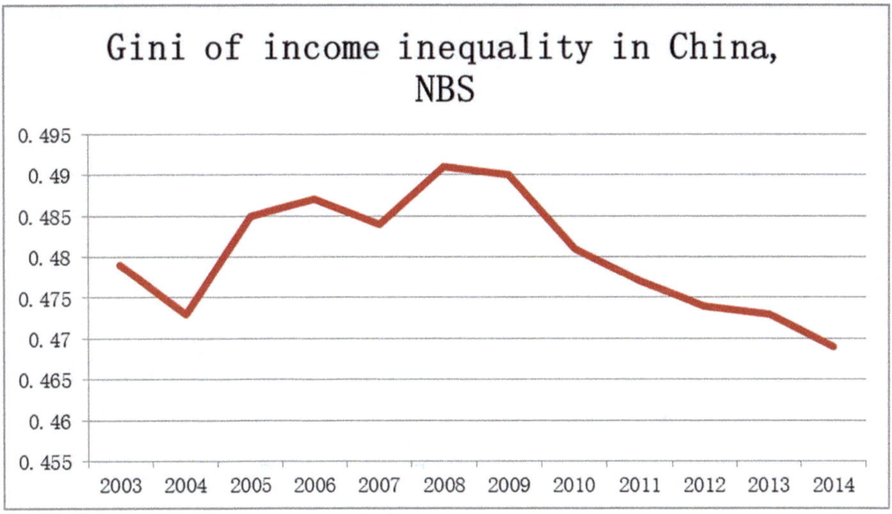

Fig. 10.3 Gini coefficient of China, 2003–2014. Source: *Statistical Communiqué of the People's Republic of China on the 2015 National Economic and Social Development*, National Bureau of Statistics

fundamentally resolved. Without fair and reasonable income distribution and redistribution, the income gap remain large and can even grow larger. Faced with these problems, we need to continue with the income distribution reform in China, and one of the policy options is to improve the redistribution function of the social security system.

10.2.2 Large Poor Population

There is no doubt that China has been successful in poverty alleviation in the past four decades. Regardless of the measurement tools, the total number of poor people in China has declined by more than 90% since the late 1970s, as shown in Fig. 10.4. Before 2010, with a excessively low poverty line for rural areas, the number of poor people and the incidence of poverty were serious underestimated. In 2011, the Chinese government raised the poverty line for rural areas to RMB 2100/person/year for the year 2010. This new poverty line is equivalent to USD 2/person/day, which was recommended by the World Bank. According to the new poverty line, the poor population in rural China was about 150 million in 2010, with a poverty incidence of 17%. In the past 5 years, the rural poor population has continued to decline, falling to less than 60 million in 2015.

However, poverty is still a major social problem in China, especially in rural areas. As we all know, in China, poverty is measured by income/consumption only, not the multidimensional poverty standard. If we measure poverty in rural China

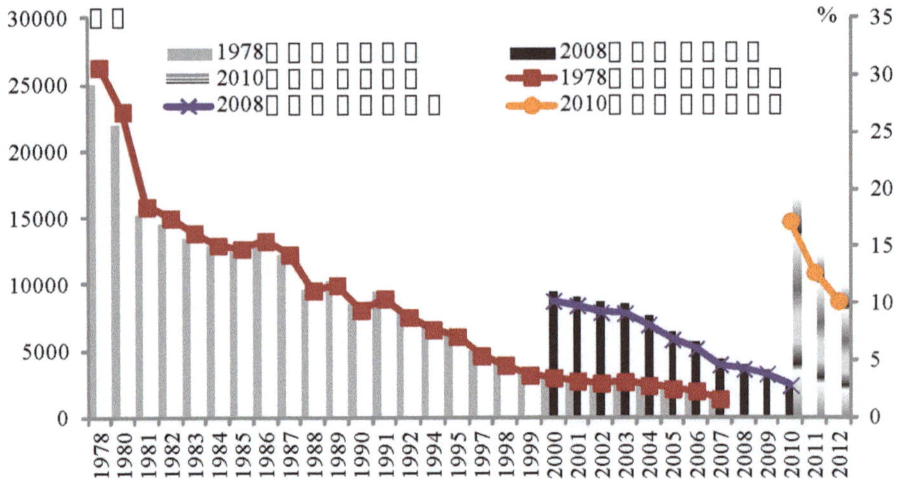

Fig. 10.4 Poor population and poverty incidence based on official poverty line. Source: China Rural Poverty Monitoring Report (all relevant years)

with multidimensional indicators, the poverty incidence will rise considerably. In addition to income/consumption poverty, many rural households can be deemed as poverty-stricken due to diseases, education needs, or housing needs.

Among all poor rural population groups, the elderly and the young deserve special attention. Like other countries, China sees a higher incidence of poverty among the elderly and the young than in other age groups. According to a research report on the structure of the rural poor population in the new situation released by Beijing Normal University, the incidence of poverty among the elderly in rural areas is now 5% higher than the average, and that among children is 10% higher than the average. To address poverty in these special groups, it is not enough to simply focus on income; healthcare and education are often key concerns.

10.2.3 A Large Number of Migrant Workers

Like other developing countries, China accelerated its urbanization process in the mid-1990s. A large number of rural workers moved to and stayed in urban areas for employment, but the vast majority of them are still migrating frequently between urban and rural areas. By 2013, close to 300 million agricultural workers were engaged in nonfarm employment (migrant workers), of whom 170 million were employed in cities (see Fig. 10.5). In addition, there are also some rural migrants not employed, such as children and the elderly. Together, the total number of migrants from rural areas to cities exceeded 200 million. China's urbanization rate is currently below 60%, which means that such a migration trend is likely to continue for

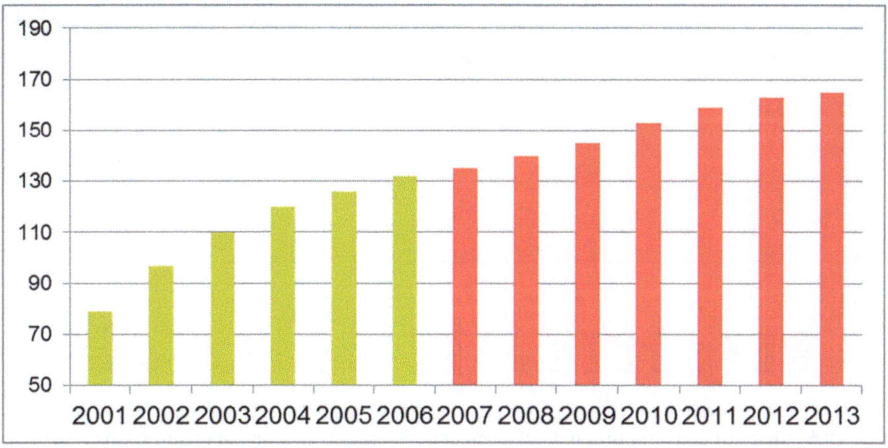

Fig. 10.5 Rural migrant workers in China (million). Source: Rural migrant worker monitoring reports of all relevant years, National Bureau of Statistics

the next 20 years.[3] Most of the migrants only have minimal education and skills, and their jobs are usually short-term with low wage. These workers are usually not covered by social security (Li, 2008; Deng & Li, 2008;). Since the migrant population's *hukou* remains in their rural hometown, they are at a disadvantage in terms of employment opportunities, salaries, social security and access to public services in the urban labor market. In the next 10 years, how to address large-scale labor migration is indeed a major challenge for the Chinese government.

10.2.4 Declining Consumption Propensity

Entering the twenty-first century, China has seen a steep drop in the share of consumption in its national income, falling from 62% in 2000 to 48% in 2010, down by 14% points over a period of 10 years (see Fig. 10.6). This has never been seen in any other country in history. Although the proportion of consumption to national income rose slightly in the past 2 years, it is still quite low. Structurally, the decline in the proportion of consumption is largely because of the rapid decline in household consumption (see Fig. 10.7). In the total consumption of the whole society, we saw the proportion of government consumption rise while that of household consumption declined. Specifically, the share of government consumption rose from 22% in the mid-1990s to 27% in 2012, while that of household consumption dropped from 78% to 73%. In household consumption, the share of urban consumption has been

[3] In 2015, more than 200 million rural laborers were engaged in agriculture, accounting for about 30% of China's total labor force. If this reduces by 1% per year, the rural labor force will still account for 20% of the total after 10 years.

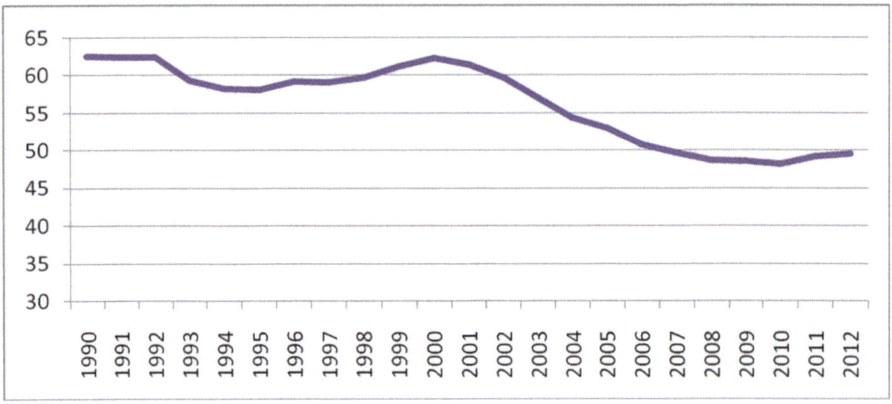

Fig. 10.6 Share of consumption in GDP (percent). Source: Based on data from *China Statistical Yearbook*

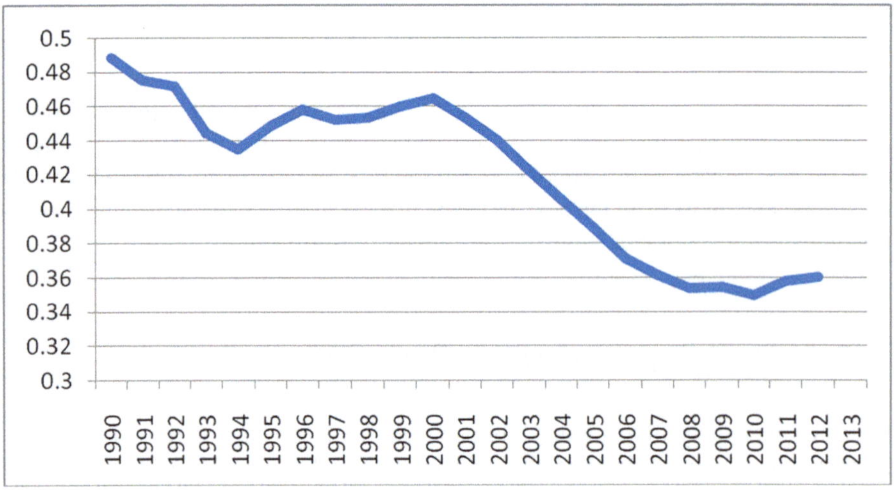

Fig. 10.7 Share of household consumption in national income. Source: Based on data from

on the rise, while that of rural consumption when down steadily. Specifically, since the 1990s, the share of urban household consumption has increased by nearly 17% points, while the share of rural household consumption has decreased by nearly 13% points (see Fig. 10.8). The reasons may be the increase in the urban population caused by urbanization on the one hand, and the relative decline in rural residents' spending capacity caused by the widening urban-rural income gap on the other hand.

Figure 10.9 shows the trend of urban and rural residents' consumption propensity since 1990 based on data from the household survey of NBS. Consumption propensity is consumption expenditure over disposable income. It is clear that the average consumption propensity of urban residents has been declining, going all the

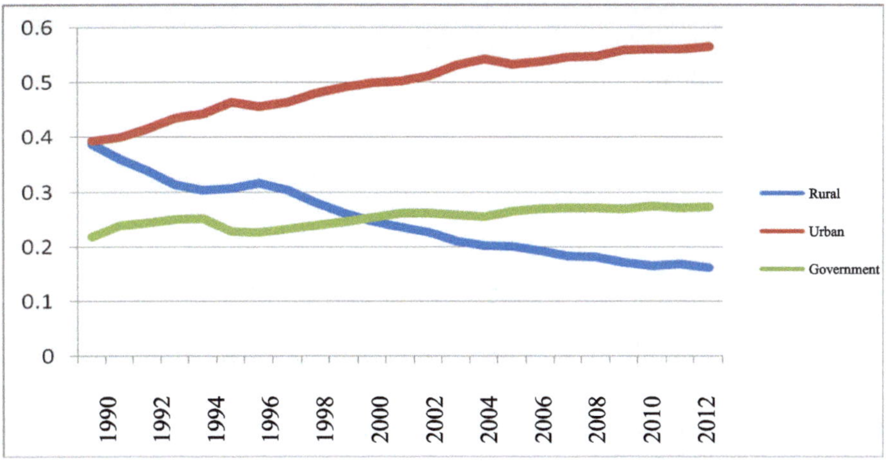

Fig. 10.8 Shares of consumption by urban residents, rural residents and government in total consumption. Source: Based on data from *China Statistical Yearbook*

way down from the 85% of 1990 to 67% in 2012, a drop of 18% points. The change in the average consumption propensity of rural residents shows a different trend. It declined significantly in the 1990s, but has been stable and slightly rising since 2000. The changes in rural residents' propensity to consume reflect the impact of income growth and the launch of social security programs in rural areas. In the 1990s, rural residents' propensity to consume declined sharply, down by nearly 15% points in 10 years. This can be explained with the following facts: (1) the slow increase in farmers' income during this period; (2) the sharp increase in farmers' tax payment; and (3) market-oriented public service delivery leading to extra financial burden for farmers. Since 2000, rural residents' consumption propensity has remained stable and rebounded slightly because their income has increased rapidly during this period on top of agricultural tax cut, agricultural subsidies, and rural social security programs like the new rural cooperative medical scheme and pension policies. On the one hand, these policy measures pushed up rural residents' income; and on the other hand, they more or less reduced their worries and raised their confidence in future life. The combined effects of these two factors are the stability and rise in rural residents' propensity to consume.

A widening income gap can also lead to a decline in residents' consumption propensity. For example, urban residents in different income groups have different average spending tendencies. The average consumption propensity of the high-income group tends to be lower than that of the low-income group. Figure 10.10 shows the changes in the average consumption propensity of urban residents by income group from 2002 to 2012. First of all, as can be predicted based on the consumption theory, regardless of income group, the average spending propensity decreases as income increases. As shown in Fig. 10.10, from 2002 to 2012, the average consumption propensity of urban residents fell by nearly 10% points.

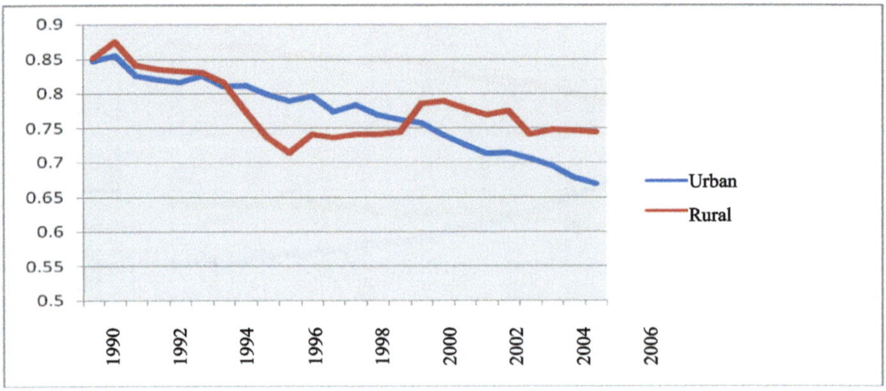

Fig. 10.9 Consumption propensity of urban and rural residents in China. Source: Based on data from *China Statistical Yearbook*

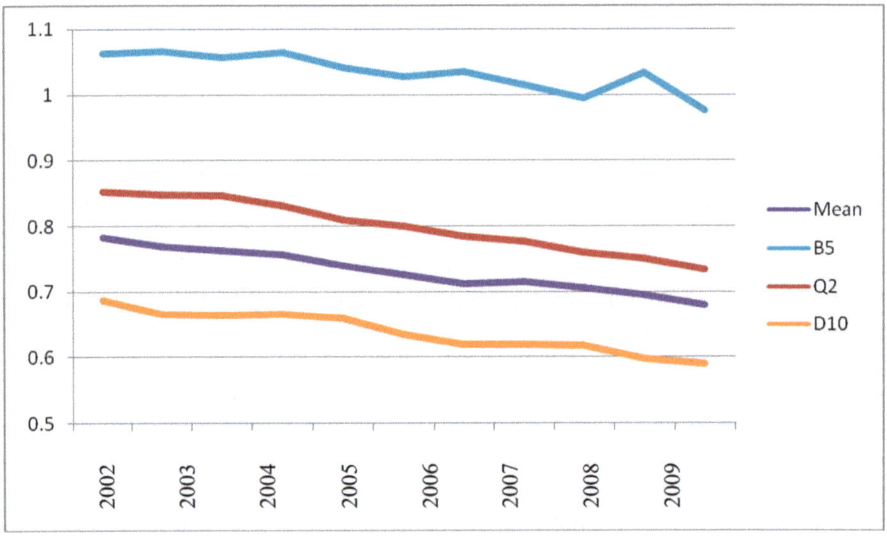

Fig. 10.10 Consumption propensity of urban residents by income group. Source: Based on data from *China Statistical Yearbook*

Specifically, the average consumption propensity of the bottom 5% in terms of income dropped by 8% points while the average consumption propensity of the top 10% decreased by 10% points. Second, the average consumption propensity is significantly different between income groups, with high-income groups much less likely to consume. As shown in Fig. 10.10, the average consumption propensity of the bottom 5% is nearly 40% points higher than that of the top 10%. This means that if we can transfer RMB10, 000 from the top 10% to the bottom 5% through income redistribution, the total expenditure of society will increase by RMB4000.

Note: Mean is the average consumption propensity of urban residents; B5 is the average consumption propensity of the bottom 5%; Q2 is the average consumption propensity of the 20% of people just above the bottom 5%; and D10 is the average consumption propensity of the top 10%.

10.2.5 Acceleration of Population Aging

In the past 20 years, China has seen its population aging at an unexpected pace, especially in the more recent years. As shown in Fig. 10.11, between 1995 and 2014, the share of population 65 years old and above to in the total population rose from 6.2% to 10.1%, up by nearly 4% points; the share of people 60 years and above rose from 9.2% to 13.7%, an increase of 4.5% points. The acceleration of population aging is even more noticeable in recent years. For example, the share of people 60 years or older in the total population increased by 2.4% points from 1995 to 2009 (14 years), and by 2.1% points in the 5 years that followed. Clearly, the acceleration of population aging means enormous pressure on economic and social development, eliminating the population dividend and requiring more and more social and economic resources for old-age care. It makes it hard for pension funds to make ends meet, brings about income inequality between generations, reveals a shortage of capital accumulation and slows economic growth.

There are also regional differences in China in terms of population aging. Data reveals that rural areas age faster than urban areas. This is because a large part of the rural labor force has moved to urban areas for job opportunities. Due to restrictions of the *hukou* system, elderly people in rural areas tend to find it difficult to relocate to urban areas and join their children who face uncertainty regarding employment outlook in urban areas. This is a major problem in rural development.

10.3 Key Functions of Social Security

Social security or welfare has the functions of insurance, poverty relief, income redistribution, and consumption smoothing. In China, social security plays an important role in stimulating domestic demand and increasing household consumption propensity, especially for low- and middle-income groups. Social security can also help regulate income distribution, alleviate poverty and maintain social stability.

10.3.1 Six Functions of Social Security

In economics and sociology, social security is widely recognized as having the following functions (Barr, 2001, 2003; Barr & Diamond, 2008):

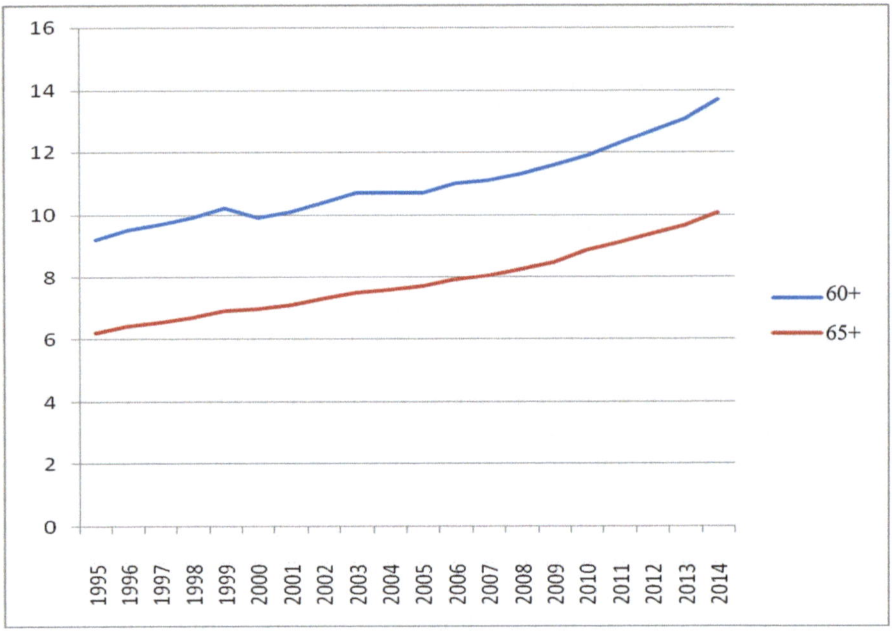

Fig. 10.11 Population aging in China (percent of elderly population). Source: Based on data from *China Statistical Yearbook 2015*

10.3.1.1 Insurance

The two major purposes of social security are to provide social insurance and relief. Social insurance usually includes social transfers such as unemployment insurance, medical insurance and retirement pension (Feldstein, 2005). For China, social security plays an important role in reducing risks resulting from uncertainties in employment, income and healthcare during the economic reform. Unemployment insurance, minimum living subsidies and medical insurance are good examples in this regard. Social insurance differs from private insurance schemes in that it is mandatory and requires more government intervention and accountability in order to avoid barriers in job hunting and ensure efficient use of medical resources. It is crucial to design a fair social security program that best integrates insurance and incentives. Most countries, either developed or developing, are trying to solve this problem according to their own situation, and China is no exception (Barr, 2003; Barr & Diamond, 2008; Feldstein, 2005).

10.3.1.2 Poverty Alleviation

The experience of China and other developing countries shows that without social security and social support, it is difficult for the poor to shake off poverty. Modern theories of poverty also point out that poverty is prone to worsening, and when poor people fall into the trap of poverty, more poverty will likely ensue (Bowles et al.,

2006). In the absence of public services, poverty, illiteracy and disease form a vicious circle. Knight et al. (2009) provide very strong evidence that children from poor and low-income families in rural China have higher dropout rates during compulsory education than those with better economic conditions. When they enter the labor market, they also have fewer opportunities to get nonfarm jobs or decent work with higher pay. As the poor population in rural China continued to decrease over the past decade, its structure changed significantly. One of the prominent features is that the number of the people who sank in poverty due to illness or disability increased. Since the beginning of the twenty-first century, China has implemented minimum living allowance programs in most urban areas, which has been effective in poverty alleviation but not in narrowing the income gap (Li & Yang, 2009). Based on relevant experience, the Chinese government began to extend the subsidy to rural areas in 2007, but with a much lower standard. We believe that China's minimum living subsidies are an effective measure in poverty alleviation and a good supplement to the traditional approach of poverty alleviation through development promotion.[4]

10.3.1.3 Income Redistribution

Social security plays its role in income redistribution. However, whether the redistribution is a priority is still controversial in the system design (Feldstein, 2005). In theory, social security has direct and indirect effects on income redistribution. The direct effect is not so obvious, but the indirect effect cannot be ignored. China's urban old-age insurance schemes have little effect on income redistribution because pensions are closely linked to salaries before retirement, but there is no doubt that the old-age insurance system has an indirect effect on income distribution within a household. As the population ages, this indirect effect will become more prominent. In the long run, we will see a greater indirect effect of medical insurance and compulsory education on income redistribution. Equal access to education opportunities is critical for narrowing the income gap among peers or within the same generation. Over the past decade, China education play a greater role in narrowing the wage gap in urban areas, but the significant inequality in access to education opportunities among urban residents is also important factor (Li, 2008). At the same time, social security programs, such as income subsidies and free or more affordable education, usually have a positive effect on income redistribution when low-income people receive most of the benefits of these programs.

[4] For more detailed discussion on the supplementary effect of minimum living allowance on Jiangxi's rural poverty reduction, see the "Rural Minimum Living Subsidy and Poverty Alleviation: Same or Complementary Effect?". http://www.fupin.gansu.gov.cn/zwzx/1181004710d3661.html

10.3.1.4 Consumption Smoothing

Social security policies, such as old-age insurance, have a significant effect on personal consumption smoothing in the long run. Therefore, they are also known as the piggy bank (Barr, 2003). Chinese families, especially rural low-income households, often encounter income fluctuations due to unemployment, fluctuating market prices, diseases and natural disasters. Income fluctuations are a major cause of temporary poverty among the rural population (Whalley & Yue, 2009). Income fluctuations inevitably cause consumption fluctuations. Therefore, social security policies such as unemployment insurance, medical insurance, and minimum living allowance are critical for consumption smoothing, especially for low-income households.

10.3.1.5 Consumption Stimulation

This function has a long-term significance particularly for countries like China, where the consumption propensity falls continuously. China's export-oriented industries were hit very hard by the international financial crisis, and the shares of exports dropped significantly by the end of 2008. Recently, Chinese economists and sociologists have called for higher government spending on social security and public services to reduce consumers' risks and financial uncertainties throughout their life cycles, so as to increase consumption propensity (Cai & Du, 2009). Although there is no strong evidence to support that the lack of social security is a major reason for the declining consumption propensity in China, some surveys suggest that Chinese households' savings are mainly for children's education, future medical expenses and the purchase of housing.[5]

10.3.1.6 Societal Stabilizer

This should be considered as an important and essential function of China's social security system. Many studies have concluded that criminal activities and social conflicts are highly related to unemployment, income inequality and poverty (Fajnzylber et al., 2008, 2002). This connection is especially strong in countries where there is no social security or insufficient welfare programs, and China is currently one of these countries. Therefore, it is very important for China to expand the coverage of the existing social security policies so as to reduce social conflicts and maintain social stability, which is also conducive to a harmonious economic and social environment for the implementation of the 13th Five-Year Plan.

---

[5] See the discussions regarding "Why Chinese People Save Money" on Xinhuanet: http://news.xinhuanet.com/fortune/2006-04/10/content_4405567.html

10.3.2 Three Basic Principles

The strategic goals of China's social security for the next 10 years and their relationship with the overall development plans of China must be clearly defined. An appropriate system should have the following three features, or follow the three basic principles: First, it should have full coverage for the entire population, whether they are young or old, rural or urban residents, formal or informal workers, employers or employees. Second, it should be transferable. Any self-paid social security program or insurance policy should be transferable along with job changes or cross-regional migration. Third, it should feature sustainability. The level of social security should remain within the government's financial capacity, but it should rise with economic growth. China's social security expenditure is generally lower than many other countries, including most developing countries (CDRF, 2009).

10.4 Income Redistribution Effect of China's Social Security System

This section focuses on the effect of the social security system in China. This study, based on data collected from the 2013 household survey conducted by the China Institute for Income Distribution, Beijing Normal University, estimates China's national income gap, and then calculates the effect of income redistribution generated by different social security policies (for old-age care, healthcare, housing, minimum living allowance, etc.) Based on the results, the income redistribution effect of the social security programs is then evaluated.

Table 10.1 shows the calculated income redistribution effects of taxes, fees and transfer payments based on the National Resident Income Survey data (CHIP2013) collected in 2013 by the Beijing Normal University Income Distribution Task Force. The calculation followed the international convention for household disposable income calculation:

$$\textbf{Disposable income} = \textbf{market income} - \textbf{taxes and fees} + \textbf{transfer income} \\ \left(\text{including public and private transfers}\right)$$

When estimating the redistribution effect of taxes/fees and transfers, we use the Gini coefficient as an indicator of the income gap. First, we calculate the Gini coefficient with market income (usually known as primary distribution) and then produce another Gini coefficient after deducting taxes and fees from the market income, and adding to it transfers. The difference between the two Gini coefficients is regarded as the redistribution effect.

Table 10.1 shows that in 2013, the Gini coefficient based on market income was approximately 0.52, and the Gini coefficient based on disposable income was 0.44. The difference is 8% points. That is to say, measured by the Gini coefficient, the income gap fell by 14.7% after redistribution. Specifically, taxes and fees did not narrow the income gap but slightly widened it; public transfers reduced the gap by nearly 9% points, which was the most significant; and private transfers reduced the gap by nearly 6% points, making it also an effective means of redistribution.

Table 10.2 lists out a breakdown of the income redistribution effects of taxes and fees and public transfers. Personal income tax was the only type of tax that narrowed the income gap, yet only very mildly, pushing down the Gini coefficient by less than 1%. Among all types of social security, unemployment insurance was the only one with a minimal effect of narrowing the income gap; while all other programs widen the income gap. For example, the old-age insurance and the medical insurance increased the income gap by 0.13% and 0.24%, respectively. This means that social insurance contributions are somewhat regressive. Although some social insurance contributions (such as old-age insurance and medical insurance for urban employees) are proportional to wages, when viewed against household income, these insurance schemes are obviously regressive. In other words, the share of these contributions in household income is smaller in high-income households than in low-income households.

In the category of public transfers, all items served to narrow the income gap to different degrees. Pensions of urban employees have a clear redistribution effect, narrowing the income gap by nearly 6%. The old-age insurance for urban and rural residents, and other old-age insurance income also helped narrow the income gap, but were much less effective. The three combined only reduced the Gini coefficient by less than 1.5%. Urban and rural minimum living subsidies, social assistance programs, and policy subsidies, which can also be categorized as social welfare policies, helped narrow the income gap, but only with minimal effect. As shown in Table 10.2, the combined effect of these only drove down the Gini coefficient by less than 1%. Finally, various agricultural subsidies (including grain subsidies) also helped narrow the income gap, bringing a 0.61% decrease in the Gini coefficient. Since this part of the subsidy mainly benefits rural residents, it has a positive effect on narrowing the urban-rural income inequality.

How much is the impact of various taxes and fees and social security policies on the income redistribution within urban and rural areas? To answer this question, we

Table 10.1 Redistribution effect of taxes, fees and transfer payments in China, 2013

	Gini Coefficient	Change	Change rate (&)
Market income	0.51740		
- Taxes and fees	0.51767	0.00027	0.05
+ Public transfers	0.47203	−0.04564	−8.82
+ Private transfers	0.44135	−0.03069	−5.93
= Disposable income	0.44135		

Source: Based on CHIP data 2013

Table 10.2 Redistribution effect of taxes, fees and public transfer payments in China, 2013

	Gini coefficient	Change	Change rate (%)
Market income	0.51740		
- Taxes and fees	0.51767	0.00027	0.05
- Old-age insurance contribution	0.51808	0.00068	0.13
- Medical insurance contribution	0.51931	0.00123	0.24
- unemployment insurance contribution	0.51905	−0.00025	−0.05
- Other fees	0.51914	0.00008	0.02
- Personal income tax	0.51767	−0.00147	−0.28
+ Public transfers	0.47203	−0.04564	−8.82
+ Retirement pensions	0.48691	−0.03076	−5.95
+ Old-age insurance payment for urban residents	0.48366	−0.00325	−0.63
+ Old-age insurance payment for rural residents	0.48098	−0.00269	−0.52
+ Other old-age care payments	0.48040	−0.00058	−0.11
+ Minimum living allowance	0.47848	−0.00192	−0.37
+ Social assistance	0.47741	−0.00107	−0.21
+ Policy subsidies	0.47657	−0.00084	−0.16
+ Rural medical expense reimbursement	0.47568	−0.00090	−0.17
+ Income in kind from governments and social organizations	0.47519	−0.00049	−0.09
+ Agricultural subsidies	0.47203	−0.00315	−0.61
+ Private transfers	0.44135	−0.03069	−5.93
Disposable income	0.44135		

Source: Based on data of CHIP 2013

need to examine the difference between Gini coefficients based on market income and disposable income, which is presented in Table 10.3. The Gini coefficient based on market income for urban residents in 2013 was 0.453 and that based on disposable income was down to 0.349. If the impact of private transfers is excluded, the urban Gini coefficient dropped by 9.5% points, or 21%. Apparently, the current tax and social security policies have a clear regulatory effect on income distribution among urban residents. However, a closer look will reveal that taxes and fees had very small effects, and even widened the income gap. This is mainly because the old-age insurance premiums and medical insurance premiums widened the gap, while the personal income tax was not sufficient to offset their influence.

Among the transfers, retirement pensions had the biggest impact on income distribution. As shown in Table 10.3, pensions for urban employees reduced the Gini coefficient by 19.2%; old-age insurance for urban residents also reduced it by 1.6%. Other transfer payments have a very limited effect on income redistribution, reducing the Gini coefficient by less than 1%.

Table 10.4 shows the income redistribution effect of taxes and fees and social security in rural China. In general, their effect of social redistribution in rural areas is significantly smaller than that in urban areas. Taxes and public transfers only reduced the rural Gini coefficient by 4.9% compared to 21% in urban areas. Similar

Table 10.3 Redistribution effect of taxes, fees and social security policies in urban China, 2013

	Gini coefficient	Change	Change rate (%)
Market income	0.45295		
- Taxes and fees	0.45502	0.00206	0.45
- Old-age insurance contribution	0.45574	0.00278	0.61
- Medical insurance contribution	0.45690	0.00116	0.26
- unemployment insurance contribution	0.45683	−0.00007	−0.01
- Other fees	0.45698	0.00015	0.03
- Personal income tax	0.45502	−0.00197	−0.43
+ Public transfers	0.35745	−0.09757	−21.54
+ Retirement pensions	0.36813	−0.08689	−19.18
+ Old-age insurance payment for urban residents	0.36101	−0.00712	−1.57
+ Old-age insurance payment for rural residents	0.36044	−0.00057	−0.13
+ Other old-age care payments	0.35989	−0.00055	−0.12
+ Minimum living allowance	0.35827	−0.00162	−0.36
+ Social assistance	0.35769	−0.00058	−0.13
+ Policy subsidies	0.35733	−0.00036	−0.08
+ Rural medical expense reimbursement	0.35778	0.00045	0.10
+ Income in kind from governments and social organizations	0.35762	−0.00017	−0.03
+ Agricultural subsidies	0.35745	−0.00017	−0.03
+ Private transfers	0.34868	−0.00877	−1.94
Disposable income	0.34868		

Source: Based on data of CHIP 2013

to the case of urban areas, taxes and fees widened rather than narrowed the income gap, as the rural Gini coefficient based on market income increased by 1.23% (see Table 10.4). Due to the seriously under-developed old-age support system in rural areas, even with the new social old-age insurance for rural residents put in place, pensions still only accounted for a very small share in rural household income. Therefore, the redistribution effect of pensions was very limited in rural China, only closing the income gap by 1%. Of course, there are more types of transfers in rural areas than in urban areas. In addition to the minimum living allowance programs, rural residents were also entitled to other subsidies, such as grain subsidies. These transfers played a role in narrowing the income gap in rural areas. As shown in Table 10.4, various agricultural subsidies reduced the Gini coefficient by about 1.34%.

The redistribution effect of private transfers is noteworthy in rural China. A major part of the private transfers in rural areas is the income sent home by family members who work elsewhere. In 2013, private transfers reduced the rural Gini coefficient by 12.24%, twice the effect of public transfers. Of course, the two are largely interchangeable. In other words, the increase in public transfers will chip out private transfers.

Table 10.4 Redistribution effect of taxes, fees and social security policies in rural China, 2013

	Gini coefficient	Change	Change rate (%)
Market income	0.46435		
- Taxes and fees	0.47005	0.00570	1.23
- Old-age insurance contribution	0.46684	0.00250	0.54
- Medical insurance contribution	0.47004	0.00320	0.69
- unemployment insurance contribution	0.46998	−0.00005	0.01
- Other fees	0.47013	0.00015	−0.03
- Personal income tax	0.47005	−0.00009	−0.02
+ Public transfers	0.44161	−0.02843	−6.12
+ Retirement pensions	0.46452	−0.00552	−1.19
+ Old-age insurance payment for urban residents	0.46330	−0.00123	−0.26
+ Old-age insurance payment for rural residents	0.45838	−0.00492	−1.06
+ Other old-age care payments	0.45781	−0.00057	−0.12
+ Minimum living allowance	0.45474	−0.00306	−0.46
+ Social assistance	0.45288	−0.00186	−0.40
+ Policy subsidies	0.45127	−0.00160	−0.36
+ Rural medical expense reimbursement	0.44864	−0.00263	−0.57
+ Income in kind from governments and social organizations	0.44781	−0.00083	−0.18
+ Agricultural subsidies	0.44161	−0.00620	−1.34
+ Private transfers	0.38479	−0.05683	−12.24
Disposable income	0.38479		

Source: Based on data of CHIP 2013

10.5 A Comparative Study: China and European Countries

As a developing country, China established its social security system only not quite long ago and is still making changes and improvement to it. Therefore, compared with those in European countries, China's social security system has a weak redistribution function.

European countries, especially those in Northern and Western Europe, have had social security and social welfare systems for over a century, and developed a comprehensive policy framework that helps reduce inequality, alleviate poverty, and maintain social stability. However, excessive social security and welfare also has certain negative effects, as it will likely hamper the improvement of efficiency or even become a heavy social burden. Since the 1980s, European countries have carried out various reforms in their social security and welfare systems, introducing active labor market policies to reduce the negative effects of excessive social security and welfare. However, European social security and welfare systems, though having gone through continuous reforms, still have a strong income redistribution function, which plays a positive role in narrowing the income gap and promoting income equality.

Social security and welfare help regulate income distribution in two ways: contributions and public transfers. Social security contribution, similar to personal income tax, adopts progressive rates. The higher the income, the higher the contribution. Thus, it is effective in narrowing the income gap. Public transfers are made in various social security and welfare programs, and are often tilted towards low-income households, thus helping narrow the income gap. Figure 10.12 shows the impact of social security contributions and public transfers on income distribution in four European countries and the United States. It is not difficult to see that the income gaps are large in these countries at primary distribution. In all of these countries, except for Sweden, the Gini coefficients based on primary distribution all exceed 0.4, and that of the United States and the United Kingdom are even close to 0.5. After social security contributions and transfers are taken into consideration, the gap of disposable income is significantly smaller. Specifically, the income gap in Denmark falls from 0.42 to below 0.3 and that of the United Kingdom from 0.47 to 0.34. Figure 10.12 also shows the different effects of social security contributions and transfer payments. Different from the United States, European countries see a greater impact from transfers than from social security contributions. For example, the income redistribution effect of transfer payment accounts for 78% of the total effect of social security, while the contributions only accounts for 22% in France. In comparison, the income redistribution effect generated by transfer payments in the United States accounts for only 20% of the total effect of social security, while the contributions accounts for 80%. China is more similar to European countries in this aspect. The social security contributions have a very limited impact, while public transfer payments play a greater role in redistribution.

As mentioned above, China's social security and welfare system has only a minor effect on income redistribution that we see the Gini of the market income gap slightly decreased. So, what is the case of European countries in comparison? Figure 10.13 shows China and major European countries' Gini coefficients of the market income and disposable income gaps. It is clear that some European countries have a bigger difference between the Gini of market income (initial distribution) and the Gini of disposable income (redistribution), the latter is significantly lower than the former. This means that the income redistribution system, including the social security and welfare programs, has played a significant role in regulating and narrowing the income gap. In contrast, China has a minor Ginin difference between the market income and disposable income, indicating the limited effect of China's redistribution policy. The difference between Britain and China is even more pronounced. The UK's market income gap is much higher than that of China. After redistribution, the UK's disposable income gap drops significantly, to a point much lower than that of China (see Fig. 10.13).

Figure 10.14 clearly illustrates the difference in income redistribution between China and European countries. In major European countries, to what extent does social security and welfare reduce income gaps? As shown in Fig. 10.14, 22 European countries all see significantly smaller income gaps after social security and welfare programs are taken into consideration. Specifically, Israel has the smallest decline, which is 22%; Slovenia has the sharpest decline, which is 38%. The

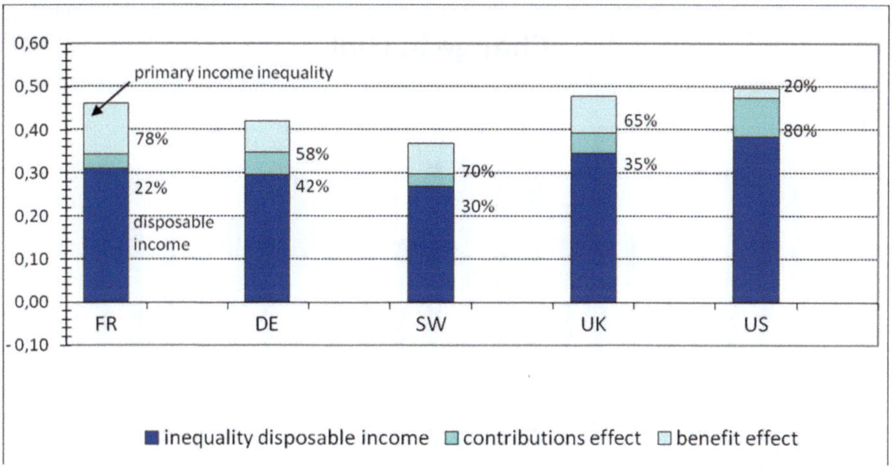

Fig. 10.12 Income redistribution effect of social security policies in four European countries and the United States. Source: Hocquet (2016). Relations between Employment and Social Security Policies in Europe: Social Protection and Employment: Partnership or Rivalry?". *Report of EU-China Social Protection Reform Project*

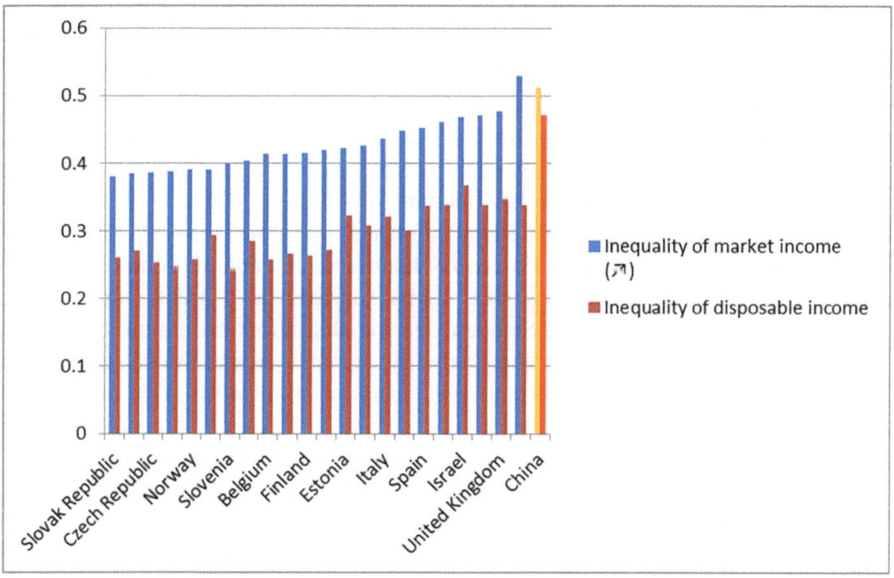

Fig. 10.13 Income redistribution effect of social security and welfare: a comparison between China and European countries. Source: Data of European countries come from Hocquet (2016) and data of China is based on CHIP 2013

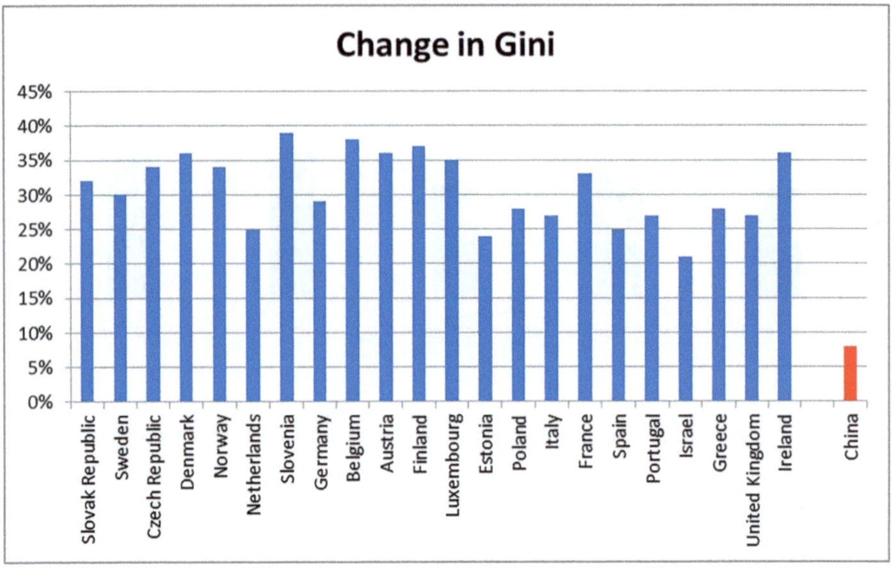

Fig. 10.14 Decrease (percent) of the income gap (Gini coefficient) as a result of social security policies. Source: Data of European countries come from Hocquet (2016) and data of China is based on CHIP 2013

average is around 30%. In contrast, China's social security and welfare system has a much less conspicuous effect on distribution, seeing only an 8% drop in the Gini coefficient of its income gap.

In addition to the transfers in the social security and welfare system, European countries also have social services such as free medical care, free education, and affordable housing to help regulate income distribution. Table 10.5 shows the income redistribution effect of European countries' social services. After adding the market value of social services on top of disposable income, the Gini coefficient decrease significantly, indicating that social services have great narrowed the income gap. Some country, like Sweden, see social services exert a greater impact on redistribution; while others, like Germany, see less impact. More specifically, free medical play a more important role, bringing about 40%–70% of the total effect. Because China has very limited research in this area, no comparison can be made here. However, from existing data, China's social services are not likely to have a strong impact on income distribution, mainly because equal access to these services remains absent. The wide gaps in access to social services between urban and rural areas, between regions, and between different groups of people, greatly weaken the effect of social services on income redistribution.

Table 10.5 Redistribution effects of public services n European countries

	Gini coefficient based on disposable income	Gini coefficient based on disposable income – market value of social services	Redistribution effect	Contribution by specific item				
				Healthcare	Education	Child care	Housing	Others
Germany	0,300	0,249	−16,9%	61,5%	30,2%	7,1%	1,8%	−0,6%
Austria	0,270	0,220	−18,5%	56,8%	34,1%	7,6%	1,6%	
Spain	0,340	0,276	−18,7%	60,4%	32,1%	5,3%	0,5%	1,6%
Finland	0,270	0,220	−18,7%	57,8%	23,0%	5,3%	0,5%	13,4%
Italy	0,320	0,259	−19,0%	48,4%	41,1%	7,9%	2,6%	
Netherlands	0,270	0,218	−19,2%	42,2%	33,3%	9,4%		15,1%
Slovakia	0,250	0,200	−19,9%	60,8%	33,7%	3,0%	2,5%	
Poland	0,320	0,256	−20,0%	43,0%	49,5%	5,5%	2,0%	
Estonia	0,310	0,246	−20,6%	56,3%	31,1%	6,8%	1,9%	3,9%
Greece	0,340	0,270	−20,6%	46,6%	28,6%	2,4%	22,3%	
Czech Republic	0,260	0,206	−20,8%	63,9%	24,5%	7,7%	3,8%	
Luxembourg	0,270	0,213	−21,1%	50,7%	36,0%	10,9%	2,4%	8,3%
Belgium	0,260	0,204	−21,7%	65,9%	20,3%	6,9%	6,9%	
Denmark	0,250	0,196	−21,8%	45,9%	26,1%	5,0%		22,9%
France	0,280	0,217	−22,5%	57,8%	25,8%	8,0%	4,9%	**3,6%**
Portugal	0,370	0,286	−22,6%	60,2%	35,4%	4,0%	0,4%	
Hungary	0,260	0,201	−22,8%	46,1%	36,0%	12,3%		5,7%
United Kingdom	0,330	0,254	−22,9%	54,6%	30,6%	3,1%	4,8%	7,0%
Ireland	0,320	0,246	−23,2%	53,9%	43,5%	0,4%	2,2%	
Sweden	0,240	0,183	−23,8%	52,1%	23,5%	6,3%	0,4%	17,6%

Source: Hocquet (2016)

10.6 Conclusions

After four decades of reform and opening up, China has made great strides in economic growth, social security and social services. However, its social security and welfare programs have not been effective in regulating income distribution. China is currently facing a series of social and economic problems, such as the widening income gap, big poor population, pressure of unemployment caused by the economic slowdown, large-scale rural migration, insufficient consumer demand, and population aging.

Many studies and experience from other countries show that an appropriate social security system has economic development and social stability as its goals. For China, the purposes of social security include insurance, poverty alleviation, income redistribution, consumption smoothing and stimulation, and social stabilization.

Fortunately, Chinese governments at all levels have realized the importance and necessity of a new social security system with wide coverage, high efficiency and sustainability (CDRF, 2009; Zheng, 2008). So far, China has basically established a social security system that covers all population groups, and in particular the old-age insurance and medical insurance policies have covered all people in urban and rural areas.

However, because of the current fragmented social security system, policies are different in urban and rural areas, and can be different for people with different employment status in cities. Since these policies are not well coordinated, different groups' contributions to and the benefits from the social security system are very different. Such differences have certain negative effects instead of positive impact in income distribution. The results of this study show that the social security and welfare system, especially the old-age insurance programs, has a positive but only minor impact on narrowing the income gap, personal income tax and social security contributions have a negative impact on income distribution, and public transfers under various social security policies, mainly old-age insurance programs, has played a positive role in narrowing the income gap.

Compared with European Union countries, China has much to do to improve its social security and welfare system as a measure to regulate income distribution. European countries have greatly reduced income inequality through social security and welfare systems. They offer highly equal access to social services, which also has helped reduce inequality in income distribution. In this regard, China has a lot to learn from them.

In the future, China's social security reform should focus more on its role in regulating income distribution. First of all, it is necessary to have progressive rates for social security contributions, linked to income level. With regard to the old-age insurance system, we should accelerate the reform of government employees' old-age insurance program, which requires no contribution from the employees and merge it with the old-age insurance system for corporate employees as soon as possible. Second, in the reform of the current fragmented social security system, we should establish a unified national social security system as soon as possible so as to reduce the difference of benefits received by different groups of people. Third, we need more social service programs. The current minimum living allowance policy needs to be more targeted and adopt higher standards. In addition, we need more welfare programs targeting the poor and low-income groups, such as child care assistance for low-income families. Finally, we should establish a simulation analysis model for the study of social security systems, especially their effect on income redistribution, so as to provide a scientific basis for policy adjustment and formulation.

References

Adelmen, I., & Sunding, D. (1987). Economic policy and income distribution in China. *Journal of Comparative Economics, 11*, 444.

Barr, N. (2001). *The welfare state as piggy bank: Information, risk, uncertainty, and the role of the state*. Oxford University Press.

Barr, N. (2003). *Preface to Chinese edition of the economics of the welfare state*. Press of Labour and Social Security.

Barr, N., & Diamond, P. (2008). *Reforming pensions, submitted to international social security review.*

Bowles, S., Durlauf, S. N., & Hoff, K. (Eds.). (2006). *Poverty Traps*. Princeton University Press.

Cai, F., & Du Y. (2009). *Blog post: Realizing the economic recovery by employment growth.* http://blog.voc.com.cn/blog.php?do=showone&uid=337&type=blog&itemid=539446

China Development Research Fund. (2009). *Social security system reform in China*. China Development Press.

Deng, Q., & Li, S. (2008). *Wage structures and inequality among local and migrant workers in urban China*. A conference paper presented in the RUMICI workshop in ANU, 10–12 December 2008.

Fajnzylber, P., Lederman, D., & Loayza, N. (2002). Inequality and violent crime. *Journal of Law and Economics, 45*, 1–39.

Fajnzylber, P., Lederman, D., & Loayza, N. (2008). What causes violent crime? *European Economic Review, 46*(7), 1323–1357.

Feldstein, M. (2005). *Rethinking social insurance*. NBER, Working Paper 11250.

Gustafsson, B., Li, S., & Sicular, T. (2008). *Income inequality and public policy in China.* Cambridge University Press.

Hocquet, J.Y. (2016). *Relations between employment and social security policies in Europe: Social protection and employment "partnership or rivalry"*. Report of EU-China Social Protection Reform Project.

Knight, J., Li, S., & Deng, Q. (2009). Education and the Poverty Trap in Rural China: Closing the Trap. *Oxford Development Studies, 38*, 1.

Li, S. (2008). *Rural migrant workers in China: Scenario, challenges and public policy*. Working Paper No. 89. Policy Integration and Statistics Department, International Labour Office, Geneva.

Li, S., & Yang, S. (2009). The impact of urban minimum living subsidy policy on income distribution and poverty in China. *Chinese Journal of Population Science (Zhongguo Renkou Kexue), 5*, 19.

Riskin, C., Zhao, R., & Li, S. (2001). *China's retreat from equality: Income distribution and economic transition*. M.E. Sharpe.

The Work Bank. (2009). *From poor areas to poor people: China's evolving poverty reduction agenda: An assessment of poverty and inequality in China*. The World Bank Office, Beijing.
Whalley, J., & Yue, X. (2009). Rural income volatility and inequality in China. *CESifo Economic Studies, 55*, 648. https://doi.org/10.1093/cesifo/ifp014
Zheng, G. (2008). *Thirty years of social security in China*. People's Publishing House.

Shi Li, professor at China Institute for Income Distribution, Beijing Normal University.

MIX
Papier aus verantwortungsvollen Quellen
Paper from responsible sources
FSC® C105338

If you have any concerns about our products,
you can contact us on
ProductSafety@springernature.com

In case Publisher is established outside the EU,
the EU authorized representative is:
Springer Nature Customer Service Center GmbH
Europaplatz 3, 69115 Heidelberg, Germany

Printed by Libri Plureos GmbH
in Hamburg, Germany